"Always Be Prepared ..."

A 'New Apologetics' Course for Catholic Secondary Schools

"Always be prepared to make a defence to anyone who calls you to account for the hope that is in you, yet do it with gentleness and reverence"
(1 Pet. 3:15).

Dr Robert M. Haddad

Nihil Obstat: Fr Peter Joseph STD

Imprimatur: +Most Reverend Anthony Fisher OP
Archbishop of Sydney
Date: 18 June 2021

The *Nihil Obstat* and *Imprimatur* are a declaration that a book or pamphlet is considered to be free from doctrinal or moral error. It is not necessarily implied that those who have granted them agree with the contents, opinions or statements expressed.

Scripture quotes taken from the **Revised Standard Version of the Bible (Second Catholic Edition)**, copyright © 2006 (Ignatius Press).

Extracts from English translation of **Catechism of the Catholic Church** for Australia copyright © June 1994 St Pauls/Libreria Editrice Vaticana.

Artist and Illustrator: **Paul Mooney, Mooney Fine Art**

Cover Design: Miguel Zaragoza

Published and distributed by Parousia Media PTY LTD
PO Box 59 Galston, NSW, 2159
Ph: +61 2 8776 8778
office@parousiamedia.com
www.parousiamedia.com

© Dr Robert M. Haddad 2021. All rights reserved. Extracts and copies of various parts or chapters of the work may be made in cases of 'fair dealing', viz., for the purpose of teaching, promoting and defending the Catholic Faith. All acknowledgments given to Dr Robert M. Haddad.

ISBN: 978-1-922660-49-7

"Always Be Prepared ..." – A 'New Apologetics' Course for Catholic Secondary Schools

CONTENTS

Dedication	6
Foreword	8
Unit Overview, Unit Objectives, Enduring Understanding	10
Notice Concerning the Personal Qualities of the 'New Apologist'	11
Notice Concerning Lesson Time Allocations	12
Lesson 1: Introduction to Apologetics	13
Lesson 2: The Existence of God and the New Atheism	18
Lesson 3: The Nature of God	25
Lesson 4: The Problem of Evil and Suffering	32
Lesson 5: Is Religion Toxic and the Cause of Evil?	38
Lesson 6: Creation and Evolution	43
Lesson 7: The Origins of Humanity	50
Lesson 8: The Material and Spiritual Nature of the Human Person	56
Lesson 9: The Reality and Nature of Divine Revelation	62
Lesson 10: The Bible: Myth or History?	68
Lesson 11: The Word of God – Scripture and Tradition	74
Lesson 12: The Judeo-Christian Story	81
Lesson 13: God as Trinity	87
Lesson 14: The Divinity of Jesus Christ	93
Lesson 15: The Bodily Resurrection of Jesus Christ	100

Lesson 16: The Foundation, Authority and Necessity of the Catholic Church and the Papacy	106
Lesson 17: The Catholic Faith and Other Religions	113
Lesson 18: The Existence of Spirits – Angels and Demons	119
Lesson 19: The Reality of Miracles	125
Lesson 20: The Compatibility of Faith and Reason	131
Lesson 21: The Existence and Knowability of Objective Truth	138
Lesson 22: The Existence and Need for Moral Absolutes	144
Lesson 23: The Existence, Nature and Importance of Natural Law	151
Lesson 24: The Relevance and Necessity of the Ten Commandments	158
Lesson 25: Law and Conscience	164
Lesson 26: The Origin and Importance of the Sacraments	170
Lesson 27: The Origin and Importance of the Mass	177
Lesson 28: The Real Presence of Christ in the Eucharist	184
Lesson 29: Marriage, Divorce and Annulments	191
Lesson 30: Beginnings of Life, Abortion, Contraception and Fertilisation Techniques	198
Lesson 31: 'Thou Shalt Not Kill': Infanticide; Euthanasia; Capital Punishment; Just War	205
Lesson 32: Marian Dogmas – Mary as Mother of God; The Immaculate Conception	212
Lesson 33: Marian Dogmas – Perpetual Virginity; Assumption Into Heaven	221
Lesson 34: The Communion of Saints	228
Lesson 35: Eternal Life with God	235
Lesson 36: Eternal Separation from God	242
Assessment Schedule	248

Dedication

To all those who have striven in recent times to restore apologetics to Catholic education.

Foreword

Apologetics is the art of providing a reasoned explanation, or defence, for one's position or beliefs to critics or inquirers. For Christians, one of the original calls to engage in apologetics was made by St Peter the Apostle, who exhorted believers to *"Always be prepared to make a defence to anyone who calls you to account for the hope that is in you"*, adding further that we should do the same *"with gentleness and reverence"* (1 Pet. 3:15). It was an apologetics closely allied to evangelisation.

Apologetics has always had a place in the life of the Church. Many great Church Fathers, Doctors and Saints throughout history engaged in apologetics to defend Catholic teaching against challenges and attacks stemming from all quarters. Figures such as Sts Athanasius, Jerome and Augustine of Hippo initially come to mind.

The English-speaking world has produced many fine apologists, including St John Henry Cardinal Newman, Archbishop Fulton J. Sheen, Hilaire Belloc, G. K. Chesterton, Frank Sheed, Frs Rumble and Carty, etc. Some of these were converts to Catholicism, some cradle Catholics. All, whether lay or clerical, loved the Catholic faith, knew its truthfulness and desired to share it with others. Their writings combined Scripture, reason, personal testimony, wit, and a bit of pugilistic flair.

However, from the 1960s onwards interest in apologetics declined significantly. For many, it had become outdated, unfashionable and irrelevant. Arguing over religious beliefs was either bad manners, offensive, or both. It now seemed best to keep one's religious beliefs to oneself, for "your truth is as good as mine." Apologetics would substantially disappear from the Catholic academy, the seminary and school curricula.

Despite its decline, apologetics would eventually make a comeback, at least in part. It was never eschewed by Vatican II (*Lumen Gentium* 10 and 11, *Dignitatis Humanae* 14, *Apostolicam Actuositatem* 6) nor by post-Conciliar Popes. Pope St John Paul II would provide the 'magna carta' for a 'new apologetics', which in essence was a return to the Scripture injunction of St Peter:

> *"… we need a new apologetic, geared to the needs of today, which keeps in mind that our task is not just to win arguments but to win souls, to engage not in ideological bickering but to vindicate and promote the Gospel … This new apologetic will also need to breathe a spirit of humanity, that compassionate humility which understands people's anxieties and questions and which is not quick to presume in them ill will or bad faith."*

Any revival of apologetics should be welcomed, especially in view of the many new and rising challenges facing the Church and the world. The need for apologetics is most acute for the young, who are highly vulnerable to the growing influence of the 'new atheism', the post-modernist denial of objective truth, the sexual revolution, fundamentalist Christianity, and proselytising Islam. Hence, the critical need to reintroduce apologetics into Catholic school curricula, to provide the young with many of the necessary answers, or at least let them know that there are answers that give Christianity, and especially Catholicism, credibility.

I therefore introduce this new resource, *Always Be Prepared*, and pray for its widespread use in Catholic schools across the world.

Dr Robert M. Haddad
Sydney, Australia
March 2021

Unit Overview, Unit Objectives, Enduring Understanding

Unit Overview

Students will explore the meaning of apologetics, the importance of apologetics in the life of the Catholic Church and the different apologetical categories and methodologies. In their exploration, students will become aware of the primary issues, questions, challenges and objections modern-day Catholics regularly encounter and learn to develop answers and responses to the same. Students will come to appreciate the 'new apologetics' and what are appropriate and inappropriate apologetic practices and attitudes.

Unit Objectives

Knowledge and Understanding
Develop an understanding of the meaning of apologetics, the different apologetical categories and methodologies, the primary issues, questions, challenges and objections modern-day Catholics regularly encounter and how to answer and respond to the same.

Skills
Develop the ability to understand, dissect and respond to the many and varied questions, challenges and objections against the Catholic faith. Develop research skills to construct responses drawing on Scripture, Church Fathers, theology, philosophy, history, literature, art, architecture, music, etc. Develop the ability to engage in apologetical conversations and debates.

Values and Attitudes
Value the importance of apologetics in the life of the Catholic Church and the need to respond to the many contemporary questions, challenges and objections, know that the Catholic Church possesses substantive answers to all questions, challenges and objections, realise the obligation incumbent on all the baptised to practise apologetics according to their circumstances, have confidence in one's potential to practise apologetics, recognise the difference between 'good' and 'bad' apologetical behaviours, practise apologetics at all times with reverence, gentleness, humility and with a genuine love for the other, and appreciate the essential role of the Holy Spirit to make the work of apologetics fruitful.

Enduring Understanding

Engaging in apologetics is an obligation incumbent upon all the baptised according to the injunction of St Peter the Apostle, *"Always be prepared to make a defence to any one who calls you to account for the hope that is in you, yet do it with gentleness and reverence"* (1 Pet. 3:15).

Notice Concerning the Personal Qualities of the 'New Apologist'

New apologetics requires a new type of Catholic apologist in order to be true to its principles and effective in practise. What, therefore, should a Catholic 'new apologist' look like?

As apologetics is essentially a religiously motivated work, it is imperative that the new apologist possesses a personal relationship with Jesus Christ crucified and risen. The best apologists are those who have a deep spiritual life, a devotion to private prayer and public worship and who actively participate in a community of faith where truth and goodness are acknowledged and practised. Apologists should be saints transformed by the message they proclaim and display undeniable holiness, as 'holy people' are the best apologetic for the truth of Catholicism/Christianity.

Apologetics, like any other activity, must be undertaken as an act of love to God and appear as God's love at work. Of all the virtues, charity most gives credibility to truth in the practical world of daily living. In dealing with others, the new apologist needs always be respectful and engaging, embodying the qualities of humanity and charity, speaking the truth in love and being good humoured towards all.

The new apologist should always have the humility to say "I don't know" when asked a question he/she cannot immediately answer and readily admit their own limitations and weaknesses. Humility must also be evident in the apologist's tone of voice and rhetoric when presenting truth and in their recognition that it is God alone who converts. An arrogant and triumphalist apologetic never wins anyone over.

The new apologist should be learned with a thorough and mature understanding of the teachings of the Catholic faith and an understanding of the positions and beliefs of their dialogue partners. New apologists ought always provide responses marked by clarity and fidelity, uncompromisingly articulating the full vision of truth. When the other questions, hesitates or even resists, the new apologist should show patience, sympathy and genuine appreciation of their good points. The new apologist should always meet the doubter's needs with respect and diplomacy, not as an argumentative and combative enemy who seeks only to critique and condemn. New apologists as friends should still make 'hard truth' claims but should propose rather than impose those truths with a pastoral wisdom.

The final element necessary for the new apologist is enthusiasm. The enthusiastic apologist is passionate and positive, confident and optimistic, displaying a manifest love and joy for the Catholic faith and truth. Enthusiastic apologists are those who display an unwavering assurance, firmness of conviction and a seriousness mixed with joy and happiness. Their message should speak joyfully of hope, mercy, peace and love, with elements of surprise and challenge. Only happy apologists are ultimately successful in the work of the new apologetics.

Notice Concerning Lesson Time Allocations

The timings indicated throughout each lesson are <u>advisory only</u>. Teachers are to make the final decision regarding time allocations for each lesson and for individual sections of each lesson. This will also depend on the capacity of the students being taught.

Lesson 1: Introduction to Apologetics

LESSON ORGANISATION

Year Level: Date: Time: Duration: Room:

Quote:
"To live without faith, without a patrimony to defend, without a steady struggle for truth, that is not living but existing" – Bl. Pier Giorgio Frassati.

Prayer:
Come, Holy Spirit, fill the hearts of your faithful and enkindle in them the fire of your love.

V. Send forth your Spirit and they shall be created.
R. And you shall renew the face of the earth.

Let us pray.
O God, who by the light of the Holy Spirit, did instruct the hearts of the faithful, grant us in the same Spirit to be truly wise and ever to rejoice in his consolation.
Through Christ our Lord. Amen.

Lesson Outcomes:

As a result of this lesson, students will be able to:

- Understand the meaning of apologetics in light of 1 Peter 3:15.
- Appreciate the history and importance of apologetics in the life of the Catholic Church.
- Comprehend the distinction between natural, Christian and Catholic apologetics.
- Discuss and evaluate the arguments for and against engaging in apologetics.
- Contrast the characteristics of the 'old apologetics' with those of the 'new.'
- Distinguish between 'good' and 'bad' apologetical practices, behaviours and attitudes.
- Recognise the most important contemporary issues that need to be addressed by apologetics.

Activity Sheets:

Activity Sheet 1, *History of Heresies.*

LESSON DELIVERY

Outcome	Time	Motivation and Introduction:	Resources/ References
Understand the meaning of apologetics in light of 1 Peter 3:15.	7 mins	Introduce yourself briefly to the students. Prayer to the Holy Spirit (or other suitable prayer). Tell the students that we are about to learn about *apologetics*. Ask the students the following questions: *Put up your hand if you have heard of the word 'apologetics'? What do you think the word means?* Take two-three responses then read out the following quote from 1 Peter 3:15: *"Always be prepared to make a defense to any one who calls you to account for the hope that is in you, yet do it with gentleness and reverence."* Explain to the students that apologetics is not about apologising, it is about providing a *reasoned explanation* for our Catholic faith. **Lesson Steps**	Sheehan, *Apologetics and Catholic Doctrine*, 17ff.
Comprehend the distinction between natural, Christian and Catholic apologetics.	10 mins	(i) Ask the students if they have ever been challenged about their Catholic faith or if they know someone who has left the Catholic faith for another religion or for no religion at all. Get the students to discuss this in small groups of two-four students before taking public responses. Take three-four responses from students. Briefly list student responses on the whiteboard under the following headings: *Natural Apologetics; Christian Apologetics; Catholic Apologetics*. Explain to the students that *natural apologetics* is primarily concerned with providing arguments for the existence of God; *Christian apologetics* is concerned with arguments that this one God is the Judeo-Christian God who has revealed himself as a Trinity of equal divine Persons, Father, Son and Holy Spirit, and that Jesus Christ is the divine Son of God who died and rose again from the dead; and *Catholic apologetics* is concerned with arguments that Jesus Christ founded one Church, namely the Catholic Church, as well as additional arguments in support of distinctive Catholic beliefs.	Sheehan, *Apologetics and Catholic Doctrine*, 22-23.

Appreciate the history and importance of apologetics in the life of the Catholic Church.	12 mins	(ii) Hand out Activity Sheet 1, *History of Heresies*. Run through the heresies that are listed, the names of the individual founder(s) of each heresy, the year each heresy began, the major challenge(s) posed by each heresy, and the respective Catholic apologists who rose to oppose each heresy. Ask the students to complete the final column designating each heresy under one of the following categories – *Natural Apologetics, Christian Apologetics* or *Catholic Apologetics*.	Dulles, *A History of Apologetics*, 27-150.
Discuss and evaluate the arguments for and against engaging in apologetics.	10 mins	(iii) Explain to the students that apologetics is not necessarily popular with everyone today. Show on a PowerPoint slide the following modern objections to apologetics: - "It is too intellectual." - "It is too defensive." - "It is arrogant to claim, 'We're right and you're wrong'." - "It is 'old fashioned', belonging to the past." - "One should not call other religions flawed or false." - "Apologetics offends non-Catholics, it amounts to a form of 'religious imperialism'." Invite students to choose <u>one</u> of these objections and compose a brief two-three sentence response. Select three students to read out their responses. Highlight to students that there are many justifications for doing apologetics but the chief one is love. All Catholics, including students, have a right to know what Catholicism really teaches and the reasons for belief in order to live out the truth as a formal member of the Church. Providing such reasons is a profound responsibility and, as Pope Benedict XVI once declared, amounts to "nothing less than an act of love." To bring a non-Catholic to the fullness of truth is an act of neighbourly love.	Kreeft & Tacelli, *Handbook of Christian Apologetics*, 20-24. Siniscalchi, "Implementing a Course in Apologetics," 115-146.
Contrast the characteristics of the 'old apologetics' with those of the 'new.'	12 mins	(iv) Introduce the term 'new apologetics.' Read aloud the following quote from Pope St John Paul II: *"We need a new apologetic, geared to the needs of today, which keeps in mind that our task is not just to win arguments but to win souls."* Highlight the two chief elements of the above quote, namely, "the needs of today" and "win souls, not arguments."	Akin, "The Golden Rule of Apologetics," 24-29. Brumley, *How Not to Share Your Faith*, 91-120.

Recognise the most important contemporary issues that need to be addressed by apologetics. Distinguish between 'good' and 'bad' apologetical practices, behaviours and attitudes.		Draw a table on the whiteboard with two columns headed *"Needs of Today"* and *"Appropriate Behaviours."* Engage the students to suggest what they believe are the apologetical needs of today and what are appropriate behaviours/attitudes modern-day apologists should display. The teacher should include some ideas of their own. Answers for *"Needs of Today"* should include addressing (new) atheism, Islam in the West, Protestantism (particularly those groups that engage in active proselytism such as Evangelicals and Pentecostals, etc.). The teacher may wish to add suggestions of their known relating to issues not so familiar to young students, such as secularism, religious indifferentism, moral relativism, and postmodernism. Spend time explaining these technical terms. Answers for *"Appropriate Behaviours"* should include listening, civility, humility, charity, friendship, compassion, understanding, honesty, fairness, integrity, enthusiasm, conviction, truth, knowledge, etc. The teacher should also mention inappropriate behaviours that once characterised 'old apologetics' and which should be avoided today, including, arrogance, triumphalism, name-calling, insults, raised voices, etc.		Gaillardetz, "Apologetics, Evangelization, and Ecumenism Today", *Origins* 35 (2005): 9-15. Kreeft & Tacelli, *Handbook of Christian Apologetics*, 23-25. Levada, "A New Apologetics for the Church in the 21st Century", 7-10.
	3 mins	**Lesson Closure**: Remind the students that all the baptised are called to engage in apologetics, that we are 'qualified' to do so because of our baptism and confirmation, that apologetics has always been an important part of the life of the Church and that there are many apologetical issues/challenges that Catholics need to address today. Finally, in the spirit of the 'new apologetics' we are called to engage in apologetics according to the original exhortation of St Peter, namely, *"with gentleness and reverence."* **Transition**: Homework: Considering the words of the Apostle in 1 Peter 3:15, should Catholics persuade or coerce others to believe the Catholic faith? Why/Why not? (1-2 paragraphs).		

Resources:
- Akin, James. "The Golden Rule of Apologetics." *Catholic Answers* (Sept.-Oct. 2016): 24-29.
- Brumley, Mark. *How Not to Share Your Faith: The Seven Deadly Sins of Apologetics and Evangelization*. El Cajon: Catholic Answers Inc., 2002, 97-120.
- Dulles, Avery. *A History of Apologetics*. San Francisco: Ignatius Press, 1999, 27-150.
- Gaillardetz, Richard R. "Apologetics, Evangelization, and Ecumenism Today." *Origins* 35 (2005): 9-15.
- Kreeft, Peter & Ronald K. Tacelli. *Handbook of Christian Apologetics: Hundreds of Answers to Crucial Questions*. Downers Grove: IVP Academic, 1994, 20-25.
- Levada, William. "A New Apologetics for the Church in the 21st Century." *Origins* 40 (2010): 7-10.
- Sheehan, Michael. *Apologetics and Catholic Doctrine*, rev. and ed. Peter M. Joseph. London: Baronius Press, 2015, 17ff. & 22-23.
- Siniscalchi, Glenn B. "Implementing a Course in Apologetics at Catholic Universities and Colleges." *Fidelitas: The Journal of the Fellowship of Catholic Scholars* (Canada) (Winter-Spring 2015): 114-149.
- *Catechism of the Catholic Church*. Libreria Editrice Vaticana: St Pauls, 1994, paras. 900, 1303.
- YOUCAT (*Youth Catechism of the Catholic Church*). San Francisco, Ignatius Press, 2010, paras. 205, 206.
- Website: Catholic Answers. "Apologetics, a theological science which has for its purpose the explanation and defense of the Christian religion." https://www.catholic.com/encyclopedia/apologetics.
- YouTube: Alison Low, "Apologetics: Introduction to Apologetics." https://www.youtube.com/watch?v=smNrFRPi7Xo.

LESSON EVALUATION (to be completed AFTER the lesson)

Assessment of lesson objectives and suggestions for improvement:
Teacher self-reflection and self-evaluation:
[OFFICIAL USE ONLY] Comments by teacher supervisor:

Lesson 2: The Existence of God and the 'New Atheism'

LESSON ORGANISATION

Year Level: Date: Time: Duration: Room:

Quote:
"An atheist is a man who has no invisible means of support" – Archbishop Fulton J. Sheen.

Prayer:
Come, Holy Spirit, fill the hearts of your faithful and enkindle in them the fire of your love.

V. Send forth your Spirit and they shall be created.
R. And you shall renew the face of the earth.

Let us pray.
O God, who by the light of the Holy Spirit, did instruct the hearts of the faithful, grant us in the same Spirit to be truly wise and ever to rejoice in his consolation.
Through Christ our Lord. Amen.

Lesson Outcomes:

As a result of this lesson, students will be able to:

- Define terms such as 'atheist' and 'agnostic.'
- Recognise well-known 'new atheists', their works, influence and popularity.
- Identity chief characteristics of the style and approach of the 'new atheists.'
- Discuss and evaluate a variety of 'new atheist' arguments against the existence of God.
- Appreciate the need for arguments for the existence of God based on reason.
- Comprehend the 'Five Ways' of St Thomas Aquinas.
- Reflect upon and analyse the conversion experience of a former atheist.

Activity Sheets:

Activity Sheet 2, *The 'Four Horsemen' of the Anti-Apocalypse.*
Activity Sheet 3, *The 'Five Ways' of St Thomas Aquinas.*
Activity Sheet 4, *The 'Five Ways' – Filling the Gaps.*

"Always Be Prepared …" – A 'New Apologetics' Course for Catholic Secondary Schools

LESSON DELIVERY

Outcome	Time	Motivation and Introduction:	Resources/ References
Define terms such as 'atheist' and 'agnostic.'	5 mins	Welcome and settle the students. Prayer to the Holy Spirit (or other suitable prayer). Tell the students that today we will be learning about atheism and the so-called 'new atheism.' Ask the students the following questions: *What does the word 'atheist' mean? What is the difference between an atheist and an agnostic?* Take two-three responses and then provide the following explanation: The words 'atheist' and 'agnostic' are originally two ancient Greek words relating respectively to 'God' and 'knowledge.' 'Theos' means God while 'gnosis' means knowledge. When you place the letter 'a' in front of a Greek word it gives the word the opposite meaning. So 'a-theos' means no God while 'a-gnosis' mean no knowledge. An atheist is someone who believes there is no God while an agnostic is someone who does not know whether any God exists or not. **Lesson Steps**	Duggan, *Beyond Reasonable Doubt*, 158-159.
Recognise well-known 'new atheists', their works, influence and popularity. Identity chief characteristics of the style and approach of the 'new atheists.'	10 mins	(i) Hand out to each student a copy of Activity Sheet 2, *The 'Four Horsemen' of the Anti-Apocalypse.* Assist students to identify the following individuals: Richard Dawkins, Christopher Hitchens, Sam Harris and Daniel Dennett. Ask the students if they have heard of any of these people or read any of their works. If so, ask the student(s) for their impressions and if they were influenced or persuaded by any of their arguments. Tell the students that these four 'new atheists' (and others) are very popular, selling millions of books, speaking to large audiences around the world, engaging in many public debates, and exerting a very large cyber and social media presence. These same 'new atheists' intentionally seek to mock and offend believers as a means of embarrassing people into abandoning their faith. On a PowerPoint slide show and read out the following examples:	Horn, "How to Respond to the New Atheism", 8-14.

		"Christianity: Sadistic God; Useless Saviour" – American Atheist Society. "I respect people; I respect humans. I do not respect religion or the idea that religion deserves respect" – Dan Merica. "Mock Christians, ridicule them in public … Don't fall for the convention that we're all too polite to talk about religion" – Richard Dawkins. "Belief in a God is a form of mental illness" – Sam Harris. "Teaching religion to children is a form of child abuse" – Christopher Hitchens. Ask students to answer the following questions: *Are the above statements acceptable behaviour for adults engaging in public debate, Yes or No? What behaviours should you display in responding to these statements?* Take two student responses.	
Discuss and evaluate a variety of 'new atheist' arguments against the existence of God.	10 mins	(ii) Present the following atheist statements/questions against belief in God. Ask students to choose one of these statements/questions and construct a 60-second response ('Pressure Challenge'). Take two student responses. - "Who made God?" - "If God exists, how come I can't see him?" - "If God loves us and wants us to be friends, why does he hide himself from us?" - "The existence of God requires scientific evidence, not arguments from religion and philosophy." - "Science now explains everything. It has done away with God." - "Adults believing in God need to get rid of faith and grow up." After taking two student responses, ask the other students if any of them have additional or alternative points of argument. Then inform the students that the best arguments for the existence of God are not found in responding to questions but in positive proofs based on reason. The best of these 'proofs' are the 'Five Ways' of the great saint and philosopher, Thomas Aquinas.	Broussard, "Hey, God, Where Are You?", 25-29. Broussard, "Why Science Can't Do Away with God", 34-38.

Appreciate the need for arguments for the existence of God based on reason.	15 mins	(iii) Before outlining the 'Five Ways' of St Thomas Aquinas explain to the students that when dialoguing with atheists/agnostics about the existence of God it is insufficient to simply present them with quotes from the Bible. Why would this be the case? (Take two-three student responses). Since atheists do not acknowledge the Bible as the written Word of God Catholics need to present proofs based on reason and from the observable world around us. On a PowerPoint slide, show the following quote from St Paul's Letter to the Romans, where he says, *"... ever since the creation of the world, the invisible existence of God and his everlasting power have been clearly seen by the mind's understanding of created things"* (1:20). Allow a few moments for students to write a brief exegesis (analysis) of this passage, identifying two-three important points to share with the rest of the class. These points should include some of the following: - That God created the world and all other things out of nothing by his infinite power. - That all created things are good for they, in differing degrees, reflect one or more of God's infinite perfections. - That a reasoned observation of creatures as regards their causes and natures should lead us to the logical conclusion that God is the first cause and designer of all things.	Broussard, "A Rational Approach to God's Existence", 36-41. Kreeft & Tacelli, *Handbook of Christian Apologetics*, 47-88.
Comprehend the 'Five Ways' of St Thomas Aquinas.		Introduce the name and person of St Thomas Aquinas. Ask if any of the students have heard of him. Outline that he was an Italian Dominican Friar (Order of Preachers founded by St Dominic Guzman) who lived during the thirteenth century and has ever since been regarded by many as the greatest philosopher and theologian in the Catholic Church's history. Hand out to each student a copy of Activity Sheet 3, *The 'Five Ways' of St Thomas Aquinas.* Explain that these 'Five Ways' together present the 'God hypothesis' as a unified and reasonable intellectual concept. Ask the students to choose one of these 'Five Ways' and reflect on its reasonableness. Allow two students to present on their chosen 'Way', outline why they chose it, why they think it makes sense, and whether they think there may exist any flaw in St Thomas' reasoning.	Feser, *Aquinas*, 65-120.

| Reflect upon and analyse the conversion experience of a former atheist. | 13 mins | (iv) Introduce the students to the person of Antony Flew. Explain that he was one of Britain's foremost atheist philosophers for over fifty years, writing many scholarly works in support of atheism. However, in 2004 he shocked the academic world by announcing his conversion to belief in an intelligent Creator, stating he was simply "following where the evidence leads." The evidence related to recent scientific discoveries that made the argument of 'intelligent design' far stronger than he originally thought. ('Intelligent Design' will be explored in more detail in a later lesson).

Show the students the following YouTube video, *Antony Flew's Conversion from Atheism* (5.09 minutes).

After viewing the video, ask students to answer the following questions:

- *What were two views Antony Flew held about life and the universe before his conversion?*
- *Why did Flew change his position to theism? How weighty was the evidence relating to DNA, complexity?*
- *How significant do you think is Flew's conversion? Why?*

Allow two-three minutes for student answers.

Finally, mention that Antony Flew did not convert to Christianity but to the God of Aristotle, that is, a God that did not interfere in the world and who provides no afterlife or resurrection. This is called *deism*. Nevertheless, Antony Flew was still sincerely journeying to the fullness of truth when he died in 2010. | Flew, *There Is ~~NOT~~ A God* ("Where the Evidence Leads"), 31-64. |
| | 3 mins | **Lesson Closure**:

Remind the students that belief in God is very reasonable and supported by strong philosophical foundations. Furthermore, while some 'new atheists' engage in mockery and ridicule of believers, modern scientific discoveries are providing additional arguments in support of belief in God. Together, philosophical and scientific arguments are the best initial arguments to present to atheists/agnostics and together propose the 'God hypothesis' as a unified and reasonable intellectual concept. | |

		Transition: Homework: Complete Activity Sheet 4, *The 'Five Ways' – Filling the Gaps.* Fill in the blank spaces from the words in the Word Bank.	
		Resources: - Broussard, Karlo. "A Rational Approach to God's Existence." *Catholic Answers* (March-April 2015): 36-41. - Broussard, Karlo. "Why Science Can't Do Away With God." *Catholic Answers* (March-April 2018): 34-38. - Broussard, Karlo. "Hey, God, Where Are You?: Explaining the Problem of Divine Hiddenness." *Catholic Answers* (July-August 2018): 25-29. - Duggan, G. H. *Beyond Reasonable Doubt.* Boston, MA: St Paul Books & Media, 1987, 55-77. - Feser, Edward. *The Last Superstition.* South Bend, Indiana: St Augustine's Press, 2008. - Feser, Edward. *Aquinas.* Oxford: One World, 2009, 65-120. - Flew, Anthony. *There Is ~~NOT~~ A God.* New York: HarperOne, 2008, 31-64. - Hahn, Scott & Benjamin Wiker. *Answering the New Atheism: Dismantling Dawkins' Case Against God.* Steubenville, Ohio: Emmaus Road Publishing, 2008. - Kreeft, Peter & Ronald K. Tacelli. *Handbook of Christian Apologetics: Hundreds of Answers to Crucial Questions.* Downers Grove: IVP Academic, 1994, 47-88. - Madrid, Patrick & Kenneth Hensley. *The Godless Delusion: A Catholic Challenge to Modern Atheism.* Huntington, Indiana: Our Sunday Visitor Publishing, 2010. - *Catechism of the Catholic Church.* Libreria Editrice Vaticana: St Pauls, 1994, paras. 2123-2134. - YOUCAT (*Youth Catechism of the Catholic Church*). San Francisco, Ignatius Press, 2010, para. 357. - Website: Horn, Trent. "How to Respond to the New Atheism." https://www.catholic.com/magazine/print-edition/how-to-respond-to-the-new-atheism. - YouTube: Flew, Antony. "Antony Flew's Conversion from Atheism." https://www.youtube.com/watch?v=MbKsIAib5YM&t=34s.	

LESSON EVALUATION (to be completed AFTER the lesson)

Assessment of lesson objectives and suggestions for improvement:
Teacher self-reflection and self-evaluation:
[OFFICIAL USE ONLY] Comments by teacher supervisor:

Lesson 3: The Nature of God

LESSON ORGANISATION

Year Level: Date: Time: Duration: Room:

Quote:
"*God loves each of us as if there were only one of us*" – St Augustine of Hippo.

Prayer:
Come, Holy Spirit, fill the hearts of your faithful and enkindle in them the fire of your love.

V. Send forth your Spirit and they shall be created.
R. And you shall renew the face of the earth.

Let us pray.
O God, who by the light of the Holy Spirit, did instruct the hearts of the faithful, grant us in the same Spirit to be truly wise and ever to rejoice in his consolation.
Through Christ our Lord. Amen.

Lesson Outcomes:

As a result of this lesson, students will be able to:

- Understand the many claims made by 'new atheists' that the Judeo-Christian God is a hidden, uncaring 'moral monster.'
- Examine the validity of the interpretations of the Old Testament made by 'new atheists.'
- Propose an alternate understanding of the Old Testament as the beginning of a progressive revelation of God's nature culminating in the life and teachings of Jesus Christ.
- Demonstrate how God possesses a personal solicitude for humanity and all creation.
- Recognise how God's love climaxes in the incarnation, wherein the "Word became flesh and dwelt among us" (John 1:14).

Activity Sheets:

Activity Sheet 5, *The 'God' of Richard Dawkins.*
Activity Sheet 6, *The Human Face of God.*

LESSON DELIVERY

Outcome	Time	Motivation and Introduction:	Resources/ References
Understand the many claims made by 'new atheists' that the Judeo-Christian God is a hidden, uncaring 'moral monster.'	7 mins	Welcome and settle the students. Prayer to the Holy Spirit (or other suitable prayer). Tell the students that today we will be looking at the nature of God, namely, whether the God of Judeo-Christianity is really good or rather a "moral monster" as claimed by the 'new atheists.' Ask the students to reflect for a couple of minutes on the following questions (Show on a PowerPoint slide): *Have you ever wondered why God doesn't reveal himself for all to see? If God really cares, why does he not intervene to stop bad things happening in the world? The God of the Old Testament on occasions seems brutal and harsh. Is he the same as the God of the New Testament?* Take two-three responses. Explain to the students that the Judeo-Christian God is best understood when we look at the Old and New Testaments together as one complete progressive revelation culminating in Jesus Christ, rather than simply looking at individual Old Testament passages/ events and interpreting them in isolation apart from the 'big picture' context. **Lesson Steps**	O'Neil & Black, *The Essential Moral Handbook: A Guide to Catholic Living*, 13-22.
Understand the many claims made by 'new atheists' that the Judeo-Christian God is a hidden, uncaring 'moral monster.' Examine the validity of the interpretations of the Old Testament made by 'new atheists.'	15 mins	(i) Remind the students that most people still believe that God is a God of love (1 John 4:8). But not all people see it that way anymore, especially modern 'new atheists.' Even though 'new atheists' do not believe in God, when they look at the Bible, especially the Old Testament, they claim to see a God who is not so loving. On a PowerPoint slide, show the students the following quotes under the heading, *The God of the New Atheists*. Inform the students that these quotes come from the writings of some of the most famous new atheists: - *"A good God would show himself to the world, not remain hidden and uncaring"* – John Schellenberg. - *"God is a 'moral monster' who allows evil and suffering in the world"* – Steven Weinberg.	Copan, *Is God a Moral Monster? Making Sense of the Old Testament God*, 20-23.

		- *"God is a 'brutal judge' who demands the stoning of people to death"* – Sam Harris. - *"God is a 'beastly character' and a 'gory father' who sanctions slavery, the inferiority of women and who demands human sacrifice"* – Christopher Hitchens. After reading through and briefly explaining the above quotes, hand out Activity Sheet 5, *The 'God' of Richard Dawkins*. This sheet contains a summarised version of a quote by the world's most popular new atheist from his book, *The God Delusion* (31):  *"The God of the Old Testament is arguably the most unpleasant character in all fiction: jealous and proud of it; a petty, unjust, unforgiving control-freak; a vindictive, bloodthirsty ethnic cleanser ..."* Ask the students to write a one-paragraph response to Richard Dawkins answering the following questions: *Do you think this is fair portrayal of God? Can the same things be said about the God of the New Testament?* Take two student responses.	
Understand the many claims made by 'new atheists' that the Judeo-Christian God is a hidden, uncaring 'moral monster.'	7 mins	(ii) Ask the students the following question, *In what ways has God revealed himself?* Invite an open class discussion. Answers may include: - Through nature. - As fire and cloud (as in the case of Moses). - Through apparitions of angels (as in the case of Abraham, Jacob, Mary). - Through the Old Testament prophets. - Through the Church and the sacraments, etc. - Through saints and miracle workers. The students may have some additional ideas to the above. Ask them to write down all responses. Then inform them that God's so-called 'hiddenness' has an important reason, namely, to enable us to live by faith. To live by faith is more pleasing in the eyes of God. As Jesus said himself, *"... you believed because you have seen me? Blessed are those who have not seen and yet believe"* (John 20:29).	Broussard, "Hey, God, Where Are You?", 25-29.

| Propose an alternate understanding of the Old Testament as the beginning of a progressive revelation of God's nature culminating in the life and teachings of Jesus Christ. | 8 mins | (iii) Ask the students the following question: *How, then, are we to understand some of the difficult things we read about God in the Old Testament, including violence, wars, massacres, etc?* Take time to hear student responses.

Explain to the students that even though it was not perfect, the Old Testament was a great improvement upon the contemporary barbarism. Furthermore, it should not be viewed alone but as part of a 'grand narrative' wherein God seeks to be reconciled with a fallen humanity. This will ultimately be achieved through the incarnation, atonement and resurrection of Jesus Christ (define these technical terms). To enable the incarnation to occur, a people had to be created and formed. These were the Hebrews. They were formed during ancient and barbaric times, being surrounded by hostile peoples and kingdoms that often sought their enslavement or destruction. For the Hebrews/Jews to survive and remain faithful over the centuries God commanded or tolerated certain actions/events which from the Christian perspective are not ideal, all for the sake of avoiding even greater evils (e.g., the extinction or apostasy of the Hebrews/Jews). This also involved the infliction of 'tough love' upon the Hebrews/Jews themselves, either to discipline and give them a distinct identity or to call them back to faithfulness with God after straying from him. We call this the 'divine pedagogy' (or 'teaching method').

The analogy is with parents and small children. Parents need, at first, to be tough with their infant children to keep them on the 'straight and narrow' and protect them. As the children grow older, the parents teach and protect them differently, using reason more than discipline. The 'higher pedagogy' with God's children begins with the coming of Jesus Christ. By the first century AD, the Jews (and the rest of the world) were in a better position to receive a higher and more perfect law, as well as the grace to live out that higher teaching. Examples of Jesus' higher teachings include loving one's enemy and the abolition of divorce and revenge. It is Jesus Christ, through his life and teachings, who brings perfection and displays the 'human face of God.' | Markos, *Apologetics for the Twenty-First Century*, 222-224.

Siniscalchi, *Retrieving Apologetics*, 215-218. |

Demonstrate how God possesses a personal solicitude for humanity and all creation.	10 mins	(iv) Exercise: Brainstorm with the students about teachings of Jesus Christ that reveal God as intimate, loving and forgiving. Answers may include, *Love your enemy, the Parable of the Lost Sheep, the Parable of the Good Shepherd, the Parable of the Good Samaritan.* Hand out Activity Sheet 6, *The Human Face of God*. Ask the students to quietly read the parable of the Prodigal Son from Luke 15:11-24 and then answer the following questions: - *Which person in this parable represents God?* - *What does this parable tell us about the type of relationship God wishes to have with us?* - *How do we know from this parable that God is always caring and never gives up on us?* - *The fact that the father "ran" towards his son when he saw him returning tells us what about the nature of God?* Take time to listen to student feedback.	O'Neil & Black, *The Essential Moral Handbook: A Guide to Catholic Living*, 7-11.
Recognise how God's love climaxes in the incarnation, wherein the "Word became flesh and dwelt among us" (John 1:14).	7 mins	(v) Inform the students that there is one event wherein God has simultaneously fully revealed himself, come intimately close to us, and shown his absolute love for us. What could this event be? After taking some student answers, tell the class that this event is the *incarnation*. What does this word mean? It means 'taking on flesh.' More specifically, it is when the "Word became flesh" (John 1:14), that is, when God became man in the person of Jesus Christ. Ask the students to write down the following: *"Fully revealed"*: Through the incarnation, we see God as a God who is "meek and humble of heart" (Matt. 11:29). *"Intimately close"*: Through the incarnation, we see a God who is not distant but a God who yearns to "dwell among us" (John 1:14). *"Absolute love"*: Through the incarnation, we see a God who out of unconditional love is willing to "lay down his life for his friends" on the Cross (John 15:13).	Schreck, *Catholic and Christian*, 7-9.

	3 mins	**Lesson Closure**:

A complete understanding of the nature of God comes only through viewing both the Old and New Testaments together as one 'grand narrative', the great rescue story initiated by God to save his children from sin. This 'rescue' involves forming and protecting a chosen people under very difficult circumstances over a long period of time and climaxes in the incarnation, when God becomes one of us and sacrifices all on the Cross out of unconditional love for us. It is the incarnation which reveals God as he truly is, the loving Father who yearns to be with us and restore us as his friends and children once more.

Transition:

Homework: Read the Gospel of John, chapter 1, verses 1-14. What do these verses reveal about God's closeness to us? How are we transformed by God becoming man in Jesus Christ? (1 paragraph). | |
| | | **Resources**:
- Broussard, Karlo. "Hey, God, Where Are You?: Explaining the Problem of Divine Hiddenness." *Catholic Answers* (July-August 2018): 25-29.
- Copan, Paul. *Is God a Moral Monster? Making Sense of the Old Testament God* (Grand Rapids, MI: Baker Books, 2011), 20-23.
- Markos, Louis. *Apologetics for the Twenty-First Century.* Wheaton, Illinois: Crossway, 2010, 222-224.
- O'Neil, Kevin J. & Peter Black. *The Essential Moral Handbook: A Guide to Catholic Living.* Liguori, Missouri: Liguori, 2004, 13-22.
- Schreck, Alan. *Catholic and Christian: An Explanation of Commonly Misunderstood Catholic Beliefs.* Cincinnati, Ohio: Servant Books, 2004, 7-9.
- Siniscalchi, Glenn B. *Retrieving Apologetics.* Eugene: Pickwick Publications, 2016, 215-218.
- *Catechism of the Catholic Church.* Libreria Editrice Vaticana: St Pauls, 1994, paras. 458, 516, 604, 776, 2658.
- YOUCAT (*Youth Catechism of the Catholic Church*). San Francisco, Ignatius Press, 2010, paras. 9, 33.
- Website: Catholic Answers: Broussard, Karlo. "Is God a Moral Monster?" https://www.catholic.com/qa/is-god-a-monster.
- YouTube: Peter Kreeft, "Is God a Moral Monster?" https://www.youtube.com/watch?v=cr25VA5RGKg. | |

LESSON EVALUATION (to be completed AFTER the lesson)

Assessment of lesson objectives and suggestions for improvement:
Teacher self-reflection and self-evaluation:
[OFFICIAL USE ONLY] Comments by teacher supervisor:

Lesson 4: The Problem of Evil and Suffering

LESSON ORGANISATION

Year Level: Date: Time: Duration: Room:

Quote:
"God Almighty would in no way permit evil in his works were he not so omnipotent and good that even out of evil he could work good" – St Augustine of Hippo.

Prayer:
Come, Holy Spirit, fill the hearts of your faithful and enkindle in them the fire of your love.

V. Send forth your Spirit and they shall be created.
R. And you shall renew the face of the earth.

Let us pray.
O God, who by the light of the Holy Spirit, did instruct the hearts of the faithful, grant us in the same Spirit to be truly wise and ever to rejoice in his consolation.
Through Christ our Lord. Amen.

Lesson Outcomes:

As a result of this lesson, students will be able to:

- Define evil and suffering as the absence of due good.
- Understand the origins of evil and suffering in the misuse of human freedom.
- Respond to atheist arguments based on evil and suffering against the existence of God.
- Appreciate that God only permits evil and suffering for the certainty of a greater good.
- Reflect on how humans can derive spiritual benefit from evil and suffering.
- Contextualise the problem of evil and suffering in the light of Christian teaching on the resurrection and eternal life.

Activity Sheets:

Activity Sheet 7, *Types of Evil and Suffering*.
Activity Sheet 8, *The Sufferings of Job*.

LESSON DELIVERY

Outcome	Time	Motivation and Introduction:	Resources/ References
	7 mins	Welcome and settle the students. Prayer to the Holy Spirit (or other suitable prayer). Tell the students that today we will be looking at the problem of evil and suffering and how it is the so-called 'rock of atheism.' Ask the students the following questions: *Have you ever thought about the existence of evil and suffering? How might the existence of evil and suffering be a 'problem' for belief in God? Have you ever questioned God about why he allows evil and suffering?* Take two-three responses. Explain to the students that the argument known as the 'rock of atheism' proceeds as follows: (a) The Judeo-Christian God is meant to be all-knowing, all-powerful and perfectly good. (b) If God were all-knowing, all-powerful and perfectly good he could and would prevent all evil and suffering. (c) Yet, evil and suffering exist in the world. (d) Therefore, an all-knowing, all-powerful and perfectly good God does not exist. Challenge: How can you respond to this reasoning? **Lesson Steps**	Walsh, *Answering the New Atheists: How Science Points to God and to the Benefits of Christianity*, 149-151.
Define evil and suffering as the absence of due good. Understand the origins of evil and suffering in the misuse of human freedom.	15 mins	(i) The first step in our response to the 'rock of atheism' is to help the students understand that evil and suffering are not things created by God but result from the absence of something good that should exist. Lead the students to complete the following exercise, identifying the absent good in each instance: <u>Evil</u> <u>Absent Good</u> Hate (Answer: Love) Greed (Answer: Generosity) Impatience (Answer: Patience) Dishonesty (Answer: Honesty)	Flader, *Question Time: 150 Questions and Answers on the Catholic Faith*, 6-7. Horn, *Why We're Catholic: Our Reasons for Faith, Hope, and Love*, 31-42.

| | | Teachers may wish to add a couple of other examples to the above.

Next, address the following question: *If evil and suffering are not things created by God, then where do they originate from?*

Before answering this question, take two-three responses from the students.

Begin your answer by acknowledging the question's difficulty, then proceed to explain that when God first created the world and humanity there was no evil and suffering; all was peace, harmony and happiness in Paradise. Evil and suffering only entered the world because of humanity's misuse of freedom – or sin. Following sin came the rupture of our relationship with God, disorder in human relationships, subjection to nature, and the loss of gifts that protected us from pain, sickness, suffering, death, etc.

All examples of evil and suffering fall under one of two categories, *moral* or *physical*. Moral evils are evils directly resulting from human actions/neglect such as lying, theft, murder, war; physical evils are evils arising from events beyond human control, such as earthquakes, cyclones, famine, etc.

Exercise: Hand out Activity Sheet 7, *Types of Evil and Suffering*. Ask the students to complete the two columns by listing examples of moral and natural evils they are aware of. | Duggan, *Beyond Reasonable Doubt*, 78-80. |
|---|---|---|---|
| Respond to atheist arguments based on evil and suffering against the existence of God. | 10 mins | (ii) Guided class discussion: Ask the students to respond to the following statement: *"There can be no all-loving, all-powerful and good God because if there were, he would prevent all evil and suffering from occurring in the first place."*

As students provide their responses, summarise their main points – for or against – in two columns on the whiteboard. Then show them the following YouTube video, *Evil, Pain & Suffering = NO GOD: Why Doesn't God STOP All Evil, Pain & Suffering?* by Jon Oleksiuk (3.11 minutes).  | |

		Re-emphasise the main argument arising from the above video, namely, that for God to prevent the possibility of all moral evil he would need to totally take away all human freedom. This would result in the abolition of humanity itself, for then humans would be reduced to the level of pre-programmed robots. *To totally take away human freedom would be a greater evil than allowing human freedom to remain and be free to choose between good and evil.* Rather than abolishing human freedom, God works with it through actual grace to enable humans to freely do good and avoid evil. In the end, humans are solely responsible for their free choices.	
Appreciate that God only permits evil and suffering for the certainty of a greater good. Reflect on how humans can derive spiritual benefit from evil and suffering.	15 mins	(iii) Highlight to the students that evil and suffering – whether from human or natural sources – invariably inflicts upon human beings much pain. The question that again arises is why a good God would allow his children to endure any level of pain if he really loves them. Explain that the 'problem of pain' is mysterious, but that God allows pain for two reasons, namely: - For our spiritual benefit; - For the certainty of a greater good. Provide the students with the following quote from C. S. Lewis that illustrates the first of these two points: *"Everyone has noticed how hard it is to turn our thoughts to God when everything is going well with us. We 'have all we want' is a terrible saying when 'all' does not include God. We find God in the interruptions"* (*The Problem of Pain*, 94). Ask the students: *What is C. S. Lewis trying to say here? What important benefit can he see arising from pain?* Take time to hear student responses. The idea of a 'greater good' can be hard to grasp because in certain circumstances it is very difficult to identify what that 'greater good' is. Hand out Activity Sheet 8, *The Sufferings of Job*. Ask the students to silently read the story of Job and answer the following questions: 1. List the pains endured by Job. 2. What spiritual benefit does Job gain from his pains?	Feser, *The Last Superstition*, 161-162. Lewis, *The Problem of Pain*, 94.

Contextualise the problem of evil and suffering in the light of Christian teaching on the resurrection and eternal life.	5 mins	3. What greater good(s) does Job eventually gain from his faithful endurance of pain? Take time to hear student responses and list them in point form on the whiteboard. (v) Invite the students to reflect on the following statement from the Nicene Creed: *"I look forward to the resurrection of the dead and the life of the world to come."* Challenge the students to identify how this article of faith proposes a solution to the problem of evil and suffering and God's goodness. Allow one-two minutes of open classroom discussion before providing the following answer: Belief in the resurrection and eternal life tells us that evil and suffering does not have the final say. Christ, by his resurrection, has conquered sin and all its consequences. We, by being faithful followers of Christ, will also one day rise again and enter into a new life where tears, mourning and death are no more (Rev. 21:4). The evil and suffering that entered into the world through our sin will only ever be temporary. On the other hand, God's solution to evil and suffering through the resurrection will be permanent. This is the ultimate proof of God's goodness.	Groothuis, *Christian Apologetics*, 644-646. Kreeft & Tacelli, *Handbook of Christian Apologetics*, 143-144.
	3 mins	**Lesson Closure:** Recall that evil and suffering are not things created by God but result from the absence of goodness that should exist. The moral/physical evils and sufferings that afflict humanity all have their origins in the misuse of human freedom, namely, sin. God merely tolerates evil. The goodness of God is not contradicted by the existence of evil and suffering; rather, God manifests his goodness in the face of evil and suffering by drawing a greater good from them and by sending Jesus Christ who, by his life, death and resurrection, ultimately conquers all the consequences of sin. **Transition:** Homework: Draw up a list of everyday sufferings you may endure/encounter. Devise a prayer offering up these sufferings to God for specific private intentions.	

Resources:
- Duggan, G. H. *Beyond Reasonable Doubt.* Boston, MA: St Paul Books & Media, 1987, 78-80.
- Feser, Edward. *The Last Superstition.* South Bend, Indiana: St Augustine's Press, 2008, 161-162.
- Flader, John. *Question Time: 150 Questions and Answers on the Catholic Faith.* Ballan, Vic.: Connor Court Publishing, 2008, 6-7.
- Groothuis, Douglas. *Christian Apologetics: A Comprehensive Case for Biblical Faith.* Downers Grove, Il.: InterVarsity Press, 2011, 614-646.
- Horn, Trent. *Why We're Catholic: Our Reasons for Faith, Hope, and Love.* El Cajon: Catholic Answers Press, 2017, 31-42.
- Kreeft, Peter & Ronald K. Tacelli. *Handbook of Christian Apologetics: Hundreds of Answers to Crucial Questions.* Downers Grove: IVP Academic, 1994, 120-146.
- Lewis, C. S. *The Problem of Pain.* London: Harper Collins Publishers, 1940, 94-96.
- Walsh, Anthony. *Answering the New Atheists: How Science Points to God and to the Benefits of Christianity.* Wilmington, Delaware: Vernon Press, 2018, 149-151.
- *Catechism of the Catholic Church.* Libreria Editrice Vaticana: St Pauls, 1994, paras. 309, 312, 313, 385, 403, 410.
- YOUCAT (*Youth Catechism of the Catholic Church*). San Francisco, Ignatius Press, 2010, paras. 285-296.
- Website: Fradd, Matthew. "The Problem of Evil." https://www.catholic.com/magazine/online-edition/the-problem-of-evil.
- YouTube: Oleksiuk, John. "Evil, Pain & Suffering = NO GOD: Why Doesn't God STOP All Evil, Pain & Suffering?" https://www.youtube.com/watch?v=cv85tvudi7Y.

LESSON EVALUATION (to be completed AFTER the lesson)

Assessment of lesson objectives and suggestions for improvement:
Teacher self-reflection and self-evaluation:
[OFFICIAL USE ONLY] Comments by teacher supervisor:

"Always Be Prepared ..." – A 'New Apologetics' Course for Catholic Secondary Schools

Lesson 5: Is Religion Toxic and the Cause of Evil?

LESSON ORGANISATION

Year Level: ____ Date: ____ Time: ____ Duration: ____ Room: ____

Quote:
"I did once say that to me art and the saints are the greatest apologetics for our faith" – Pope Benedict XVI.

Prayer:
Come, Holy Spirit, fill the hearts of your faithful and enkindle in them the fire of your love.

V. Send forth your Spirit and they shall be created.
R. And you shall renew the face of the earth.

Let us pray.
O God, who by the light of the Holy Spirit, did instruct the hearts of the faithful, grant us in the same Spirit to be truly wise and ever to rejoice in his consolation.
Through Christ our Lord. Amen.

Lesson Outcomes:

As a result of this lesson, students will be able to:

- Understand the allegations made against Catholicism/Christianity as toxic and the cause of evil.
- Explore Catholic/Christian teachings as to their moral/ethical nature, or otherwise.
- Identify individual examples of great Catholic/Christian religious figures and intellects.
- Appreciate Catholicism's/Christianity's positive contribution to the well-being and advancement of humanity and the world.
- Distinguish between evils occasioned in the name of God/Catholicism and the formal teachings/apologies/pronouncements of the Catholic Church.

Activity Sheets:

Activity Sheet 9, *Saints and Scholars.*
Activity Sheet 10, *Great Beauty and Service.*
Activity Sheet 11, *Pope Says Sorry for Sins of Church.*

LESSON DELIVERY

Outcome	Time	Motivation and Introduction:	Resources/ References
Understand the allegations made against Catholicism/ Christianity as toxic and the cause of evil.	7 mins	Welcome and settle the students. Prayer to the Holy Spirit (or other suitable prayer). Tell the students that today we will be looking at the accusation that religion, Catholicism/Christianity in particular, is 'toxic' and a cause of evil. This accusation has become more widespread since the '9/11' terrorist attacks in 2001. Provide the students with the following quote as an example of such an allegation: *"Christians have been guilty of abusing, oppressing, enslaving, insulting, tormenting, torturing and killing people in the name of God for centuries, all based on their own theological reading of the Bible"* – Sam Harris, *Letter to a Christian Nation* (27). Ask the students what allegations they have heard/are aware of against the Catholic Church/Christianity re being the cause of evil, etc. Take student answers and list them on the whiteboard. Answers may include: - Violence. - Wars/crusades. - Inquisitions. - Slavery. - Intolerance/bigotry. - Oppression of women. - Sexual abuse crisis. - Irrational/anti-science. Explain to the students that Catholics/Christians have made several serious errors/mistakes in the past but just to focus on these errors, etc., without acknowledging the overall positive contribution of Catholicism/Christianity to society and the world over the centuries is both unhistorical and unjust. **Lesson Steps**	Graham, *Apologetics Without Apology: Speaking of God in a World Troubled by Religion*, 107-109. Siniscalchi, *Retrieving Apologetics*, 215-227.
Explore Catholic/Christian teachings as to their moral/ ethical nature, or otherwise.	10 mins	(i) A response to the allegation that Catholicism/Christianity is toxic/a cause of evil needs to begin with an exploration of its core moral/ethical teachings. This will afford the most accurate basis on which to judge its value, whether positive or negative.	*Catechism of the Catholic Church*, Paras. 1789, 1971, 2055, 2058.

		Ask the students to create a chart with the heading *Principal Christian Moral and Ethical Teachings*. Brainstorm with the students about the core moral/ethical teachings that characterise Christianity. Provide the students with the first example of such teachings, namely, the Ten Commandments. Other examples of moral/ ethical teachings include: - The Sermon on the Mount, e.g., *"Love your enemies and pray for those who persecute you"* (Matt. 6:44). - The Beatitudes, e.g., *"Blessed are the peace makers …"* (Matt. 5:3-12). - The 'Golden Rule' – *"Do to others as you would have them do to you"* (Luke 6:31). - The Great Commandment – *"Love one another as I have loved you"* (John 13:34). After assisting students to complete the above chart, explain that evils committed by Christians over the centuries were in direct contradiction to Christian moral/ethical teachings, not inspired or caused by any of them.	YOUCAT (*Youth Catechism of the Catholic Church*), paras. 283, 349.
Identify individual examples of great Catholic/Christian religious figures and intellects.	10 mins	(ii) Inform the students that the positive contribution of Catholicism/Christianity to the world and humanity over twenty centuries has been enormous; however, it is not as well known as it ought to be. While atheism portrays religion and religious people as either corrupt, ignorant or superstitious, there are countless examples of believers who have been outstanding both in their holiness and intellectual contribution to the world. Exercise: Hand out Activity Sheet 9, *Saints and Scholars*. Assist the students to match the name of the Catholic saint/scholar in Column A with the achievement in Column B. The first one is done to help start off the students.	Benedictine Monks of St Augustine's Abbey, *The Book of Saints*.
Appreciate Catholicism's/ Christianity's positive contribution to the well-being and advancement of humanity and the world.	10 mins	(iii) Explain to the students that in addition to producing great saints and scholars, Catholicism/Christianity has inspired many other eminent benefits for humanity in the following areas: - Education; health care; art; architecture; music. Produce and show the students a PowerPoint presentation that highlights the achievements of Catholicism/Christianity in the above areas. Spend five-seven minutes outlining the specifics of	Borngässer and Toman, *Cathedrals and Churches of Europe*. Manion and Vines, *Illuminated Manuscripts in Australian Collections*.

		these achievements. See Activity Sheet 10, *Great Beauty and Service* for material to assist in the production of the PowerPoint presentation. Other images may be added.	
Distinguish between evils occasioned in the name of God/ Catholicism and formal teachings/ apologies/ pronouncements of the Catholic Church.	15 mins	(iv) Refer students back to the argument that evils committed by Christians over the centuries were in direct contradiction to Christian moral/ethical teachings, not inspired or caused by any of them. Afterwards, inform the students that in recent decades the Church has admitted many of these evils and issued formal apologies for such. During the pontificate of Pope St John Paul II (1978-2005) many such apologies were made. Hand out to each student a copy of Activity Sheet 11, *Pope Says Sorry for Sins of Church*. Ask students to quietly read through the newspaper article and then lead them through an open class discussion based on the following questions: (a) What was the year of St John Paul II's apology? Why do you think he chose to do this momentous act in that year? (b) What sins did St John Paul II specifically ask forgiveness for? (c) What is the significance of asking for forgiveness for sins "committed in the service of truth"? How could truth have been better served? (d) Do you think St John Paul II's apology improved the image of the Catholic Church? Why/Why not? In conclusion, the classroom teacher may note how millions of Catholics/Christians, particularly in the twentieth century, were victims of wars and persecutions inspired by atheistic ideologies, e.g., Communism/Nazism, receiving no apology for their sufferings.	Rory Carroll, "Pope Says Sorry for Sins of Church."
	3 mins	**Lesson Closure**: Remind the students that in judging the goodness or otherwise of Catholicism/Christianity it should be done by reference to the moral and ethical teachings of Jesus Christ, rather than by the failings of various followers over the centuries. Any assessment should also include a willingness to acknowledge its countless positive contributions to humanity made by innumerable saints and scholars in all sorts of fields. Where evils were perpetrated, these should be honestly and frankly acknowledged and forgiveness asked for, as Pope St John Paul II did over one hundred times during his pontificate. Christians, in turn, have also often suffered unjustly.	

		Transition: Homework: Choose one of the persons listed in Column A from Activity Sheet 9 (*Saints and Scholars*) and write 200 words about their contributions to the Church, the world, or humanity.	
		Resources:<ul><li>Benedictine Monks of St Augustine's Abbey, Ramsgate. *The Book of Saints*. London: A&C Black, 1989.</li><li>Borngässer, Barbara and Rolf Toman. *Cathedrals and Churches of Europe*. Potsdam: H.F. Ullmann Publishing, 2015.</li><li>Carroll, Rory. "Pope Says Sorry for Sins of Church." https://www.theguardian.com/world/2000/mar/13/catholicism.religion.</li><li>Graham, Elaine. *Apologetics Without Apology: Speaking of God in a World Troubled by Religion.* Eugene: Cascade Books, 2017, 107-109.</li><li>Manion, Margaret M. and Vera F. Vines. *Illuminated Manuscripts in Australian Collections.* Melbourne: Thames and Hudson, 1984.</li><li>Siniscalchi, Glenn B. *Retrieving Apologetics*. Eugene: Pickwick Publications, 2016, 215-227.</li><li>*Catechism of the Catholic Church*. Libreria Editrice Vaticana: St Pauls, 1994, paras. 1789, 1971, 2055, 2058.</li><li>YOUCAT (*Youth Catechism of the Catholic Church*). San Francisco, Ignatius Press, 2010, paras. 283, 349.</li><li>Lucie-Smith, Fr Alexander. "Does Catholicism cause wars? Not if it is true Catholicism." https://catholicherald.co.uk/commentandblogs/2013/04/25/does-catholicism-cause-wars-not-if-it-is-true-catholicism/.</li><li>YouTube: Catholic News Service, "Pope apologizes for past sins of Christians." https://www.youtube.com/watch?v=x7fjyq6cFtg.</li></ul>	

LESSON EVALUATION (to be completed AFTER the lesson)

Assessment of lesson objectives and suggestions for improvement:
Teacher self-reflection and self-evaluation:
[OFFICIAL USE ONLY] Comments by teacher supervisor:

"Always Be Prepared …" – A 'New Apologetics' Course for Catholic Secondary Schools

Lesson 6: <u>Creation and Evolution</u>

LESSON ORGANISATION

Year Level: Date: Time: Duration: Room:

Quote:
"Faith is like a bright ray of sunlight. It enables us to see God in all things as well as all things in God" – St Francis de Sales.

Prayer:
Come, Holy Spirit, fill the hearts of your faithful and enkindle in them the fire of your love.

V. Send forth your Spirit and they shall be created.
R. And you shall renew the face of the earth.

Let us pray.
O God, who by the light of the Holy Spirit, did instruct the hearts of the faithful, grant us in the same Spirit to be truly wise and ever to rejoice in his consolation.
Through Christ our Lord. Amen.

Lesson Outcomes:

As a result of this lesson, students will be able to:

- Appreciate the compatibility of science and the Genesis account of creation.
- Evaluate and understand scientific evidence pointing to the universe having a beginning.
- Contrast the various arguments for how and why the universe had a beginning.
- Identify evidence pointing to a rational designer for the universe.
- Distinguish and evaluate the various arguments for and against the competing views of 'natural selection' versus 'punctuated equilibrium.'

Activity Sheets:

Activity Sheet 12, *Fr George Lemaître and the 'Big Bang.'*
Activity Sheet 13, *The Anthropic Principle.*
Activity Sheet 14, *The 'Cambrian Explosion.'*

LESSON DELIVERY

Outcome	Time	Motivation and Introduction:	Resources/ References
Appreciate the compatibility of science and the Genesis account of creation.	12 mins	Welcome and settle the students. Prayer to the Holy Spirit (or other suitable prayer). Tell the students that today we will look at various theories/ opinions regarding the origin of the universe and life. Outline to the students that many people today believe that science and religion are incompatible and offer two competing and irreconcilable views concerning the origin of the universe and life. On the one hand, atheistic evolutionists assert that the universe came into existence by itself with the 'Big Bang' 13.8 billion years ago and life came later through random chance processes and natural selection. In contrast, 'creationist' Christians insist that according to the book of Genesis the universe and life are only 6,000 years old, that they were created immediately by God over a six-day period, and that evolution through natural selection is unbiblical and impossible. Ask the students the following question: *Is there perhaps a third, alternate way, to the above two viewpoints?* Take one or two answers. Show the students the following YouTube video, *Creation and Evolution* by Catholic Central (6.51 minutes).  After viewing the video, ask the students to write down what they believe is the 'third way' for Catholics re the origin of the universe and life. (Answer: Genesis is not to be read as a literal scientific history book but as a book that contains essential truths about God as the creator of the universe and first cause of all life and that evolution, if true, is a mechanism created by God to continue the development of the universe and life after the initial creation.)	Holden & Pinsent, *Apologia: Catholic Answers to Today's Questions*, 11-13.
Evaluate and understand scientific evidence pointing to the universe having a beginning.	10 mins	**Lesson Steps** (i) Inform the students that at the beginning of the 20th century it was the established science that the universe was eternal, meaning that it always existed, it had no beginning and was	Spitzer, *New Proofs for the Existence of God*, 13-23.

		unchanging (the 'Steady State Theory'). Having no beginning, therefore, it was not created by God or any other being. This was the position of the famous astronomer Prof. Fred Hoyle, an agnostic. This all began to change in 1927 when a Belgian Catholic priest by the name of Fr George Lemaître announced that the universe was expanding and had a definite calculable beginning from a single point, or 'singularity.' Hand out Activity Sheet 12, *Fr George Lemaître and the 'Big Bang.'* Choose students to read aloud about Fr Lemaître and his scientific contribution and answer the following questions: *What was the core discovery made by Fr Lemaître? Why do you think some scientists were initially hostile to his conclusions?*	Wiker, *The Catholic Church & Science*, 85-100.
Contrast the various arguments for how and why the universe had a beginning.	10 mins	(ii) Even though all scientists today believe that the universe had a beginning, there are radically different opinions as to the 'how' and 'why.' Read out the following statement from the famous scientist Stephen Hawking: *"Because there is a law such as gravity, the universe can and will create itself from nothing. Spontaneous creation is the reason there is something rather than nothing"* – The Grand Design (2010, 180). Stephen Hawking finds support for his view on 'spontaneous creation' from other scientists such as Lawrence Krauss, who believes in multiple universes (or 'Multiverse Theory'). Like Hawking, Krauss believes that universes can and always will spontaneously appear from nothing due to fluctuations in the so-called 'quantum vacuum.' Classroom discussion: Brainstorm with the class about the content of Hawking's statement. *What is Hawking trying to say? Is there any problem with what he is saying?* Conclude this discussion by introducing and explaining the *Kalam Cosmological Argument* (show on a PowerPoint slide): *Everything that begins to exist requires a cause for its beginning.* *The world began to exist.* *Therefore, the world had a cause for its beginning* (namely, God).	Robinson, *The Realist Guide to Religion and Science*, 374-380.

		In other words, something cannot come from nothing; only nothing comes from nothing (*ex nihilo nihil*).	
		On the other hand, Hawking and Krauss argue that everything comes from nothing: "Nothing is God and God is nothing." However, to say that something has power when it really does not is the essence of superstition. To say that nothingness possesses the power to create is the greatest superstition.	
Identify evidence pointing to a rational designer for the universe.	10 mins	(iii) Another argument on behalf of a universe created by a rational designer is the so-called 'anthropic principle' (from the Greek word *anthropos*, meaning human). According to this argument, the universe is so finely tuned that if any of its fundamental forces were differently calibrated, life as we know it would not exist. Looking at our universe, it gives the appearance that it was deliberately arranged by some super-intellect for human life (the 'Big Bloom'); otherwise, it came to be through a series of random events against the most incredible odds. Fred Hoyle himself once observed, *"A common-sense interpretation of the facts suggests that a super intellect has monkeyed with physics, as well as chemistry and biology, and that there are no blind forces worth speaking about in nature."*	Hahn & Wiker, *Answering the New Atheism*, 23-51. Horn, *Answering Atheism*, 147-176. Robinson, *The Realist Guide to Religion and Science*, 382-383. Wiker, *The Catholic Church & Science*, 89-91.
		Produce and show the students a PowerPoint presentation that highlights examples of 'anthropic coincidences.' Spend five-six minutes outlining the specifics of these coincidences. See Activity Sheet 13, *The Anthropic Principle* for material to assist in the production of this PowerPoint presentation. Highlight the odds against such coincidences occurring randomly in nature.	
		The counter-argument against the anthropic principle is the concept of 'multiverse' advocated by Lawrence Krauss. This is the belief in innumerable other universes each with their own peculiar settings. Our own universe happens to be one which by chance had the right settings for life.	
		Explain to the students, however, that the concept of the multiverse is beyond scientific observation, meaning there is and can never be any evidence for it. Furthermore, even if multiverse theory were true it still leaves unanswered the question of first causality, namely, how were all the universes created in the first place.	

Distinguish and evaluate the various arguments for and against the competing views of 'natural selection' versus 'punctuated equilibrium.'	12 mins	(iv) Allied to the theory of spontaneous creation is the Darwinian theory of evolution through natural selection. Explain to the students that, put simply, this involves one species developing into another superior species through chance random positive mutations over lengthy periods of time. Those creatures that develop superior characteristics due to positive mutations tend, through natural selection, to survive over those that do not ('survival of the fittest'), passing on the newly acquired traits to the next generation. Posit to the students that there are three options here: (a) Evolution replaces God as the cause and developer of life. (b) God is the first cause of all life and embeds in all life-forms the innate ability to develop and improve. (c) Evolution on a 'micro' scale is possible allowing for minor changes within a species but impossible on a 'macro' scale, that is, enabling one species to develop into a new superior species. It is important to inform the students that since Pope Pius XII in 1950 (*Humani Generis*) Catholics are free to believe either (b) or (c) above. Only atheistic evolution is 'off-limits.' For a theist, whether evolution is fact or fiction is more a philosophical or scientific question than a religious one. Case study: Return to the PowerPoint presentation. Show the students the slides relating to *The 'Cambrian Explosion.'* Spend five-six minutes outlining to students the concept of 'punctuated equilibrium' as a viable alternative to atheistic and theistic theories of evolution. See Activity Sheet 14 for material to assist in the production of these slides. Highlight how the sudden emergence of multiple life forms during the Cambrian Explosion challenges the Darwinian model of slow evolutionary change over long periods of time.	Meyer *et al*, *Explore Evolution*, 22-32. Purcell, *From Big Bang to Big Mystery*, 125-127. Robinson, *The Realist Guide to Religion and Science*, 457-462.
	3 mins	**Lesson Closure:** Remind the students that the universe and all life within it have their origins in God. God is the first cause of both. Nevertheless, he has embedded within the universe and all creatures an ability to develop and improve. 'Big Bang' and Darwinian evolution theories cannot replace God as the first cause of all things as they cannot	

explain why there was a beginning and how species suddenly appear complete in the fossil record. Nevertheless, 'Big Bang' theory supports the Christian notion of a created universe and micro-evolutionary changes within species is unquestionable. The 'Anthropic Principle' and 'Punctuated Equilibrium' are viable theories on behalf of a universe finely tuned for life by God and life being a product of God's direct creative activity.

Transition:

Homework: If macro-evolution (one species developing into another superior species through chance random positive mutations over lengthy periods of time) was eventually proven as undoubted science would that challenge your belief in God? Why/Why not? (1-2 paragraphs).

Resources:
- Hahn, Scott & Benjamin Wiker. *Answering the New Atheism: Dismantling Dawkins' Case Against God.* Steubenville, Ohio: Emmaus Road Publishing, 2008, 23-51.
- Holden, Marcus & Andrew Pinsent. *Apologia: Catholic Answers to Today's Questions.* London: Catholic Truth Society, 2010, 11-13.
- Horn, Trent. *Answering Atheism: How to Make the Case for God with Logic and Charity.* San Diego: Catholic Answers Press, 2013, 147-176.
- Meyer, Stephen, Paul Nelson, Jonathon Moneymaker, Scott Minnich & Ralph Seelke. *Explore Evolution.* Melbourne: Hill House Publishers, 2009, 22-32.
- Purcell, Brendan. *From Big Bang to Big Mystery: Human Origins in the Light of Creation and Evolution.* Dublin, Ireland: Veritas Publications, 2011, 125-127.
- Robinson, Paul. *The Realist Guide to Religion and Science.* Leominster, United Kingdom: Gracewing, 2018, 374-380.
- Spitzer, Robert J. *New Proofs for the Existence of God: Contributions of Contemporary Physics and Philosophy.* Grand Rapids, Michigan: Eerdmans Publishing Co., 2010, 13-23.
- Wiker, Benjamin. *The Catholic Church & Science: Answering the Questions, Exposing the Myths.* Charlotte, New Carolina: TAN Books and Publishers, 2011, 85-100.
- *Catechism of the Catholic Church.* Libreria Editrice Vaticana: St Pauls, 1994, paras. 282-324.
- YOUCAT (*Youth Catechism of the Catholic Church*). San Francisco, Ignatius Press, 2010, paras. 42, 43, 368, 444.

		<ul><li>Website: Catholic Answers. "Genesis and Creation." https://www.catholic.com/tract/creation-and-genesis.</li><li>YouTube: Catholic Central. "Creation and Evolution." https://www.youtube.com/watch?v=B_sE07heyy4.</li></ul>

LESSON EVALUATION (to be completed AFTER the lesson)

Assessment of lesson objectives and suggestions for improvement:
Teacher self-reflection and self-evaluation:
[OFFICIAL USE ONLY] Comments by teacher supervisor:

Lesson 7: The Origins of Humanity

LESSON ORGANISATION

Year Level: _____ Date: _____ Time: _____ Duration: _____ Room: _____

Quote:
"After God had created Adam, Adam experienced a strong sense of love, when God sent sleep over him. And God created a figure to love for the man out of his rib, and so the woman is the love of man" – St Hildegard of Bingen.

Prayer:
Come, Holy Spirit, fill the hearts of your faithful and enkindle in them the fire of your love.

V. Send forth your Spirit and they shall be created.
R. And you shall renew the face of the earth.

Let us pray.
O God, who by the light of the Holy Spirit, did instruct the hearts of the faithful, grant us in the same Spirit to be truly wise and ever to rejoice in his consolation.
Through Christ our Lord. Amen.

Lesson Outcomes:

As a result of this lesson, students will be able to:

- Contend for an historical Adam and Eve specially created by God from which all humans have their origin.
- Appreciate how modern genetics establishes the foundation and unity of the human family in one pair of original parents.
- Demonstrate how modern humans are unique creatures unconnected with previously existing or contemporary species.
- Advocate that the human soul, in contrast to the human body, cannot evolve due to its spiritual nature.

Activity Sheets:

Activity Sheet 15, *'African Adam' and 'Mitochondrial Eve.'*
Activity Sheet 16, *Adam and Eve: Evolved or Specially Created?*

LESSON DELIVERY

Outcome	Time	Motivation and Introduction:	Resources/ References
Contend for an historical Adam and Eve specially created by God from which all humans have their origin.	7 mins	Welcome and settle the students. Prayer to the Holy Spirit (or other suitable prayer). Tell the students that today we will be looking at the question of human origins. This is a highly controversial topic and one that is confusing for many Catholics, especially younger ones. This topic is highly controversial because most scientists today consider the biblical account of Adam and Eve to be no more than a myth. Read to the students the following quote from the 'new atheist', Sam Harris: *"Scientific evidence shows that the Adam and Eve of the Bible could not have existed. There is no genetic data or evidence of any human bottleneck as few as two people. There are simply too many different genes for that to be possible"* – "No Adam, No Eve." The topic is confusing for many Catholics because they regularly hear about 'cave men' such as Homo Erectus, Neanderthal Man, Cro-Magnon Man, etc., and then ask the question, *So where do Adam and Eve fit in?* Inform the students that there is a reasonable answer to this question and that it is not a case of 'Cave men v/s Adam and Eve.' The Catholic Church does not place science and religion in opposition. The answer is 'both/and' rather than 'either/or.' We will now proceed to explore this answer. **Lesson Steps**	Trasancos, "How do Adam and Eve fit with Evolution?" (Website).
Contend for an historical Adam and Eve specially created by God from which all humans have their origin.	10 mins	(i) Scripture exegesis: Invite the students to read from the book of Genesis, chapter 2, verses 4-9 & 15-24 relating to the creation of man and woman. Afterwards, in open class discussion ask them to identify and write down the essential points arising from the text. These points should include: - God formed the man (Adam) immediately from the dust of the earth. - God "breathed" into the man the "breath of life" to become a "living being."	Ratzinger, 'In the Beginning', 41-49. Walton, *The Lost World of Adam and Eve*, 96-103.

		- God placed the man in the garden of Eden to till and keep it. - It was not good that man should be alone. - God caused a deep sleep to fall upon the man and while he slept took from his side a rib from which was formed the woman (Eve). - The man and woman share the same "flesh" and "bones." - The man and woman become "one flesh" through marriage. Sum up the Genesis account by stating that God directly created man and woman, that man and woman both share the same human nature (body and soul), and that from their "one flesh" union they are the first parents of all future generations.	
Appreciate how modern genetics establishes the foundation and unity of the human family in one pair of original parents.	12 mins	(ii) Next, challenge the students by asking the following question: *Knowing what we now know from human history, science and genetics, is there anything in Genesis 2 about the creation of man and woman that is problematic or unbelievable?* Student objections may include: - The creation story of Adam and Eve does not seem to square with what we know about cave men, etc. - If all humans come from Adam and Eve, then their children must have committed incest. - How can genetically different races (Caucasian, Negro, Oriental, etc.) come from the same parents? Hand out to the students Activity Sheet 15, *'African Adam' and 'Mitochondrial Eve.'* How does the information in this sheet address the above objections and/or support the Genesis account of humanity's origin from a single set of parents (monogenism)?	Purcell, *From Big Bang to Big Mystery*, 320-332.
Demonstrate how modern humans are unique creatures unconnected with previously existing or contemporary species.	15 mins	(iii) Classroom discussion: Having established the possibility of humanity's origins from a single set of parents, the next question to consider relates to the origin of Adam and Eve. Did they evolve from pre-humans (cave men) or were they directly created by God as unique and completely separate creatures? Hand out Activity Sheet 16, *Adam and Eve: Evolved or Specially Created?*	Robinson, *The Realist Guide to Religion and Science*, 475-486. Sheehan, *Apologetics and Catholic Doctrine*, 359-370.

Advocate that the human soul, in contrast to the human body, cannot evolve due to its spiritual nature.	10 mins	Ask the students to read the arguments as outlined on the sheet and in the space provided write their reasons for which of the two positions they prefer. Select four students who would like to present their arguments to the class and be willing to be cross-examined by the other students. (iv) Emphasise that no matter whether the human body evolved or not, humans are still unique creatures specially created by God. This is because they have *souls*. Define for the students the term 'soul' ("the principle of life in a being"). All plants, animals and humans have life; therefore, they all have souls. However, human souls are *spiritual*, meaning they are directly created and infused by God and can live on after the death of the body. Ask the students to reflect on the following question: *If human souls are directly created and infused by God, what are the implications for human evolution?* Guide student discussion and list responses on the whiteboard. Points to consider: - Evolution deals with the development of parts, but the human soul has no parts. - Evolution deals with the development of material bodies, but the human soul is spiritual, not material. - Being spiritual and possessing no parts, the human soul could not have evolved. - Without evolution, the human soul must be specially and directly created. - Only God can create. - Therefore, all human souls are directly created by God. - At most, only the human body could have evolved.	Walton, *The Lost World of Adam and Eve*, 190-197. Rice, *50 Questions on the Natural Law*, 155-158. Sheehan, *Apologetics and Catholic Doctrine*, 359-370.
	3 mins	**Lesson Closure**: Genesis 2 provides important fundamentals concerning the origins of humanity, namely, that man and woman are specially created by God, body and soul, and share the same human nature. Catholics may still believe the Genesis account of human creation but since 1950 (Pius XII *Humani Generis*) are	

free to explore the question of the evolution of the human body from pre-human 'cave men.' However, whatever position one may take regarding the human body the Church remains unambiguous that the human soul, being spiritual, is not a product of evolution but is specially created and infused by God. It also is Catholic doctrine that Adam and Eve are the first parents of all humans (monogenism), ensuring the unity of humanity as one family. This latter point finds support in the latest findings of modern genetics.

Transition:

Homework: Would it affect your faith in Christianity if the evolution of the human body were ever proven to be a fact? Why/Why not? (1-2 paragraphs).

Resources:
- Purcell, Brendan. *From Big Bang to Big Mystery: Human Origins in the Light of Creation and Evolution.* Dublin, Ireland: Veritas Publications, 2011, 320-332.
- Ratzinger, Joseph. *'In the Beginning ...' A Catholic Understanding of the Creation and the Fall.* New York, NY: T&T Clark, 1990, 41-49.
- Rice, Charles. *50 Questions on the Natural Law: What it is and Why We Need it.* San Francisco: Ignatius Press, 1993, 155-158.
- Robinson, Paul. *The Realist Guide to Religion and Science.* Leominster, United Kingdom: Gracewing, 2018, 475-486.
- Sheehan, Michael. *Apologetics and Catholic Doctrine*, rev. and ed. Peter M. Joseph. London: Baronius Press, 2015, 359-370.
- Trasancos, Stacey, "How do Adam and Eve fit with Evolution?" https://www.ncregister.com/blog/trasancos/how-do-adam-and-eve-fit-with-evolution.
- Walton, John H. *The Lost World of Adam and Eve.* Downers Grove, Ill.: Intervarsity Press, 2015, 96-103 & 190-197.
- *Catechism of the Catholic Church.* Libreria Editrice Vaticana: St Pauls, 1994, paras. 360, 366, 369.
- YOUCAT (*Youth Catechism of the Catholic Church*). San Francisco, Ignatius Press, 2010, paras. 56, 63.
- Website: Trasancos, Stacey. "Human Origins: Which is it? Science or Theology?" https://www.catholic.com/magazine/online-edition/human-origins-which-is-it-science-or-theology.
- YouTube: Staples, Tim. "How do we know Adam and Eve existed?" https://www.youtube.com/watch?v=i8N3uL_6NKM.

LESSON EVALUATION (to be completed AFTER the lesson)

Assessment of lesson objectives and suggestions for improvement:
Teacher self-reflection and self-evaluation:
[OFFICIAL USE ONLY] Comments by teacher supervisor:

Lesson 8: The Material and Spiritual Nature of the Human Person

LESSON ORGANISATION

Year Level: Date: Time: Duration: Room:

Quote:
"The human person is a unique composite – a unity of spirit and matter, soul and body, fashioned in the image of God and destined to live forever" – Pope St John Paul II.

Prayer:
Come, Holy Spirit, fill the hearts of your faithful and enkindle in them the fire of your love.

V. Send forth your Spirit and they shall be created.
R. And you shall renew the face of the earth.

Let us pray.
O God, who by the light of the Holy Spirit, did instruct the hearts of the faithful, grant us in the same Spirit to be truly wise and ever to rejoice in his consolation.
Through Christ our Lord. Amen.

Lesson Outcomes:

As a result of this lesson, students will be able to:

- Recognise that man and woman are beings created in the image and likeness of God (*imago Dei*).
- Contrast the theistic view of the human person with the views of 'new atheists.'
- Understand and articulate the theistic view of the human person as a being possessing a spiritual soul that is the principle of life, consciousness, intelligence, freedom and personality.
- Appreciate that human beings through their intellects can understand objective meaning and purpose.
- Comprehend the arguments for life after death and that humans are destined for eternal life in God.

Activity Sheets:

Activity Sheet 17, *The Human Person: Material, Spiritual, or Both?*

LESSON DELIVERY

Outcome	Time	Motivation and Introduction:	Resources/ References
Contrast the theistic view of the human person with the views of 'new atheists.'	8 mins	Welcome and settle the students. Prayer to the Holy Spirit (or other suitable prayer). Tell the students that today we will be learning about the Catholic/Christian view of the nature of the human person and contrasting that view with the views of atheists. Explain to the students that with the rise of atheism in Western societies there now exist two starkly contrasting views about the the human person, the meaning and purpose of human life, and the ultimate destiny of all humans. Produce and show the students a PowerPoint presentation entitled *'The Human Person'* with two columns, one headed 'The Theistic View' the other headed 'The Atheist View.' Ask the students to reproduce the table inserting the points as listed below. Briefly explain each of the points, highlighting the contrasting views and the significance of the differences. | *The Human Person*	
---	---
The Theistic/Catholic View	**The Atheistic/Post-Modern View**
Created by God in his image and likeness.	A product of evolution through natural selection.
Possesses a body and soul.	Possesses only a body.
Has senses and intellect to know and understand.	Is only an intelligent machine. Senses and intellect untrustworthy.
Possesses a free will.	Has no freedom. Free will is illusory.
Has an eternal destiny in the afterlife.	Has no afterlife beyond the grave.	 **Lesson Steps**	Brown, "Developments in the New Atheism", 259-268. Schreck, *Catholic and Christian*, 16-17.
Recognise that man and woman are beings created in the image and likeness of God (*imago Dei*).	10 mins	(i) Ask the students if they have heard of the term 'image of God.' After noting student responses, inform the class that the term 'image of God' comes originally from the Bible. Ask one of the students to read Genesis 1:27: *"So God created man in his own image, in the image of God he created them; male and female he created them."* Exercise: Ask the students to imagine that they were present at	Ratzinger, *'In the Beginning'*, 44-49. Flader, *The Creed: A Tour of the Catechism*, 81-82.

| | | the creation of the first man and woman. Ask them to write down what they believe they would have seen. In what ways were the first man and woman in the 'image of God'? Choose two students to read out their answers.

After listening to student answers, inform them that the meaning of 'image of God' has two important aspects. The first relates to humans as individuals. Each person is gifted by God with two natural spiritual powers. The first of these is intelligence. With intelligence, humans can know and understand things in their nature and purpose. The second spiritual power is free will. With freedom, humans have the power to make choices, to love or hate. Having intelligence and freedom enables humans to more perfectly reflect God who is infinite intellect and will. (NB: While providing this answer make clear to the students that 'image of God' has nothing to do with humans physically looking like God).

The second aspect concerning 'image of God' relates to humans as social beings. As male and female, humans are in intimate relationship with each other and through this relationship become fruitful in bearing a 'third person', or children. This reflects God in his Trinitarian life. The Father eternally begets the Son; the Father and the Son mutually know each other; from this mutual knowledge proceeds a mutual love. This mutual love is a 'third person', or the Holy Spirit.

Summarise the above for the students on a PowerPoint slide under the headings of 'Image of God', 'Intellect', 'Will', 'Relationship', 'Fruitfulness.' | Purcell, *From Big Bang to Big Mystery*, 293-303. |
|---|---|---|---|
| Understand and articulate the theistic view of the human person as a being possessing a spiritual soul that is the principle of life, consciousness, intelligence, freedom and personality. | 15 mins | (ii) Remind the students that 'new atheists', piece by piece, are attempting to reconstruct the traditional picture of the human person, human nature, powers and ultimate destiny. Refer the students back to the table *'The Human Person'* and the points contained in the column headed 'The Atheist View.'

Hand out Activity Sheet 17, *The Human Person: Material, Spiritual, or Both?* Ask the students to read through the list of human activities and identify which ones are physical/material and which are spiritual/immaterial activities. Afterwards, chose one student to read the 'Conclusion' and allow time for discussion. | Robinson, *The Realist Guide to Religion and Science*, 4-10.

Sheehan, *Apologetics and Catholic Doctrine*, 62-70. |

Appreciate that human beings through their intellects can understand objective meaning and purpose.	10 mins	(iii) On a PowerPoint slide show the students the following quote from the atheist philosopher Bertrand Russell:

"Man's origin, his growth, his hopes and fears, his loves and his beliefs, are but the outcome of accidental collocations of atoms."

Explain to the students that if Bertrand Russell is correct and everything is only the "outcome of accidental collocations of atoms" then most of human experience – including any sense of objective meaning and purpose – is an illusion.

Ask the students to write a 3-point response to Russell under the heading, *Meaning and Purpose: How do I know they really exist?* Choose three students to each read out one response. Some points that may assist student responses include:
- Humans through their senses and intellects are inherently 'wired' to accurately understand things in their nature and purpose.
- Everything around us has a self-evident purpose, e.g., money has the purpose of enabling buying and selling; food has the purpose to nourish and sustain life. It follows that humans should also have meaning and purpose.
- There does exist *objective* meaning and purpose that corresponds with the reality of what a thing is and what it is meant to do. Objective meaning and purpose is what humans instinctively desire and seek.
- Humans can create their own *subjective* meaning and purpose, but this is at the level of opinion or sentiment and may not correspond to reality.

Conclude by telling the students that objective meaning and purpose cannot exist unless it is purposely given by some kind of external intelligence, which Christians call God. Without an objective purpose-giver such as God, then life becomes absurd, without ultimate significance, value, or purpose. | Nelson, "A Purposeful Kind of World" (Website).

Rice, *50 Questions on the Natural Law*, 121-124. |
| Comprehend the arguments for life after death and that humans are destined for eternal life in God. | 10 mins | (iv) Show the students the following YouTube video, *The Immortality of the Soul* by Tim Staples of Catholic Answers (4.31 minutes).  | |

| | | Tim Staples provides a number of proofs for the immortality of the soul. Ask the students to write down two of these proofs.

Conclude by telling the students that death is the separation of the soul from the body. After this occurs, the body decomposes, breaking up into its component parts. The human soul, however, being spiritual, does not have component parts and, therefore, by its nature cannot decompose. It lives on in the afterlife. Scripture tells us that the soul goes to judgement (Heb. 9:27) and then has an eternal destiny with or without God. At the end of the world, the body will be resurrected and re-joined with the spiritual soul in its eternal destiny (Rom. 6:5). | |
|---|---|---|---|
| | 3 mins | **Lesson Closure**:

Remind the students that theism and atheism propose two radically opposing views of the human person, human nature, purpose and destiny. The Catholic/Christian view pre-supposes the existence of God, who created humans in his image and likeness, possessing both a material (body) and a spiritual (soul) side. The existence of the spiritual soul is evidenced by the spiritual activities humans can perform, including self-consciousness, understanding and loving. Through their power of understanding (the intellect), humans can discover the objective meaning and purpose of things, including the meaning and purpose of life. Being spiritual in nature, the human soul is not made up of component parts and, unlike the body, cannot decompose after death. This means that it lives on after death and has an eternal destiny either with or without God.

Transition:

Homework: Write a response to the following comment from physicist Lawrence Krauss, "You are all stardust … So, forget Jesus. The stars died so that you could be here today." (1-2 paragraphs). | |
| | | **Resources**:
- Brown, Neil. "Developments in the New Atheism." *The Australasian Catholic Record* 92, no. 3 (July 2015): 259-268.
- Flader, John. *The Creed: A Tour of the Catechism, Volume One.* Ballan, Victoria: Modotti Press, 2011, 81-82. | |

- Purcell, Brendan. *From Big Bang to Big Mystery: Human Origins in the Light of Creation and Evolution.* Dublin, Ireland: Veritas Publications, 2011, 293-303.
- Ratzinger, Joseph. *'In the Beginning ...' A Catholic Understanding of the Creation and the Fall.* New York, NY: T&T Clark, 1990, 44-49.
- Rice, Charles. *50 Questions on the Natural Law: What it is and Why We Need it.* San Francisco: Ignatius Press, 1993, 121-128.
- Robinson, Paul. *The Realist Guide to Religion and Science.* Leominster, United Kingdom: Gracewing, 2018, 4-10.
- Schreck, Alan. *Catholic and Christian: An Explanation of Commonly Misunderstood Catholic Beliefs.* Cincinnati, Ohio: Servant Books, 2004, 16-17.
- Sheehan, Michael. *Apologetics and Catholic Doctrine*, rev. and ed. Peter M. Joseph. London: Baronius Press, 2015, 62-70.
- *Catechism of the Catholic Church.* Libreria Editrice Vaticana: St Pauls, 1994, paras. 362-366.
- YOUCAT (*Youth Catechism of the Catholic Church*). San Francisco, Ignatius Press, 2010, paras. 62, 63.
- Website: Nelson, Matthew. "A Purposeful Kind of World." https://www.catholic.com/magazine/online-edition/a-purposeful-kind-of-world.
- YouTube: Staples, Tim. "The Immortality of the Soul." https://www.youtube.com/watch?v=WxR23-J0aps.

LESSON EVALUATION (to be completed AFTER the lesson)

Assessment of lesson objectives and suggestions for improvement:
Teacher self-reflection and self-evaluation:
[OFFICIAL USE ONLY] Comments by teacher supervisor:

Lesson 9: The Reality and Nature of Divine Revelation

LESSON ORGANISATION

Year Level: Date: Time: Duration: Room:
Quote: *"God in his goodness gives us divine revelation to know truths about him that otherwise could not be known by unaided human reason alone"* – St Thomas Aquinas. **Prayer:** Come, Holy Spirit, fill the hearts of your faithful and enkindle in them the fire of your love. V. Send forth your Spirit and they shall be created. R. And you shall renew the face of the earth. Let us pray. O God, who by the light of the Holy Spirit, did instruct the hearts of the faithful, grant us in the same Spirit to be truly wise and ever to rejoice in his consolation. Through Christ our Lord. Amen.
Lesson Outcomes: As a result of this lesson, students will be able to: - Understand the distinction between general (natural) and special (public) revelation. - Appreciate why human beings need special revelation. - Identify how God is concerned to contact human beings and has specially revealed himself to chosen and historically identifiable individuals over millennia. - Value God's special revelation as reasonable, worthy of an intelligent and caring God, and beneficial to humanity. - Recognise that God reveals himself to humanity most perfectly in Jesus Christ.
Activity Sheets: Activity Sheet 18, *Revealed Religion*. Activity Sheet 19, *God's Plan of Loving Goodness*.

LESSON DELIVERY

Outcome	Time	Motivation and Introduction:	Resources/ References
Understand the distinction between general (natural) and special (public) revelation.	7 mins	Welcome and settle the students. Prayer to the Holy Spirit (or other suitable prayer). Tell the students that today we will be learning about the reality, need for, and value of divine revelation. Atheists, because they do not believe in God, naturally do not believe in any so-called 'divine revelation.' However, there are others – such as deists – who while they believe in God do not believe that he has revealed himself specially to human beings. They hold that God is impersonal, not interested in talking to or engaging humanity, or too different and powerful to be bothered with engaging insignificant beings such as humans. For them, the only form of divine revelation that is worthy or reliable is the 'book of nature.' Inform the students that nature is certainly a valid form of God's revelation, but in addition to nature God has also specially revealed himself publicly to humanity. On a PowerPoint slide, outline the following two paragraphs from the *Catechism of the Catholic Church*: Para. 32: *As St Paul says to the gentiles: for what can be known about God is plain to them, because he has shown it to them. Ever since the creation of the world his invisible nature, namely, his eternal power and deity, has been clearly perceived in the things that have been made.* Para. 50: *... But there is another order of knowledge which man cannot possibly arrive at by his own powers: the order of divine Revelation. Through an utterly free decision, God has revealed himself and given himself to man.* Conclude by affirming that the two 'modes' of revelation (natural /general and special/public), though different, both originate from God and complement each other without contradiction. Together, they give humanity knowledge of everything necessary for life, happiness and salvation.	Duggan, *Beyond Reasonable Doubt*, 81. Ward, *The Christian Idea of God*, 213-221.

		Lesson Steps	
Appreciate why human beings need special revelation.	12 mins	(i) Inform the students that the study of general/natural revelation is called philosophy, while the study of special/public revelation is called theology. Both are necessary to get the 'full picture' about God and the Christian life. Show the students the following YouTube video, *Why St Thomas Aquinas Says We Need Divine Revelation* by Scott M. Sullivan (3.41 minutes). Ask them to note  the three reasons why divine (special) revelation is necessary and the three reasons why philosophy is important. Choose two students to read out their answers. Afterwards, display and explain these reasons on a PowerPoint slide as follows: Divine Revelation is necessary because: - Some important truths about God cannot be known by unaided reason at all, e.g., the Trinity. - Philosophical knowledge of God can only be attained by a few, after much study, and often mixed with some error. - Divine revelation is a more secure and easier way to come to the knowledge of God. Philosophy is important because: - It can prove the truths that are foundational for faith, e.g., the existence of God. - It can help clarify teachings of theology. - It can be used to refute opponents of the faith.	Rice, *50 Questions on the Natural Law*, 147-151.
Identify how God is concerned to contact human beings and has specially revealed himself to chosen and historically identifiable individuals over millennia.	10 mins	(ii) God's special revelation to humanity is found principally in the holy books collectively called 'The Bible.' Hand out to the students Activity Sheet 18, *Revealed Religion*. Ask the students to look at four recorded instances when God specially revealed himself to humanity. Read the words of God in these four instances and answer the question, *What was God's ultimate purpose in speaking to Adam, Abraham, Moses and David?* Take two student answers. Afterwards, provide the following answer: God spoke to humanity to reveal his plan to form a family – a chosen people – through whom he would one day come into the world in the person of Jesus Christ. Without this revelation such a plan would have been unknowable to humanity.	Clovis, *A Biblical Search for the Church Christ Founded*, 6-10.

Value God's special revelation as reasonable, worthy of an intelligent and caring God, and beneficial to humanity.	13 mins	(iii) Remind the students that some (deists) regard the notion of special revelation as something unbefitting a God who is infinitely perfect and superior to human beings. For these same people, it is "unreasonable" to expect such a God to bother himself with "lowly" human beings. Still others (atheists) claim that nothing God has allegedly revealed is of real benefit to humans in any case. From the Christian perspective, however, the reality is very different. Exercise: Invite the students to divide into pairs and brainstorm any revealed teachings that they think are reasonable and beneficial to humanity. Write appropriate student responses on the whiteboard. Responses may include any of the following: - The Ten Commandments (e.g., "Thou shalt not steal/lie": Exod. 20). - The Beatitudes (e.g., "Blessed are the peacemakers": Matt. 5:9). - The 'Golden Rule' ("Do unto others as you would have them do unto you": Matt. 7:12). - "Turn the other cheek" (Matt. 5:39). - Forgive "seventy times seven" (Matt. 18:22). Afterwards, on a PowerPoint slide present and explain the following as another example of beneficial special revelation: The teaching on the Trinity is the most extraordinary example of special revelation. We only know about the Trinity because it was revealed by Jesus himself. It reveals that God is a 'community of persons' living a life of infinite knowledge and love. It is, therefore, a teaching that contains a social and moral dimension. It teaches humans that if they want to be like God – and therefore truly human – they ought to be persons of selfless communal love. It is in knowing who God truly is that we come to know who we truly should be.	Rice, *50 Questions on the Natural Law*, 152-155.
Recognise that God reveals himself to humanity most perfectly in Jesus Christ.	10 mins	(iv) Challenge: Ask the students to answer the following questions: *What is the most perfect way God has revealed himself to humanity? How does this 'perfect' revelation reveal his love for humanity?* Take three student responses. Student answers may include: - Through the Old Testament Prophets. - Through the Bible.	Clovis, *A Biblical Search for the Church Christ Founded*, 9-10. Flader, *The Creed: A Tour of the Catechism*, 28-29.

- Through the Church.
- Through the Sacraments.
- Through Bishops and Priests
- Through the examples of modern holy people.

Acknowledge these and any other appropriate answers as ways God does reveal himself to humanity, however, they are all secondary and limited forms of revelation compared to God's ultimate self-revelation — the person of Jesus Christ.

God reveals his plan of love and salvation for humanity in phases over many centuries, through patriarchs, kings and prophets. This revelation reaches its climax in Jesus Christ. Hand out to the students Activity Sheet 19, *God's Plan of Loving Goodness*. There are two columns headed, (a) *How God reveals himself in Jesus Christ* and (b) *How God reveals his love for humanity in Jesus Christ*. Invite the students to complete these two columns with the statements from the Word Bank. (Answers: 2, 3, 6, 8, 9 into Column A; 1, 4, 5, 7, 10 into Column B).

3 mins

Lesson Closure:

Sum up for the students that the God of Judeo-Christianity is one who loves us and has revealed himself to us via two modes, general (natural) and special (public) revelation. Special revelation illustrates God's love and care for us and has been given in stages to chosen individuals over millennia to enable us to more easily and accurately know truths about him. God's special revelation reaches a climax and is expressed most perfectly in Jesus Christ, who is the "Word made flesh" and who came to "dwell among us." There is no further authentic special revelation to come after Jesus Christ.

Transition:

Homework: Search through the Bible and write down two examples of God's special revelation (apart from those outlined in the Activity Sheets) that you believe are of value or importance to humanity.

Resources:
- Clovis, Linus F. *A Biblical Search for the Church Christ Founded.* Leominster, United Kingdom: Gracewing, 2012, 6-10.

		<ul><li>Duggan, G. H. *Beyond Reasonable Doubt*. Boston, MA: St Paul Books & Media, 1987, 81.</li><li>Flader, John. *The Creed: A Tour of the Catechism, Volume One*. Ballan, Victoria: Modotti Press, 2011, 28-29.</li><li>Rice, Charles. *50 Questions on the Natural Law: What it is and Why We Need it*. San Francisco: Ignatius Press, 1993, 147-151.</li><li>Ward, Keith. *The Christian Idea of God: A Philosophical Foundation for Faith*. Cambridge: Cambridge University Press, 2017, 213-221.</li><li>*Catechism of the Catholic Church*. Libreria Editrice Vaticana: St Pauls, 1994, paras. 32, 50, 55-58, 64-66.</li><li>YOUCAT (*Youth Catechism of the Catholic Church*). San Francisco, Ignatius Press, 2010, paras. 7-10.</li><li>Website: Akin, James. "Revelation: Public and Private." https://www.catholic.com/magazine/print-edition/revelation-public-and-private.</li><li>YouTube: Sullivan, Scott M. "Why St Thomas Aquinas Says We Need Divine Revelation." https://www.youtube.com/watch?v=Wsf5wTcVzCE.</li></ul>

LESSON EVALUATION (to be completed AFTER the lesson)

Assessment of lesson objectives and suggestions for improvement:
Teacher self-reflection and self-evaluation:
[OFFICIAL USE ONLY] Comments by teacher supervisor:

Lesson 10: The Bible: Myth or History?

LESSON ORGANISATION

Year Level: **Date:** **Time:** **Duration:** **Room:**

Quote:
"Ignorance of the Scriptures is ignorance of Christ" – St Jerome.

Prayer:
Come, Holy Spirit, fill the hearts of your faithful and enkindle in them the fire of your love.

V. Send forth your Spirit and they shall be created.
R. And you shall renew the face of the earth.

Let us pray.
O God, who by the light of the Holy Spirit, did instruct the hearts of the faithful, grant us in the same Spirit to be truly wise and ever to rejoice in his consolation.
Through Christ our Lord. Amen.

Lesson Outcomes:

As a result of this lesson, students will be able to:

- Understand claims made against the historical reliability of the Bible.
- Adduce historical/archaeological evidence for the existence of Abraham, Moses, Jesus, etc.
- Articulate reasons in support of the reliability of the Gospel accounts concerning the person and life of Jesus Christ.
- Reconcile alleged historical and textual contradictions/inconsistencies in the New Testament.
- Identify ancient manuscripts/codices that evidence the accurate transmission of Scripture texts over the centuries.

Activity Sheets:

Activity Sheet 20, *Abraham, Moses and Jesus – Did They Exist?*
Activity Sheet 21, *Manuscript Evidence in Support of the Bible.*

"Always Be Prepared …" – A 'New Apologetics' Course for Catholic Secondary Schools

LESSON DELIVERY

Outcome	Time	Motivation and Introduction:	Resources/ References
Understand claims made against the historical reliability of the Bible	7 mins	Welcome and settle the students. Prayer to the Holy Spirit (or other suitable prayer). Tell the students that today we will be looking at whether the Bible is historically reliable or rather a collection of myths/inaccuracies, contradictions, etc. Inform the students that until the late eighteenth-century Catholics/Christians generally did not question the historical reliability of the Bible, believing it to be inspired and inerrant (without error). Since the time of the 'Enlightenment', however, many scholars/critics have come forward to challenge the reliability of the Bible. On a PowerPoint slide present the following list of objections raised by these scholars/critics against the historical reliability of the Bible: - Persons such as Abraham, Moses and Jesus are only mythical figures who never really existed at all. - The Gospel accounts of Jesus were not written by contemporary eyewitnesses and contain myths, additions and exaggerations. - The Bible contains errors, contradictions and inconsistencies within itself and with known history. - The original Bible manuscripts have all been lost and copyists have not accurately transmitted them over the centuries. **Lesson Steps**	Crean, *A Catholic Replies to Professor Dawkins*, 62-63. Duggan, *Beyond Reasonable Doubt*, 87-93. Kreeft & Tacelli, *Handbook of Christian Apologetics*, 199-203. Sheehan, *Apologetics and Catholic Doctrine*, 268-272.
Adduce historical/ archaeological evidence for the existence of Abraham, Moses, Jesus, etc.	15 mins	(i) Hand out to the students a copy of Activity Sheet 20, *Abraham, Moses and Jesus – Did They Exist?* Choose students to read the notes outlining the arguments against the existence of Abraham, Moses and Jesus, as well as the counterarguments. Then ask the students to answer the following question: *What do you think is the most convincing argument for the existence of Jesus and why?* Take two student responses.	Bergsma & Petrie, *A Catholic Introduction to the Bible*, 148-150, 188-189.

		After taking two student answers, tell the students that perhaps the most convincing evidence for the existence of Jesus is the emergence of a community of believers from the AD 30s onwards, the time traditionally attributed to the public life, death and resurrection of Jesus. You cannot have an effect (a community) without a cause (Jesus).	Blomberg, *The Historical Reliability of the Gospels*, 196-201.
Articulate reasons in support of the reliability of the Gospel accounts concerning the person and life of Jesus Christ.	10 mins	(ii) Question: *What evidence exists for the authenticity and reliability of the Gospels concerning the person and life of Jesus Christ?* On a PowerPoint slide list the following points about the four Gospels and their authors: - The ancient Church believed without controversy that the Gospels were written by Matthew, Mark, Luke and John. - The Gospels illustrate a detailed knowledge of the social, religious and political situation in Palestine in the first half of the first century AD while the Jerusalem Temple still existed. - The four Gospel authors were all willing to mention matters that discredited themselves and the other disciples – their lack of understanding, jealousies, cowardice, betrayals. - The four Gospel authors gained no worldly benefit from preaching about Jesus and were all willing to suffer and die for the truths contained in the Gospels. Classroom discussion: *What do each of these four points tell us about the Gospels and their authors?* While soliciting student responses guide them towards the following conclusions: - The Gospels are reliable because they were written by men who witnessed the main events in Jesus' life, not by later unconnected strangers. - The Gospels are reliable because they were written in the first century AD, close to the events associated with Jesus. - The Gospels are reliable because they were written by men who were willing to write the truth even if such maligned their own character. - The Gospels are reliable because it is unreasonable for people to willingly suffer and die for something they know is not true.	Blomberg, *The Historical Reliability of the Gospels*, 160-161. Crean, *A Catholic Replies to Professor Dawkins*, 66-73. Duggan, *Beyond Reasonable Doubt*, 96-110. Petrie, *The Case for Jesus*, 1-54, 84-101.

Reconcile alleged historical and textual contradictions/ inconsistencies in the New Testament.	10 mins	(iii) Ask the students if they have ever heard that the Bible contains errors and, if so, what may be some examples? Inform them that many modern Biblical scholars claim that there are errors, or at least contradictions/inconsistencies. On a PowerPoint slide provide the following ten examples of alleged 'errors': - The different versions of Jesus' family tree. - The 'unhistorical' date of Quirinius' census of Judea. - Whether Jesus preached about the "Kingdom of God" or the "Kingdom of Heaven." - Whether Jesus' famous sermon occurred on a mount or on a plain. - Whether Jesus sent out the disciples to preach carrying or not carrying walking staffs. - Whether Jesus freed one or two men of demonic possession in Gerasa. - Whether Jesus cured one or two blind men in Jericho. - Whether Jesus cleansed the Temple at the beginning or at the end of his public ministry. - The differing accounts as to which weekday the Last Supper was celebrated. - The contradictory words written above Jesus on the Cross. Tell the students that the Church formally teaches that "the books of Scripture firmly, faithfully, and without error teach the truth" that God wanted us to know and that all the above *apparent* contradictions/inconsistencies can be reconciled. Example reconciliation exercise: Ask the students to look at the following verses of Scripture relating to the words written above Jesus on the Cross and note how they are different. Ask them to then write one-two paragraphs giving their opinion as to whether the differences are substantial and how they may, or may not, be reconciled (Take two student responses): Matt. 27:37: "This is Jesus, the King of the Jews." Mark 15:26: "The King of the Jews." Luke 23:38: "This is the King of the Jews." John 19:19: "Jesus of Nazareth, the King of the Jews." Answer: There are no contradictions or errors between the above verses. They essentially say the same thing (Jesus is King). The difference in presentation is an example of the highly individualised manner the Gospel writers treated the subject.	Blomberg, *The Historical Reliability of the Gospels*, 115-116, 175, 195.

Identify ancient manuscripts/ codices that evidence the accurate transmission of Scripture texts over the centuries.	10 mins	(iv) The next question relates to whether the books of the Bible have been accurately transmitted by copyists over the centuries. Some modern scholars also doubt this. Hand out Activity Sheet 21, *Manuscript Evidence in Support of the Bible*. Choose students to read the evidence in support of the faithful transmission of the Bible. Discuss how this evidence compares to manuscripts of other ancient non-biblical texts.	Crean, *A Catholic Replies to Professor Dawkins*, 63-66. Duggan, *Beyond Reasonable Doubt*, 92-93.
	3 mins	**Lesson Closure:** Remind the students that the reliability of the Bible continues to be contested by many people for many different reasons. Nevertheless, whether it be the existence of Abraham, Moses or Jesus, alleged errors, inconsistencies or historical contradictions, or doubts over the textual transmission over the centuries, there are many viable arguments to defend the Bible. Not all questions can be easily answered, but there are sufficient answers to dismiss the scepticism of Biblical critics as largely unjustified. **Transition:** Homework: For archaeological evidence in support of the Gospels, watch the following YouTube video, *Historical Evidence for Gospel Accounts* by Fr Robert Spitzer (4.29 minutes). 	
		Resources: <ul><li>Bergsma, John and Brant Petrie. *A Catholic Introduction to the Bible. Volume 1, The Old Testament.* San Francisco: Ignatius Press, 2018, 148-150, 188-189.</li><li>Blomberg, Craig. *The Historical Reliability of the Gospels.* Downers Grove, Illinois: InterVarsity Press, 1987, 160-161, 196-201.</li><li>Crean, Thomas. *A Catholic Replies to Professor Dawkins.* Oxford: Family Publications, 2007, 62-63, 66-73.</li><li>Duggan, G. H. *Beyond Reasonable Doubt.* Boston, MA: St Paul Books & Media, 1987, 87-93, 96-110.</li><li>Kreeft, Peter & Ronald K. Tacelli. *Handbook of Christian Apologetics: Hundreds of Answers to Crucial Questions.* Downers Grove: IVP Academic, 1994, 199-203.</li><li>Sheehan, Michael. *Apologetics and Catholic Doctrine*, rev. and ed. Peter M. Joseph. London: Baronius Press, 2015, 268-272.</li></ul>	

		<ul><li>*Catechism of the Catholic Church*. Libreria Editrice Vaticana: St Pauls, 1994, paras. 105-107.</li><li>YOUCAT (*Youth Catechism of the Catholic Church*). San Francisco, Ignatius Press, 2010, paras. 14-15.</li><li>Website: Olson, Carl E. "Are the Gospels Myth?" https://www.catholic.com/magazine/print-edition/are-the-gospels-myth.</li><li>YouTube: Spitzer, Robert. "Historical Evidence for Gospel Accounts." https://www.youtube.com/watch?v=d-LHOe_v4KQ.</li></ul>

LESSON EVALUATION (to be completed AFTER the lesson)

Assessment of lesson objectives and suggestions for improvement:
Teacher self-reflection and self-evaluation:
[OFFICIAL USE ONLY] Comments by teacher supervisor:

"Always Be Prepared …" – A 'New Apologetics' Course for Catholic Secondary Schools

Lesson 11: <u>The Word of God – Scripture and Tradition</u>

LESSON ORGANISATION

Year Level: Date: Time: Duration: Room:

Quote:
"It is the truth revealed through Scripture and Tradition and articulated by the Church's Magisterium that sets us free" – Pope Benedict XVI.

Prayer:
Come, Holy Spirit, fill the hearts of your faithful and enkindle in them the fire of your love.

V. Send forth your Spirit and they shall be created.
R. And you shall renew the face of the earth.

Let us pray.
O God, who by the light of the Holy Spirit, did instruct the hearts of the faithful, grant us in the same Spirit to be truly wise and ever to rejoice in his consolation.
Through Christ our Lord. Amen.

Lesson Outcomes:

As a result of this lesson, students will be able to:

- Understand that the 'Word of God' consists of both the written Scriptures and Apostolic Tradition.
- Appreciate that Apostolic Tradition derives from Christ and is part of the original 'deposit of faith' left with the Apostles.
- Identify the different 'modes' through which Scripture and Apostolic Tradition are passed on.
- Recognise the relationship between and compatibility of Scripture, Apostolic Tradition and the Church's Magisterium.
- Illustrate using examples how Catholic practices/teachings contained in Apostolic Tradition have material support in written Scripture.

Activity Sheets:

Activity Sheet 22, *Debating Boettner.*

LESSON DELIVERY

Outcome	Time	Motivation and Introduction:	Resources/ References
Understand that the 'Word of God' consists of both the written Scriptures and Apostolic Tradition.	7 mins	Welcome and settle the students. Prayer to the Holy Spirit (or other suitable prayer). Tell the students that today we will be looking at what is meant by the 'Word of God.' Ordinarily, when Christians hear the phrase 'Word of God' they immediately think of the Bible and all the Old and New Testament books. Both Catholics and non-Catholic Christians (Protestants) accept the Bible as the Word of God (NB: Catholics have seven extra Old Testament books). However, Catholics also adhere to something called 'Apostolic Tradition.' On the other hand, many non-Catholic Christians, adhering to the principle of *sola scriptura* (the 'Bible alone'), reject all forms of tradition and cite the following words of Jesus and St Paul in support (show on a PowerPoint slide): *"And why do you transgress the commandment of God for the sake of your tradition?"* (Matt. 15:3). *"See to it that no one makes a prey of you by philosophy and empty deceit, according to human tradition, according to the elemental spirits of the universe, and not according to Christ"* (Col. 2:8). For these same non-Catholic Christians, the Bible alone is the sole 'rule of faith' and contains everything necessary for salvation, a view they believe is approved by the following words of St Paul: *"All scripture is inspired by God and is profitable for teaching, for reproof, for correction, and for the training in righteousness, that the man of God may be complete ..."* (2 Tim. 3:16-17). On the other hand, Catholics cite the following verse from St Paul, where he urges Christians to adhere to written and oral traditions: *"Stand firm and hold to the traditions which you were taught by us, either by word of mouth or by letter"* (2 Thess. 2:15). For Catholics, only those traditions that directly contradict Scripture are condemned; Apostolic Tradition is not such a tradition.	Armstrong, *A Biblical Defense of Catholicism*, 3-24. Keating, *Catholicism and Fundamentalism*, 134-141. Miller, *The Bible and the Church*, 51-68.

		Lesson Steps	
Appreciate that Apostolic Tradition derives from Christ and is part of the original 'deposit of faith' left with the Apostles.	12 mins	(i) Inform the students that the word 'tradition' comes from the Greek, *paradosis*. This word passes into Latin as *traditio*, meaning 'handing on.' Catholics believe Jesus handed on the faith "once and for all to the saints" (Jude 3). This was the first 'tradition' and was done not in writing but by word of mouth to the Apostles and the first Christians. Over the next few decades, the Holy Spirit inspired a number of Apostles and Evangelists to put down in writing some of the original *paradosis*. As a result, part of the original *paradosis* became embedded in what we now call the Gospels/letters of the New Testament. Catholics call this the *written* Word of God. Importantly, the rest of the *paradosis* not embedded in writing remained with the Church as the *unwritten* Word of God. Show the students the following YouTube video, *Sacred Tradition* by Joan Watson of Three Minute Theology (3.51 minutes). Ask them to answer the following questions (choose various students to read out their answers):  - *How did the early Christians spread the Gospel?* - *What does St Paul ask Christians to "hold on to" in 2 Thess. 2:15?* - *How did illiterate Christians in the early centuries hear the Word of God?* - *What is the role of the 'Magisterium'?*	Horn, *The Case for Catholicism*, 35-36. Salza, *The Biblical Basis for the Catholic Faith*, 26-27.
Identify the different 'modes' through which Scripture and Apostolic Tradition are passed on.	10 mins	(ii) Classroom discussion: *While it is obvious that Scripture is handed on in written form (the books of the Bible), what are the 'modes' by which the contents of Apostolic Tradition are passed on?* Give the students a few minutes to consider this question among themselves before taking responses. Under the heading "Modes of Tradition" record appropriate student responses on the whiteboard. List "word of mouth" (2 Thess. 2:15) as the first mode. Guide student discussion to consider the following other modes and provide an explanation for each: - Prayer (private and liturgical). - Art; Architecture; Music. - Writings of the Church Fathers, Doctors and Saints. - Decrees of Church Councils; Church catechisms.	Flader, *The Creed: A Tour of the Catechism*, 30. Salza, *The Biblical Basis for the Catholic Faith*, 35-36.

Recognise the relationship between and compatibility of Scripture, Apostolic Tradition and the Church's Magisterium.	15 mins	Point out to the students that Apostolic Tradition is not limited to 'oral' tradition but is passed on through many other and different modes. Direct the students to record the above list in their books. (iii) Revisit common objections against Apostolic Tradition. Hand out Activity Sheet 22, *Debating Boettner*. Invite the students to respond to the following quote from a famous anti-Catholic writer by the name of Loraine Boettner:  *"The Church of Rome is following a set of traditions ... which by her own pronouncements she has elevated to equal authority with, or even superiority over the Word of God ... to justify doctrines and practices which have no basis in Scripture, or which are in violation of Scripture"* (Roman Catholicism, 93). Task 1: Together with the students tease out the main assertions of Loraine Boettner, namely: - The Catholic Church says Tradition is equal to Scripture. - The Catholic Church says Tradition is superior to Scripture. - Catholics use Tradition to justify doctrines that are not in or contrary to Scripture. Task 2: Ask the students: *How would you respond to Boettner's accusations?* (In three points). Assist the students with some prompts. After taking two-three responses, show and explain the following on a PowerPoint slide: - The Catholic Church says Apostolic Tradition and the written Scriptures together form the original 'deposit of faith.' - Yes, the Catholic Church says Apostolic Tradition is equal to Scripture in authority. - No, the Catholic Church does not say that Apostolic Tradition is superior to Scripture. - The Catholic Church says that all doctrines contained in Apostolic Tradition are *materially* found in Scripture, meaning there is support for these same doctrines in Scripture. - The Catholic Church says there is no contradiction between the contents of Scripture and Apostolic Tradition. - Certain traditions that are not Apostolic – disciplinary, liturgical or devotional – can be changed or abandoned.	*Catechism of the Catholic Church*, Paras. 80-87. Ray, *Crossing the Tiber*, 49-57. Shea, *Not by Scripture Alone*, 169-210.

Illustrate using examples how Catholic practices/ teachings contained in Apostolic Tradition have material support in written Scripture.	10 mins	- The Catholic Church says it is the role of the Magisterium (teaching authority of the Church) – not private individuals – to define and interpret Scripture and Apostolic Tradition. - The Catholic Church says that Scripture alone is never formally sufficient to know the true Word of God; Scripture, Apostolic Tradition and the authority of the Magisterium are needed for 'formal' sufficiency. (iv) Exercise: Invite the students to investigate one Catholic practice and one Catholic teaching that is found in Tradition but not explicitly in Scripture. Choose the 'Sign of the Cross' and Mary's assumption into heaven. Work with the students to answer the following questions: (a) *Is this practice/belief mentioned explicitly in Scripture?* (Answer: No/No). (b) *Is silence in Scripture sufficient to disqualify a practice or belief?* (Answer: No. Not everything about Christianity was ever intended to be put down in writing. See John 21:25). (c) *Is there anything about the practice/belief that contradicts Scripture?* (Answer: No as regards the 'Sign of the Cross.' But critics of the assumption assert that if Mary was a normal sinner she would have died and been buried like any normal Jew/Christian). (d) *Is there anything in Scripture that materially supports the practice/belief?* (Answer: Yes. The 'Sign of the Cross' reminds Christians of the Cross upon which Jesus was crucified and the words "in the name of the Father and of the Son and of the Holy Spirit" reminds Christians of the Trinity and the baptismal formula in Matt. 28:19. Concerning the assumption, Scripture says nothing about how Mary left the world and there are precedents of other people being taken up into heaven body and soul, e.g., Enoch [Gen. 5:21-24] and Elijah [2 Kings 2:11] while the woman appearing in heaven and "clothed with the sun" in Rev. 12 is in the image of Mary). (e) *Where do we find this practice/belief in Apostolic Tradition?* (Answer: The 'Sign of the Cross' is practised in all the liturgies of the Church and in private prayer; the assumption of Mary is found in the writings of the Church Fathers as early as the late fourth century AD [e.g., St Epiphanius of Salamis; St Jerome]).	Horn, *The Case for Catholicism*, 331-339. Salza, *The Biblical Basis for the Catholic Faith*, 26-27.

	3 mins	**Lesson Closure:** Sum up for the students that the 'Word of God' consists of both the written Scriptures and Apostolic Tradition. Together, they form the 'deposit of faith' given "once and for all to the saints" by Christ himself. While Jesus condemns "traditions of men" that contradict the Scriptures, Apostolic Tradition is consistent with Scripture and the two support and interpret each other. The Church is the final arbiter possessing the authority to define what is authentic Scripture and Tradition and interpret the true Word of God. **Transition:** Homework: Besides 2 Thess. 2:15, there are a number of other verses in the New Testament that speak favourably of tradition. Ask the students to look up 1 Cor. 11:1-2 and 2 Thess. 3:6 and write out these verses in their workbooks. What traditions is St Paul asking Christians in these verses to maintain/live by?	
		Resources:<ul><li>Armstrong, Dave. *A Biblical Defense of Catholicism.* Manchester, NH: Sophia Institute Press, 2003, 3-24.</li><li>Flader, John. *The Creed: A Tour of the Catechism, Volume One.* Ballan, Victoria: Modotti Press, 2011, 30.</li><li>Horn, Trent. *The Case for Catholicism: Answers to Classic and Contemporary Protestant Objections.* San Francisco: Ignatius Press, 2017, 35-36, 331-339.</li><li>Keating, Karl. *Catholicism and Fundamentalism.* San Francisco: Ignatius Press, 1988, 134-141.</li><li>Miller, Daniel. "The Bible and the Church." In *Answering the Anti-Catholic Challenge: A Response to Ray Galea,* ed. Robert M. Haddad. Ballan, Victoria: Modotti Press, 2012, 51-68.</li><li>Ray, Stephen K. *Crossing the Tiber: Evangelical Protestants Discover the Historic Church.* San Francisco: Ignatius Press, 1997, 49-57.</li><li>Salza, John. *The Biblical Basis for the Catholic Faith.* Huntingdon, Indiana: Our Sunday Visitor Publishing, 2005, 26-27, 35-36.</li><li>Shea, Mark P. "What is the Relationship Between Scripture and Tradition?" in *Not by Scripture Alone,* ed. Robert A. Sungenis, 169-210. Santa Barbara, CA: Queenship Publishing Company, 1997.</li><li>*Catechism of the Catholic Church.* Libreria Editrice Vaticana: St Pauls, 1994, paras. 80-87.</li></ul>	

		<ul><li>YOUCAT (*Youth Catechism of the Catholic Church*). San Francisco, Ignatius Press, 2010, para. 12.</li><li>Website: Catholic Answers. "Scripture and Tradition." https://www.catholic.com/tract/scripture-and-tradition.</li><li>YouTube: Watson, Joan. "Sacred Tradition." https://www.youtube.com/watch?v=kpdy4QJZ-GU.</li></ul>

LESSON EVALUATION (to be completed AFTER the lesson)

Assessment of lesson objectives and suggestions for improvement:
Teacher self-reflection and self-evaluation:
[OFFICIAL USE ONLY] Comments by teacher supervisor:

Lesson 12: The Judeo-Christian Story

LESSON ORGANISATION

Year Level: Date: Time: Duration: Room:

Quote:
"Human history is the long terrible story of man trying to find something other than God which will make him happy" – C. S. Lewis.

Prayer:
Come, Holy Spirit, fill the hearts of your faithful and enkindle in them the fire of your love.

V. Send forth your Spirit and they shall be created.
R. And you shall renew the face of the earth.

Let us pray.
O God, who by the light of the Holy Spirit, did instruct the hearts of the faithful, grant us in the same Spirit to be truly wise and ever to rejoice in his consolation.
Through Christ our Lord. Amen.

Lesson Outcomes:

As a result of this lesson, students will be able to:

- Understand the importance and purpose of 'grand narratives.'
- Identify and understand the different narrative types – 'meta', 'midi', 'mini.'
- Articulate the Judeo-Christian story/narrative in four parts – Creation, Fall, Redemption, Parousia.
- Recognise the differences between the Judeo-Christian story/narrative and alternative secular, 'mini', 'midi' narratives.
- Appreciate how the Judeo-Christian story/narrative helps believers understand life's 'big questions.'

Activity Sheets:

Activity Sheet 23, *Paradise Lost and Regained.*
Activity Sheet 24, *Comparing the Narratives.*

LESSON DELIVERY

Outcome	Time	Motivation and Introduction:	Resources/ References
Understand the importance and purpose of 'grand narratives.'	7 mins	Welcome and settle the students. Prayer to the Holy Spirit (or other suitable prayer). Tell the students that today we will be looking at the importance of the Judeo-Christian story as a 'grand' or 'meta' narrative that provides ultimate meaning and purpose to life. Elaborate that a 'grand' or 'meta' narrative is a story that supplies a unified vision of the world with shared beliefs, binding values and a universal interpretation of history and human destiny. In the Judeo-Christian grand narrative, the purpose of life is to know, love and serve God in this world and to attain eternal life with him in the next (heaven). The challenge young people face today is two-fold: the rise of secularism and the so-called 'post-modern' denial of grand narratives. With the rise of secularism, the Judeo-Christian grand narrative is being replaced with the grand narrative of 'naturalism', a universe of matter and energy without God and spiritual purpose; with post-modernism, the Judeo-Christian grand narrative is being replaced by scepticism. Define scepticism as the denial of truth and/or the inability of humans to know truth. If there is no truth, or if we cannot know truth, then grand narratives of whatever kind have no foundation and ultimately fall apart. There is no master or normative narrative, even a secular one. Without a grand narrative, individuals create their own personal 'mini' or 'midi' narratives which often time lack a spiritual dimension and/or ultimate purpose and do not provide answers to life's 'big questions.' **Lesson Steps**	Madrid & Hensley, *The Godless Delusion*, 25-30. Rowland, *Catholic Theology*, 161.
Identify and understand the different narrative types – 'meta', 'midi', 'mini.'	15 mins	(i) On a PowerPoint slide, provide the students with the following definitions: (a) Secular world view: This world and everything in it is meaningful as it is. There is no ultimate significance beyond the immediate experience of everyday life. Hence, there is no need for any transformative spirituality.	Savage, *Making Sense of Generation Y*, 37-38.

(b) 'Meta' narrative: A story on a grand scale explaining the world and the meaning, purpose and end of life.
(c) 'Midi' narrative: A modest, communal world view that is only concerned with the here and now and our place among our immediate family and friends.
(d) 'Mini' narrative: An individualistic world view focussed merely on oneself and whatever brings personal joy, happiness and success in the here and now.

(c) and (d) are spiritualities for this world, rather than a future heaven.

Show the students the following YouTube video, *How We Create Narratives* by Jordan Peterson (3.12 minutes). Ask them to answer the following questions (choose various students to read out their answers):
- *What is the most basic narrative?*
  (Answer: "I was here and I'm trying to go there." The story of journey).
- *Narratives are trying to teach young people what?*
  (Answer: How to comprehend their existence).
- *What are the three elements of a cultural narrative?*
  (Answer: Paradise; Paradise Lost; Paradise Re-Gained).
- *What do these three elements remind us of?*
  (Answer: The Christian story of Creation, the Fall and the Redemption).

| Articulate the Judeo-Christian story/narrative in four parts – Creation, Fall, Redemption, Parousia. | 10 mins | (ii) Ask the students the following question: *What are the main parts of the Judeo-Christian story, or meta narrative?* Take two-three student responses.

Hand out Activity Sheet 23, *Paradise Lost and Regained*. Explain how the Judeo-Christian narrative is a grand story in four parts that encapsulates the original creation (Paradise), original sin and expulsion (Paradise Lost), the redemption through Jesus' death and resurrection (Paradise Regained), and Jesus' second coming and last judgement (Paradise Confirmed). Emphasise that the Judeo-Christian narrative remains relevant as it is a story that spans the whole history of humanity, continues to this day, and has a future still to be realised. | Ratzinger, *'In the Beginning'*, 71-77.

Schreck, *Catholic and Christian*, 205-219. |

Recognise the differences between the Judeo-Christian story/narrative and alternative secular, 'mini', 'midi' narratives.	10 mins	(iii) The next question relates to the differences between the Judeo-Christian meta-narrative and alternative secular, 'mini' or 'midi' narratives. Exercise: Hand out Activity Sheet 24, *Comparing the Narratives*. 'Column A' lists the chief characteristics of secular, 'mini' and 'midi' narratives. Work with the students to complete Column B, which should list the opposing Judeo-Christian characteristic for each point in Column A. At the end of the exercise the two respective columns should look something as follows: | Column A – Secular, 'mini', 'midi' narratives	Column B – Judeo-Christian narrative
---	---
The universe brought itself into existence.	The universe is created and designed by God.
Humans are the product of evolution/natural selection.	Humans are created in the image and likeness of God.
Good education, medicine/science conquers sin and death.	Christ conquers sin and death.
Life is cold, harsh and uncaring.	God's providence cares for all persons and things.
There is no meaning or purpose to life.	Life has an ultimate meaning and purpose.
We create our own meaning and purpose.	God gives meaning and purpose.
Life is just about family, friends and myself.	Humans are one family, children of God.
Life is about me and my own pleasure.	Life is about service, sacrifice, love of self and others.
'You only live once.'	This life is a preparation for the next.
Humans can solve all their problems.	Humans should turn to God in times of need.
Pain and suffering are evils that should be avoided.	There is spiritual value to pain and suffering.
Life ends with death and the grave.	There is eternal life in heaven.	 There are many more points that could be placed in both columns. Conclude this section by stating that humans naturally desire a unified vision that provides meaning and purpose to all aspects of life and that the Judeo-Christian meta-narrative more than any other meets this fundamental human need.	O'Shea, *Educating in Christ*, 204-205.
Appreciate how the Judeo-Christian story/narrative helps believers to understand life's 'big questions.'	10 mins	(iv) Divide the classroom into groups of four students each. Ask the students to brainstorm and feedback on the following question: *What does the Judeo-Christian meta-narrative help us understand when it comes to the 'big questions' of life?* Collate on the whiteboard any reasonable responses, adding some of your own. By the end of this discussion the students should have noted down the following points: - How and why the world exists. - The goodness of creation. - How evil and suffering entered the world. - Humans are not alone or abandoned by God. - God as a God of love, mercy and forgiveness. - God's plan for human redemption. - How goodness ultimately overcomes evil.	Madrid & Hensley, *The Godless Delusion*, 21-24. Weidenkopf, *The Real Story of Catholic History*, 311-313.

		- How pain and suffering can have spiritual value. - Humans are made for love; the real meaning of love. - Life as something more than the pursuit of pleasure and material gain. - How humanity has an eternal destiny beyond the grave. Conclude by telling the students that the Judeo-Christian meta-narrative is a classic example of a narrative that provides a comprehensive understanding of the world, the meaning of life and our place in it. Each of us has a specific role in the Judeo-Christian meta-narrative given to us by God (i.e., vocation), one that is the source of happiness in this world and eternal life in the next.	
	3 mins	**Lesson Closure**: Remind the students that humans have a natural desire to understand the meaning and purpose of life and their specific place in it. There are many universal narratives that attempt to provide meaning and purpose – with or without God – and others that are limited or personalised. Among the competing narratives, the Judeo-Christian narrative is the most valuable because it is universal, combines the secular and spiritual, sequences the human story, provides meaning and purpose, answers the 'big questions', and points each individual to an ultimate and eternal destiny with God. **Transition**: Homework: Ask the students to consider what particular part they play in the Judeo-Christian meta-narrative (their vocation) and how they can discern what that may be (via prayer).	
		Resources: - Madrid, Patrick & Kenneth Hensley. *The Godless Delusion: A Catholic Challenge to Modern Atheism*. Huntington, Indiana: Our Sunday Visitor Publishing, 2010, 21-30. - O'Shea, Gerard. *Educating in Christ: A Practical Handbook*. Brooklyn, New York: Angelico Press, 2018, 204-205. - Ratzinger, Joseph. *'In the Beginning …' A Catholic Understanding of the Creation and the Fall*. New York, NY: T&T Clark, 1990, 71-77.	

- Rowland, Tracey. *Catholic Theology.* London: Bloomsbury T&T Clark, 2017, 161.
- Savage, Sara, Sylvia Collins Mayo, Bob Mayo with Graham Cray. *Making Sense of Generation Y: The World View of 15-25-Year-Olds.* London: Church House Publishing, 2006, 37-38.
- Schreck, Alan. *Catholic and Christian: An Explanation of Commonly Misunderstood Catholic Beliefs.* Cincinnati, Ohio: Servant Books, 2004, 205-219.
- Weidenkopf, Steve. *The Real Story of Catholic History.* El Cajon, California: Catholic Answers Press, 2017, 311-313.
- *Catechism of the Catholic Church.* Libreria Editrice Vaticana: St Pauls, 1994, paras. 1 & 68.
- YOUCAT (*Youth Catechism of the Catholic Church*). San Francisco, Ignatius Press, 2010, para. 1.
- Website: Selmys, Melinda. "What is Postmodernism?" https://www.catholic.com/magazine/print-edition/what-is-postmodernism.
- YouTube: Peterson, Jordan. "How We Create Narratives." https://www.youtube.com/watch?v=URBQGEX4g-Q&t=9s.

LESSON EVALUATION (to be completed AFTER the lesson)

Assessment of lesson objectives and suggestions for improvement:
Teacher self-reflection and self-evaluation:
[OFFICIAL USE ONLY] Comments by teacher supervisor:

Lesson 13: God as Trinity

LESSON ORGANISATION

Year Level:	Date:	Time:	Duration:	Room:

Quote:
"God is above all things as Father, for he is principle and source; he is through all things through the Word; and he is in all things in the Holy Spirit" – St Athanasius of Alexandria.

Prayer:
Come, Holy Spirit, fill the hearts of your faithful and enkindle in them the fire of your love.

V. Send forth your Spirit and they shall be created.
R. And you shall renew the face of the earth.

Let us pray.
O God, who by the light of the Holy Spirit, did instruct the hearts of the faithful, grant us in the same Spirit to be truly wise and ever to rejoice in his consolation.
Through Christ our Lord. Amen.

Lesson Outcomes:

As a result of this lesson, students will be able to:

- Critique the portrayal of Trinitarian beliefs in the works of anti-Trinitarian critics.
- Reflect on passages in the Old and New Testaments that afford evidence in support of the doctrine of the Trinity.
- Examine how the doctrine of the Trinity is portrayed in art and symbol.
- Understand and articulate the Trinity as a 'communion of love' wherein God knows and loves himself.
- Analyse official Catholic creedal statements relating to the Trinity.

Activity Sheets:

Activity Sheet 25, *Understanding the Trinity*.
Activity Sheet 26, *Comparing the Creeds*.

LESSON DELIVERY

Outcome	Time	Motivation and Introduction:	Resources/ References
Critique the portrayal of Trinitarian beliefs in the works of anti-Trinitarian critics.	10 mins	Welcome and settle the students. Prayer to the Holy Spirit (or other suitable prayer). Tell the students that today we will learn about *God as Trinity*. Ask the students the following questions: *Put up your hand if you have heard of the word 'Trinity'?; What do you think the word means?* Take two-three responses. Explain to the students that there are many people, both theists and atheists, who reject or even ridicule the idea of the Trinity. On a PowerPoint slide, provide the students with the following three examples, the first a Jehovah's Witnesses critique, the second an Islamic critique, the third an atheist one: *"Jehovah is one, Jesus Christ is his creature Son, and the Holy Spirit is Jehovah's active force. The doctrine of a Trinity is unchristian and of pagan origin"* – The Watchtower Bible & Tract Society. *"Unbelievers are those that say: 'Allah is one of three.' There is but one God ... those of them that disbelieve shall be sternly punished"* – The Koran, Sura 5. *"God is simultaneously himself and his son (and a ghost). Makes sense"* – Richard Dawkins. Ask the students to analyse the above critiques and in open class discussion identify anything they find interesting, compelling or objectionable. Afterwards, explain to the students that there are good responses to any critique of the Trinity but that ultimately the Trinity is a *mystery*, that is, something we can have some knowledge of but not complete knowledge. That is because only God can know everything about himself.	Holden & Pinsent, *Apologia: Catholic Answers to Today's Questions*, 31-34. Horn, *Why We're Catholic: Our Reasons for Faith, Hope, and Love*, 59-65.
Reflect on passages in the Old and New Testaments that afford evidence in support of the doctrine of the Trinity.	10 mins	**Lesson Steps** (i) Inform the students that the word 'Trinity' is not in the Bible, either in the Old or New Testaments. For some, this means that	Sheehan, *Apologetics and Catholic Doctrine*, 318-327.

| | | the Trinity as a doctrine is not Christian (e.g., Jehovah's Witnesses). Nevertheless, while the word 'Trinity' is not explicitly in the Bible it is arguable that the doctrine of the Trinity is at least *materially* present therein. Where?

On a PowerPoint slide display the following quotes from the Bible:

"Then God said, 'Let us make man in our image, after our likeness' … So God created man in his own image, in the image of God he created him …" (Gen. 1:26-27).

"Then the Lord God said, 'Behold, the man has become like one of us, knowing good and evil'" (Gen. 3:22).

"And the angel said to her, 'The Holy Spirit will come upon you, and the power of the Most High will overshadow you; therefore the child to be born will be called holy, the Son of God'" (Luke 1:34-35).

"And when he came up out of the water, immediately he saw the heavens opened and the Spirit descending upon him like a dove; and a voice came from heaven, 'You are my beloved Son; with you I am well pleased'" (Mark 1:10-11).

"Go therefore and make disciples of all nations, baptizing them in the name of the Father and of the Son and of the Holy Spirit, teaching them to observe all that I have commanded you; and behold, I am with you always, to the close of the age" (Matt. 28:19-20).

Ask the students to choose one of the above quotes and identify the evidence for God as Trinity. Ask one student per quote to present their answer to the class. Provide additional commentary or clarification, if necessary, to student answers.

In conclusion, inform the students that the Trinity is a 'strict mystery', meaning that it was not possible to know this truth about God unless it was specially revealed, as Jesus Christ did in the above quote recorded in the Gospel of Matthew. | Staples, "Defending the Trinity", 30-34. |

Examine how the doctrine of the Trinity is portrayed in art and symbol.	15 mins	(ii) Show the students the following YouTube video, *The Trinity* by Catholic Central (5.44 minutes).  Afterwards, explain to the students that for some the Trinity is untrue because "It doesn't make sense." The following are two common objections: - "How can God be one and three at the same time?" - "If the Father is God and the Son is God and the Holy Spirit is God then we really have three Gods, not one. The Trinity sounds like a disguised form of polytheism." (Belief in many Gods). Exercise: Symbols/pictures can be a helpful way to understand the Trinity. Hand out Activity Sheet 25, *Understanding the Trinity*. Ask the students to look at each of the symbols/pictures. Choose two and outline how each provides an insight(s) into understanding the Trinity. *Are these symbols/pictures adequate to explain the mystery of the Trinity? Why/Why not?*		Fradd, "How Not to Share the Trinity", 34-39.
Understand and articulate the Trinity as a 'communion of love' wherein God knows and loves himself.	7 mins	(iii) Another way to explain and understand the Trinity is to portray it as a 'communion of love' between persons. What does this mean? On a PowerPoint slide provide the students with the following explanation: As humans, we know ourselves, but the knowledge we have of ourselves is limited and imperfect. God the Father also knows himself, but God's knowledge of himself is infinite and perfect. Being infinite and perfect, God's knowledge of himself is equal to himself and must therefore be divine in essence. The New Testament calls God's knowledge of himself the "Word", or the Second Person of the Blessed Trinity. God the Father and the Word share mutual knowledge of each other. This mutual knowledge brings forth mutual love, a love that is infinite and eternal. Like God's knowledge of himself, God's love of himself is equal to himself and likewise must also be divine in essence. This mutual love between the Father and the Word the New Testament calls the "Holy Spirit", or the Third Person of the Blessed Trinity.		O'Neil & Black, *The Essential Moral Handbook: A Guide to Catholic Living*, 6-7.

Analyse official Catholic creedal statements relating to the Trinity.	10 mins	Question: The Trinitarian 'communion of love' wherein two Persons know and love each other and generate a third reflects which human institution? (Answer: The family) (iv) Hand out Activity Sheet 26, *Comparing the Creeds*. Ask the students to read through the two Creeds – the Apostles' and Nicene Creeds – and identify the differences between them. Highlight which parts of the Nicene Creed relate to God as Trinity, that is, identifies the Father, Son and Holy Spirit as Divine Persons. Explain the significance of these passages and the historical reasons for their inclusion.	Sheed, *Theology and Sanity*, 54-61.
	3 mins	**Lesson Closure:** Sum up for the students that the Trinity is a 'strict mystery' that we only know about because Jesus Christ has revealed it, as evidenced in various passages in the New Testament. While revealed, it is still difficult to understand, though art and symbols can provide helpful insights into the mystery. The Nicene Creed is another vehicle that assists believers to understand the Trinity as three Divine Persons and their relationship to each other. One of the best ways to understand the Trinity is by visualising it as a 'communion of love' between the Father and the Son that generates a third Person, the Holy Spirit. Ultimately, only God can fully know and understand himself as Trinity as only the infinite can fully know and understand the infinite. **Transition:** Homework: Research the term 'perichoresis.' How does it help to understand the relationship of the three Persons in the Trinity to each other? (1-2 paragraphs).	
		Resources: • Fradd, Matthew. "How Not to Share the Trinity." *Catholic Answers* (March-April 2014): 34-39. • Holden, Marcus & Andrew Pinsent. *Apologia: Catholic Answers to Today's Questions*. London: Catholic Truth Society, 2010, 31-34. • Horn, Trent. *Why We're Catholic: Our Reasons for Faith, Hope, and Love*. El Cajon: Catholic Answers Press, 2017, 59-65.	

		<ul><li>O'Neil, Kevin J. & Peter Black. *The Essential Moral Handbook: A Guide to Catholic Living.* Liguori, Missouri: Liguori, 2004, 6-7.</li><li>Sheed, Frank J. *Theology and Sanity.* London: Sheed & Ward, 1973, 54-61.</li><li>Sheehan, Michael. *Apologetics and Catholic Doctrine*, rev. and ed. Peter M. Joseph. London: Baronius Press, 2015, 318-327.</li><li>Staples, Tim. "Defending the Trinity." *Catholic Answers* (July-August 2014): 30-34.</li><li>*Catechism of the Catholic Church.* Libreria Editrice Vaticana: St Pauls, 1994, paras. 202, 232, 234, 252.</li><li>YOUCAT (*Youth Catechism of the Catholic Church*). San Francisco, Ignatius Press, 2010, paras. 35, 36.</li><li>Website: Catholic Answers. "Why the Trinity is Three Persons." https://www.catholic.com/qa/why-the-trinity-is-three-persons.</li><li>YouTube: Catholic Central. "The Trinity." https://www.youtube.com/watch?v=wkYM9OvX7f8.</li></ul>

LESSON EVALUATION (to be completed AFTER the lesson)

Assessment of lesson objectives and suggestions for improvement:
Teacher self-reflection and self-evaluation:
[OFFICIAL USE ONLY] Comments by teacher supervisor:

Lesson 14: The Divinity of Jesus Christ

LESSON ORGANISATION

Year Level: Date: Time: Duration: Room:

Quote:
"Therefore, the Word of God came in person, so that, being the image of the Father, he would be able to recreate humanity afresh in that image" – St Athanasius of Alexandria.

Prayer:
Come, Holy Spirit, fill the hearts of your faithful and enkindle in them the fire of your love.

V. Send forth your Spirit and they shall be created.
R. And you shall renew the face of the earth.

Let us pray.
O God, who by the light of the Holy Spirit, did instruct the hearts of the faithful, grant us in the same Spirit to be truly wise and ever to rejoice in his consolation.
Through Christ our Lord. Amen.

Lesson Outcomes:

As a result of this lesson, students will be able to:

- Discuss the challenges posed by those who deny the divinity of Jesus Christ.
- Be familiar with verses from the Old and New Testaments that support belief in the divinity of Christ.
- Determine the personal trustworthiness of Christ against his claims to be divine.
- Support the historical reliability of Scripture texts testifying to the divinity of Christ.
- Explore the writings of Church Fathers that evidence the divinity of Christ.
- Present evidence from outside the Bible supporting the historical existence of Christ.

Activity Sheets:

Activity Sheet 27, *Jesus: God, Man, or Both?*

LESSON DELIVERY

Outcome	Time	Motivation and Introduction:	Resources/ References
Discuss the challenges posed by those who deny the divinity of Jesus Christ.	7 mins	Welcome and settle the students. Prayer to the Holy Spirit (or other suitable prayer). Tell the students that today we will be learning about the divinity of Christ, that is, how Jesus is both true God and true man. Ask the students the following questions: *Have you ever been visited at your home by a member of the Jehovah's Witnesses? Has anyone of the Islamic faith spoken to you about Jesus? Has anyone heard of or read 'The Da Vinci Code'?* Take two-three responses and then on a PowerPoint slide outline the following: Belief in the divinity of Jesus Christ has been challenged since ancient times and is still controversial today: - Jehovah's Witnesses believe Jesus was the Archangel Michael in human form. - Moslems believe Jesus was only a human messenger of God, or prophet. - Dan Brown – author of *The Da Vinci Code* – believes Jesus was a great man but was later made into the 'Son of God' by the Council of Nicaea in AD 325. - 'Mythicists' believe Jesus was only a fictional figure who never really existed. Ask the students if they have heard any of the above claims about Jesus Christ. Then ask if there are any other claims they have heard which undermine or deny the divinity of Christ. **Lesson Steps**	Coffey, *The Gospel According to Jehovah's Witnesses*, 28-54. Horn, "Did Jesus Exist?", 16-21. Jomier, *The Bible and the Qur'an*, 65-74.
Be familiar with verses from the Old and New Testaments that support belief in the divinity of Christ.	10 mins	(i) Explain to the students that many who deny the divinity of Christ do so by quoting verses from the Bible in support. Hand out Activity Sheet 27, *Jesus: God, Man, or Both?* Choose individual students to read through the various quotes from the Old and New Testaments and identify which ones apparently support or oppose the divinity of Christ. Provide the students with a 'Catholic' explanation for those quotes that seem to suggest that Jesus Christ was no more than a creature /man/prophet.	Kreeft & Tacelli, *Handbook of Christian Apologetics*, 173-174. Petrie, *The Case for Jesus*, 119-136.

| Determine the personal trustworthiness of Christ against his claims to be divine. | 15 mins | (ii) Jesus Christ never made any direct statement claiming to be God (e.g., "I am God") but he did on various occasions say things that *by implication* amounted to such a claim. On a PowerPoint slide provide the following quotes from the Gospel of John as examples of such statements:

- *"… the Father loves the Son and has given all things into his hands"* (John 3:35).
- *"… whatever the Father does, the Son does likewise"* (John 5:19).
- *"Truly, truly, I say to you, before Abraham was, I am"* (John 8:58).
- *"I and the Father are one"* (John 10:30).
- *"… the Father is in me and I am in the Father"* (John 10:37-38).
- *"Let not your hearts be troubled; believe in God, believe also in me"* (John 14:1).
- *"All that the Father has is mine"* (John 16:15).

Inform the students that there are two matters to consider with respect to the above quotes: (i) whether Jesus was personally trustworthy; and (ii) whether the Gospel of John is a reliable historical record of what Jesus said.

Exercise: C. S. Lewis posed the first question in the following terms (the so-called 'Trilemma'): "Was Jesus of Nazareth a liar, lunatic or Lord?" Ask the students to write a one-two paragraph response to this question from what they know about Jesus' life, sayings, miracles, etc. Allow two students to read their responses to the class. During and after these readings the teacher may choose to highlight the following teachings/actions of Jesus as evidence that he was neither a liar nor lunatic: 

- His teaching to love our neighbour and our enemies.
- His teaching on turning the other cheek.
- His teaching on forgiving a brother seventy times seven.
- His teachings on the Prodigal Son and the Good Shepherd.
- His showing mercy to the poor and repentant.
- His keeping continued company with the poor/powerless.
- His fleeing from those who tried to make him King. | Kreeft, *Fundamentals of the Faith*, 59-63. |

Support the historical reliability of Scripture texts testifying to the divinity of Christ.		The second question relates to the historical reliability of the Gospel of John in its current form. Inform the students that we know it is identical to the most ancient copies we possess dating back to the second century AD, including the following: - *John Wylands manuscript* – early 2nd century. - *Codex Bodmar* – 2nd century. - *Codex Vaticanus* – 4th century. - *Codex Sinaiticus* – 4th century. - *Codex Bezae* – 5th century. - *Codex Ephraimi* – 5th century. - *Codex Amiatinus* – 7th century. Ask the students the following question: *What are the implications of the above?* After taking two-three responses provide the following answer: What this means is that there is no evidence of tampering or alteration of the original text, reinforcing the integrity of the Gospel of John and the authenticity of Jesus' words contained therein. Also, it is difficult to question the genuineness of St John himself, considering that the historical record shows he was willing to suffer persecution and even death for what he believed and taught.	Duggan, *Beyond Reasonable Doubt*, 99-105. Holden & Pinsent, *Apologia: Catholic Answers to Today's Questions*, 22-25.
Explore the writings of Church Fathers that evidence the divinity of Christ.	10 mins	(iii) Ask the students the following question: *Does anyone remember what Dan Brown in his book 'The Da Vinci Code' said about Jesus?* After taking one-two responses read to the students the following: *"The divinity of Jesus was first raised and established at the Council of Nicaea in AD 325."* From what they have already learnt from this lesson, challenge the students to respond to the above statement. Take one-two responses. Any responses will probably quote verses from Scripture which were written well before AD 325. Inform the students that there is another way to respond to Dan Brown, namely, by quoting extracts from the writings of the 'Church Fathers.' These are writers, lay-men, bishops, saints or doctors who wrote about or defended Christianity between	Olson & Miesel, *The Da Vinci Hoax*, 116-122.

| | | the years AD 100 and AD 749. Invite the students to state if they know the names of any of these Fathers, particularly any who wrote before AD 325.

On a PowerPoint slide provide the following three quotes from 'pre-Nicene' Church Fathers:

St Ignatius of Antioch (c. AD 110):
"To those who are united in flesh and in spirit by every commandment of his, who are filled with the grace of God without wavering, and who are filtered clear of every foreign stain, I wish an unalloyed joy in Jesus Christ, our God."

St Melito of Sardis (c. AD 177):
"Being God and likewise perfect man, (Jesus) gave positive indications of his two natures: of his Deity, by the miracles during the three years following after his Baptism; of his humanity, in the thirty years which came before his Baptism."

St Irenaeus of Lyons (c. AD 180):
"Nevertheless, what cannot be said of anyone else who ever lived, that (Jesus) is himself in his own right God and Lord and Eternal King and Only-begotten and Incarnate Word, proclaimed as such by all the Prophets and by the Apostles and by the Spirit himself."

Exercise: Ask the students the following questions: *Why are each of these quotes important for refuting Dan Brown's claims? How do they specifically speak of Jesus Christ's divinity and humanity?* Answers should highlight their pre-AD 325 authorship and terms such as "God", "perfect man", "two natures", "deity", "humanity", "Lord", "Eternal King", "Only-begotten", "Incarnate Word." | |
| Present evidence from outside the Bible supporting the historical existence of Christ. | 10 mins | (iv) Tell the students that the idea of 'mythicism' is slowly becoming popular. This is the belief that Jesus is simply a myth invented by Christians and that there is no historical evidence for his existence outside of the Bible. One recent popular book promoting mythicism is *The Christ Myth: The Greatest Story Ever Sold* by Acharya S. | Horn, "Four Reasons I Think Jesus Really Existed" (Video). |

		Show the students the following YouTube video, *Is Jesus a Myth?* by Karlo Broussard of Catholic Answers (2.34 minutes). Afterwards, ask the students to answer the following questions (allow time for classroom discussion): 	
		- *What are the Christian sources for Jesus' existence?* - *What are two non-Christian sources for Jesus' existence? Are they convincing?* - *Why is it important to have non-Christian sources for Jesus' existence?*	
	3 mins	**Lesson Closure**: Sum up for the students that there is ample evidence for Jesus' existence and divinity in and outside the Bible. As for the Bible's integrity, ancient manuscripts evidence a consistency that negates any suggestion of later tampering, while evidence of Jesus' character precludes any possibility of him being a liar or fraud. Furthermore, the writings of the very early Church Fathers straightforwardly debunk modern theories that Jesus' divinity was only "invented" by the Council of Nicaea in AD 325. Consequently, Christians can still, like St Thomas the Apostle, confidently declare that Jesus Christ is "Lord and God." **Transition**: Homework: Look up the Roman historian Suetonius and what reference he made to the Christians in his book, *Lives of the Caesars*. What is interesting about his reference to Christ?	
		Resources: • Coffey, John F. *The Gospel According to Jehovah's Witnesses.* Melbourne: The Polding Press, 1979, 28-54. • Duggan, G. H. *Beyond Reasonable Doubt.* Boston, MA: St Paul Books & Media, 1987, 99-105. • Holden, Marcus & Andrew Pinsent. *Apologia: Catholic Answers to Today's Questions.* London: Catholic Truth Society, 2010, 23-25. • Horn, Trent. "Did Jesus Exist?" *Catholic Answers* (May-June 2013): 16-21.	

		<ul><li>Jomier, Jacques. *The Bible and the Qur'an.* San Francisco: Ignatius Press, 2002, 65-74.</li><li>Kreeft, Peter. *Fundamentals of the Faith: Essays in Christian Apologetics.* San Francisco: Ignatius Press, 1988, 59-63.</li><li>Kreeft, Peter & Ronald K. Tacelli. *Handbook of Christian Apologetics: Hundreds of Answers to Crucial Questions.* Downers Grove: IVP Academic, 1994, 173-174.</li><li>Olson, Carl E. & Sandra Miesel. *The Da Vinci Hoax.* San Francisco: Ignatius Press, 2004, 116-122.</li><li>Petrie, Brant. *The Case for Jesus: The Biblical and Historical Evidence for Christ.* New York: Image, 2016, 1-54, 84-101, 119-136.</li><li>*Catechism of the Catholic Church.* Libreria Editrice Vaticana: St Pauls, 1994, paras. 456, 461-463, 479, 485, 488, 497, 723.</li><li>YOUCAT (*Youth Catechism of the Catholic Church*). San Francisco, Ignatius Press, 2010, para. 39.</li><li>Website: Horn, Trent. "Four Reasons I Think Jesus Really Existed." https://www.catholic.com/magazine/online-edition/four-reasons-i-think-jesus-really-existed.</li><li>YouTube: Broussard, Karlo. "Is Jesus a Myth?" https://www.youtube.com/watch?v=iKdG05w9WLA.</li></ul>

LESSON EVALUATION (to be completed AFTER the lesson)

Assessment of lesson objectives and suggestions for improvement:
Teacher self-reflection and self-evaluation:
[OFFICIAL USE ONLY] Comments by teacher supervisor:

Lesson 15: The Bodily Resurrection of Jesus Christ

LESSON ORGANISATION

Year Level: _____ Date: _____ Time: _____ Duration: _____ Room: _____

Quote:
"Let no one mourn that he has fallen again and again; for forgiveness has risen from the grave" – St John Chrysostom.

Prayer:
Come, Holy Spirit, fill the hearts of your faithful and enkindle in them the fire of your love.

V. Send forth your Spirit and they shall be created.
R. And you shall renew the face of the earth.

Let us pray.
O God, who by the light of the Holy Spirit, did instruct the hearts of the faithful, grant us in the same Spirit to be truly wise and ever to rejoice in his consolation.
Through Christ our Lord. Amen.

Lesson Outcomes:

As a result of this lesson, students will be able to:

- Recognise the various objections to the resurrection of Jesus Christ.
- Understand the central importance of the resurrection of Christ to Christianity.
- Be familiar with verses from the New Testament testifying to the resurrection of Christ and the variety of witnesses.
- Affirm the personal integrity and reliability of the Gospel authors and the transformative impact of the resurrection upon those who witnessed the same.
- Respond to the various theories questioning the resurrection of Christ.

Activity Sheets:

Activity Sheet 28, *Who Saw Jesus Christ Risen?*
Activity Sheet 29, *Theories Denying the Resurrection of Jesus.*

LESSON DELIVERY

Outcome	Time	Motivation and Introduction:	Resources/ References
Recognise the various objections to the resurrection of Jesus Christ.	10 mins	Welcome and settle the students. Prayer to the Holy Spirit (or other suitable prayer). Tell the students that today we will be looking at the resurrection of Jesus Christ from the dead and the many objections to this belief. The objections to the resurrection of Christ are many and varied. On a PowerPoint slide outline the following: - Moslems believe that someone else died on the Cross in the place of Christ. Christ avoided death by being lifted up into the presence of Allah (Sura 4:157-158). - 'Critical' biblical scholars doubt the resurrection accounts in the Gospels as dubious on the grounds that they were written many years after the death of Christ. - Sceptics prefer natural explanations for what happened to Christ's body, for example, that it was stolen or left as food for scavenging animals. - Atheists mock the accounts of Christ's resurrection as little more than fairy tales. They claim that Christ's body simply decomposed like any other dead body. Classroom discussion: Why is it important for Christianity that Jesus Christ rose from the dead? After taking two-three responses outline the following: - It validates Jesus Christ as the Messiah and the divine Son of God. - If 'Gospel' means "good news", then a Gospel without the resurrection is no Gospel at all. - It reinforces the hope of our own future resurrection and triumph over death (1 Cor. 15:14-19). **Lesson Steps**	Duggan, *Beyond Reasonable Doubt*, 141-143.
Understand the central importance of the resurrection of Christ to Christianity.			
Be familiar with verses from the New Testament testifying to the resurrection of Christ and the variety of witnesses.	10 mins	(i) Hand out Activity Sheet 28, *Who Saw Jesus Christ Risen?* This sheet outlines the New Testament verses that record appearances of the Risen Jesus and those who claimed to have seen him. Ask the students to answer the following questions:	Sheehan, *Apologetics and Catholic Doctrine*, 113-122.

Affirm the personal integrity and reliability of the Gospel authors and the transformative impact of the resurrection upon those who witnessed the same.	12 mins	- At least how many people saw Jesus Christ after his resurrection? - How many times was the Risen Christ seen by more than one person at the same time? - What different places and times was the Risen Christ seen? - Which witnesses were Apostles, and which were not? - Which witness was not initially a follower of Jesus? *What does the above variety say about the reliability of the eyewitness accounts?* (ii) Emphasise to the students that while the Gospel accounts mention that there were many witnesses to Christ's resurrection there is an important counter-claim that needs to be addressed, namely, that the Apostles stole the dead body of Jesus and then for years afterwards went around telling others that he had risen from the dead. This is the so-called 'fraud theory.' Activity: Ask the students to imagine that the 'fraud theory' is true. If so, list what they think the Apostles would have hoped to gain by promoting such a fraud. Allow for an open class discussion. Possible answers could include: - Material possessions (lands, gold, money). - Fame/social prestige. - Glamorous marriages. - Political power. Highlight, however, that there is no historical evidence that the Apostles or Gospel writers gained any of the above advantages. To the contrary, the evidence indicates that the opposite was the case with the Apostles, etc., enduring the following: - Loss of domestic security. - Hunger. - Rejection/ridicule. - Difficult long-distance journeys. - Shipwreck. - Imprisonment. - Torture. - Exile. - Execution/martyrdom.	Crean, *A Catholic Replies to Professor Dawkins*, 76-77. Kreeft & Tacelli, *Handbook of Christian Apologetics*, 184-186. Rice, *50 Questions on the Natural Law*, 178-179.

Respond to the various theories questioning the resurrection of Jesus Christ.		To accentuate the point, mention that there is also no record that any of the Apostles, etc., later 'spilled the beans' and exposed the alleged conspiracy voluntarily or under cross-examination. Rather, they persevered in their preaching of the Risen Christ despite the above difficulties and did so with a level of courage and selflessness they did not possess while Jesus was with them. This transformation testifies to their sincerity and integrity and provides further evidence that they were witnesses to a powerful and life-changing event.	
Respond to the various theories questioning the resurrection of Jesus Christ.	10 mins	(iii) Inform the students that besides the 'fraud theory' there are many other theories denying the resurrection of Christ. They include the following three: - The 'Swoon Theory.' - The 'Trash Theory.' - The 'Hallucination Theory.' Hand out Activity Sheet 29, *Theories Denying the Resurrection of Jesus*. Ask the students to draw a line matching the Title in Column A with the Theory in Column B and the Rebuttal in Column C.	Horn, *Why We're Catholic: Our Reasons for Faith, Hope, and Love*, 51-58. Longenecker, "Atheists and Easter Apologetics", 18-23.
Respond to the various theories questioning the resurrection of Christ.	10 mins	(iv) Show the students the following YouTube video, *How Do We Know the Tomb was Empty?* by Karlo Broussard of Catholic Answers (3.25 minutes). Afterwards, ask the students to answer the following questions (allow time for classroom discussion): - *How many different sources testify to Jesus' tomb being empty?* - *Why is it important that Jesus' tomb should be empty?* - *Do the Gospel accounts of the empty tomb satisfy modern standards of historical proof?*	
	3 mins	**Lesson Closure**: Remind the students that the resurrection of Christ remains the central pillar of Christianity. It continues to be a highly contested belief from multiple perspectives, nevertheless, the Gospel accounts have stood the test of time and meet all the accepted	

historical standards of attestation. The integrity of the many and varied witnesses also remains incontestable and the fact that so many of them were willing to suffer and die for their witness adds weight to their credibility. Of the various theories opposing Christ's resurrection, all of them can be challenged from the historical record and none carry enough persuasive weight to overturn the Gospel accounts.

Transition:

Homework: What would your immediate response be if you saw a news story claiming that the bones of Jesus have been discovered? (One-two paragraphs).

Resources:
- Crean, Thomas. *A Catholic Replies to Professor Dawkins.* Oxford: Family Publications, 2007, 76-77.
- Duggan, G. H. *Beyond Reasonable Doubt.* Boston, MA: St Paul Books & Media, 1987, 141-143.
- Horn, Trent. *Why We're Catholic: Our Reasons for Faith, Hope, and Love.* El Cajon: Catholic Answers Press, 2017, 51-58.
- Kreeft, Peter & Ronald K. Tacelli. *Handbook of Christian Apologetics: Hundreds of Answers to Crucial Questions.* Downers Grove: IVP Academic, 1994, 184-186.
- Longenecker, Dwight. "Atheists and Easter Apologetics." *Catholic Answers* (March-April 2014): 18-23.
- Rice, Charles. *50 Questions on the Natural Law: What it is and Why We Need it.* San Francisco: Ignatius Press, 1993, 178-179.
- Sheehan, Michael. *Apologetics and Catholic Doctrine*, rev. and ed. Peter M. Joseph. London: Baronius Press, 2015, 113-122.
- *Catechism of the Catholic Church.* Libreria Editrice Vaticana: St Pauls, 1994, paras. 638-646, 651-656.
- YOUCAT (*Youth Catechism of the Catholic Church*). San Francisco, Ignatius Press, 2010, paras. 104-108.
- Website: Harrison, Brian. "Explaining Away Jesus' Resurrection." https://www.catholic.com/magazine/print-edition/explaining-away-jesus-resurrection-1.
- YouTube: Broussard, Karlo. "How Do We Know the Tomb Was Empty?" https://www.youtube.com/watch?v=C6myazD-fV4.

LESSON EVALUATION (to be completed AFTER the lesson)

Assessment of lesson objectives and suggestions for improvement:
Teacher self-reflection and self-evaluation:
[OFFICIAL USE ONLY] Comments by teacher supervisor:

Lesson 16: The Foundation, Authority and Necessity of the Catholic Church and the Papacy

LESSON ORGANISATION

Year Level: Date: Time: Duration: Room:

Quote:
"We honour Christ if we honour the Pope; we dishonour Christ if we dishonour the Pope" – St Catherine of Siena.

Prayer:
Come, Holy Spirit, fill the hearts of your faithful and enkindle in them the fire of your love.

V. Send forth your Spirit and they shall be created.
R. And you shall renew the face of the earth.

Let us pray.
O God, who by the light of the Holy Spirit, did instruct the hearts of the faithful, grant us in the same Spirit to be truly wise and ever to rejoice in his consolation.
Through Christ our Lord. Amen.

Lesson Outcomes:

As a result of this lesson, students will be able to:

- Appreciate the reality and need for external authority outside of ourselves.
- Recognise and analyse scriptural evidence that Jesus Christ founded a church with authority to teach, govern and sanctify.
- Demonstrate from the Gospels that Christ bestowed upon St Peter primacy over the other disciples and exclusive power and authority through the "keys."
- Define terms such as 'magisterium' and 'infallibility.'
- Understand how authority is passed on in the Church over the centuries.

Activity Sheets:

Activity Sheet 30, *'Infallibility' – What it Does and Does Not Mean.*

LESSON DELIVERY

Outcome	Time	Motivation and Introduction:	Resources/ References
Appreciate the reality and need for external authority outside of ourselves.	7 mins	Welcome and settle the students. Prayer to the Holy Spirit (or other suitable prayer). Tell the students that today we will look at the concept of 'external authority', that is, authority outside of ourselves, particularly the authority of the Catholic Church and the Pope. Inform the students that 'authority' is not a popular thing in the minds of many young people today. There are a variety of reasons for this. Ask the students to suggest their own reasons. Take three-four responses. Reasons may include: - Young people feel they are their own authority and resent being told by others how to think/believe/live. - Authority figures are seen as much older and out of touch with the young. - Young people do not trust authority figures due to scandal/corruption. - Young people no longer believe in 'absolutes' and hence distrust persons or organisations that claim to know and teach 'truth.' Conclude the discussion by affirming that those who believe in God usually believe that he is the ultimate authority and exercises his authority to teach, govern and sanctify his people. God most perfectly achieves this through Jesus Christ, who while on earth established a visible church with delegated authority to similarly teach, govern and sanctify believers in his name. **Lesson Steps**	Salza, *The Biblical Basis for the Catholic Faith*, 40-64. Shea, *By What Authority?*, 131-153. Sheehan, *Apologetics and Catholic Doctrine*, 134-140.
Recognise and analyse scriptural evidence that Jesus Christ founded a church with authority to teach, govern and sanctify.	10 mins	(i) Question: Did Jesus Christ really establish a church with authority to teach, govern and sanctify? If so, what is the evidence? After two-three student responses, display the following quote from Matthew's Gospel on a PowerPoint slide: *"You are Peter, and on this rock I will build my church. I will give you the keys of the kingdom of heaven, and whatever you bind on earth shall be bound in heaven, and whatever you loose on earth shall be loosed in heaven"* (Matt. 16:18-19).	Clovis, *A Biblical Search for the Church Christ Founded*, 31-52. Schreck, *Catholic and Christian*, 75-87.

		Scripture exegesis: Invite the students to analyse Matt. 16:18-19 and answer the following questions: - *Which words, if any, show that Jesus started a church?* (Answer: "… on this rock I will build my church"). - *What do you think Jesus meant by the word 'church'?* - (Answer: A community of believers led by pastoral [caring] shepherds). - *What power/authority did Jesus give to this church?* (Answer: The power to "bind" and "loose"). Inform the students that the words "bind" and "loose" are ancient Jewish terms for making and unmaking laws/rules, etc., for the spiritual benefit and well-being of God's people. Then ask them the following question: *Are there any other verses in Scripture that support the idea of a church with power/authority?* Answer: Yes. Show the following on a PowerPoint slide: "… if he refuses to listen even to the church, let him be to you as a Gentile and a tax collector" (Matt. 18:17). "He who hears you hears me, and he who rejects you rejects me" (Luke 10:16). "Obey your leaders and submit to them; for they are keeping watch over your souls, as men who will have to give account" (Heb. 13:17). Question: *What are the consequences for those who refuse to "listen" or "hear", or who "reject"?*	
Demonstrate from the Gospels that Christ bestowed upon St Peter primacy over the other disciples and exclusive power and authority through the "keys."	15 mins	(ii) Return the class' focus back to Matt. 16:18-19 and ask the following question: *Normally, any organisation has a single leader that is the ultimate authority. What does Jesus say and do to St Peter in this passage?* (Answer: He changes his name from Simon to Peter (*"Rock"*) and gives him the *"keys of the kingdom of heaven"*). Show the students the following YouTube video, *The Primacy of Peter* by Joan Watson of Three Minute Theology (3.47 minutes).	Duggan, *Beyond Reasonable Doubt*, 141-143. Ray, *Crossing the Tiber*, 69-72.

		Afterwards, ask the students to answer the following questions (allow time for classroom discussion): - *Why is Jesus changing the name of Simon to Peter ("Rock")?* (Answer: To signify his new role/mission as the visible foundation of his Church on earth). - *What do you think is the significance of "the keys"?* (Answer: They signify St Peter's new power and authority to govern the Church as Christ's 'chief steward', or 'Prime Minister'). - *Listen for the terms "strengthen the brethren" and "feed the sheep." Where do these terms come from and how do they demonstrate St Peter's relationship to the rest of the Church?* (Answer: They come from Luke 22:32 and John 21:15-17 [display these two verses up on a PowerPoint slide] and they demonstrate St Peter's new responsibility to spiritually care for and feed all the other followers of Christ). Classroom discussion: Catholics believe that the power, authority and responsibility given to St Peter to "bind", "loose", "strengthen" and "feed" has been passed on over the centuries and is now held by the Pope in Rome as 'successor to St Peter.' That being the case, what are the implications of this for each of us? Dedicate up to five minutes for this discussion. Answers should relate to "listening", "hearing", "obeying." Why? For our spiritual instruction, well-being and ultimate happiness in this life and the next.	
Define terms such as 'magisterium' and 'infallibility.'	10 mins	(iii) Emphasise to the students that when speaking about authority in the Catholic Church some technical terms are used. Two examples of this are the words 'magisterium' and 'infallibility.' (Show both these words on a PowerPoint slide). Ask the students if they have heard of the term 'magisterium.' They may have heard it used in relation to modern-day judges who are called 'magistrates.' Inform the students that this word derives from the Latin 'magister', which means teacher. It highlights that the Church is our teacher (as well as our 'mother'). 'Infallibility' is a more controversial word, especially when used in relation to the Pope. Hand out Activity Sheet 30, *'Infallibility'*	Armstrong, *A Biblical Defense of Catholicism*, 211-238.

		– *What it Does and Does Not Mean*. Ask the students to tick the statements that correctly define and help understand the term 'infallibility' when used in relation to the Pope and put a cross through the statements that do not. The following are the correct answers: - Speaking 'ex cathedra', or from the Chair of Peter. - Addressing the Universal Church. - Defining a question relating to faith or morals. - Intending to settle a question once and for all. Conclude by noting that the Pope is, therefore, infallible only on rare occasions and under strict conditions.	
Understand how authority is passed on in the Church over the centuries.	10 mins	(iv) Final question: *How is power and authority passed on in the Church?* Student answers may include, through the Pope nominating his successor, or through bishops transferring their authority to their favourite priest, or through popular vote, etc. On a PowerPoint slide show the students the following: *"While they were worshipping the Lord and fasting, the Holy Spirit said, 'Set apart for me Barnabas and Saul for the work to which I have called them.' Then after fasting and praying they laid their hands on them and sent them off"* (Acts 13:2-3). Point out to the students that this verse relates to when Sts Barnabas and Paul were chosen and made ('consecrated') bishops of the Church by the Apostles. This is called 'apostolic succession.' Identify the following distinctive points: - Those who were "worshipping the Lord and fasting" were the Apostles. - The Holy Spirit asked the Apostles to "set apart" Sts Barnabas and Paul. - The Apostles "laid their hands" on Sts Barnabas and Paul. Ask the students, *At which point in Acts 13:2-3 were Sts Barnabas and Paul actually made into bishops, or successors to the Apostles?* Answer: When hands were laid upon them. Highlight that while lay people are today consulted in the appointment process of new bishops as successors to the Apostles, it is the Holy Spirit who calls and – through the laying	Schreck, *Catholic and Christian*, 32-33, 78-80.

		of hands – bestows the apostolic power and authority. This process is meant to stress that the authority of the Bishop comes solely from God.

The same can be said for the authority of the Pope. As the first Pope, St Peter's authority came directly from Jesus Christ. Inform the students that there have been 266 Popes from the time of St Peter till the present (refer the students to a list of the Popes at http://www.newadvent.org/cathen/12272b.htm). Since Jesus Christ is not currently on earth, the next best way to highlight the Pope's divine authority is to have new 'Bishops of Rome' elected by a vote of the clergy of Rome. Today, the eligible clergy of Rome who can elect a new Pope are all the Cardinals of the Church under the age of 80. |
| | 3 mins | **Lesson Closure**:

Conclude by reiterating that, while we all treasure our own individualism and independence, there is a living teaching authority external to ourselves that has been established by God, namely, the Catholic Church headed by the Pope. Summarising its power and authority, the Church and Pope possess the "keys" to bind, loose, strengthen and feed her children for their spiritual benefit. In turn, believers are called upon to listen, hear and obey the Church/Pope as mother and teacher. While the Church/Pope possess great power and authority, they are at their best when they exercise the same as humble servants of the People of God.

Transition:

Homework: Ask the students to view an ordination ceremony of bishops as an example of how power and authority is passed on in the Church from one generation to the next. An instance can be found at https://www.youtube.com/watch?v=V0jLZV_eoXw (*The Pope ordains two new Bishops in St Peter's Basilica*). |
| | | **Resources**:
  - Armstrong, Dave. *A Biblical Defense of Catholicism.* Manchester, NH: Sophia Institute Press, 2003, 211-238.
  - Clovis, Linus F. *A Biblical Search for the Church Christ Founded.* Leominster, United Kingdom: Gracewing, 2012, 31-52. |

		<ul><li>Duggan, G. H. *Beyond Reasonable Doubt.* Boston, MA: St Paul Books & Media, 1987, 202-207.</li><li>Ray, Stephen K. *Crossing the Tiber: Evangelical Protestants Discover the Historic Church.* San Francisco: Ignatius Press, 1997, 69-72.</li><li>Salza, John. *The Biblical Basis for the Catholic Faith.* Huntingdon, Indiana: Our Sunday Visitor Publishing, 2005, 40-64.</li><li>Shea, Mark P. *By What Authority?: An Evangelical Discovers Catholic Tradition.* Huntington, Indiana: Our Sunday Visitor Publishing Division, 1996, 131-153.</li><li>Sheehan, Michael. *Apologetics and Catholic Doctrine*, rev. and ed. by Peter M. Joseph. London: Baronius Press, 2015, 134-140.</li><li>Schreck, Alan. *Catholic and Christian: An Explanation of Commonly Misunderstood Catholic Beliefs.* Cincinnati, Ohio: Servant Books, 2004, 32-33, 47, 75-87.</li><li>*Catechism of the Catholic Church.* Libreria Editrice Vaticana: St Pauls, 1994, paras. 553, 862, 881, 882, 886.</li><li>YOUCAT (*Youth Catechism of the Catholic Church*). San Francisco, Ignatius Press, 2010, paras. 140-144.</li><li>Website: Knox, Ronald. "The Teaching Authority of the Church." https://www.catholic.com/magazine/print-edition/the-teaching-authority-of-the-church.</li><li>YouTube: Watson, Joan. "The Primacy of Peter." https://www.youtube.com/watch?v=ErT-XPm21NA.</li></ul>

LESSON EVALUATION (to be completed AFTER the lesson)

Assessment of lesson objectives and suggestions for improvement:
Teacher self-reflection and self-evaluation:
[OFFICIAL USE ONLY] Comments by teacher supervisor:

"Always Be Prepared …" – A 'New Apologetics' Course for Catholic Secondary Schools

Lesson 17: <u>The Catholic Faith and Other Religions</u>

LESSON ORGANISATION

Year Level: Date: Time: Duration: Room:

Quote:
"The Church respects everything in other religions that is good and true" – YOUCAT para. 136.

Prayer:
Come, Holy Spirit, fill the hearts of your faithful and enkindle in them the fire of your love.

V. Send forth your Spirit and they shall be created.
R. And you shall renew the face of the earth.

Let us pray.
O God, who by the light of the Holy Spirit, did instruct the hearts of the faithful, grant us in the same Spirit to be truly wise and ever to rejoice in his consolation.
Through Christ our Lord. Amen.

Lesson Outcomes:

As a result of this lesson, students will be able to:

- Recognise Jesus Christ as the unique mediator between God and humanity.
- Understand the necessity of belonging to the Catholic Church in God's plan of salvation.
- Appreciate the importance of peaceful co-existence between Catholicism and other religions.
- Highlight examples of commonalities and instances where different religions can cooperate for the common good.
- Acknowledge the limits of ecumenism and inter-faith cooperation.
- Value the importance of continuous ecumenical and inter-faith dialogue in the quest for ultimate unity under "one Lord and one shepherd."

Activity Sheets:

Activity Sheet 31, *Commonalities and Common Good.*
Activity Sheet 32, *The 'Non-Negotiables.'*

LESSON DELIVERY

Outcome	Time	Motivation and Introduction:	Resources/ References
Recognise Jesus Christ as the unique mediator between God and humanity. Understand the necessity of belonging to the Catholic Church in God's plan of salvation.	5 mins	Welcome and settle the students. Prayer to the Holy Spirit (or other suitable prayer). Tell the students that today we will be looking at the uniqueness of the Catholic religion and its relationship to other religions. Inform the students that the idea of religious 'uniqueness' is a very controversial one in the context of today's culture and attitudes. Ask the students why they may think that is the case. Take two responses. Answers may include the following: - Such a claim can appear to be proud, arrogant, offensive and intolerant. - Such a claim is contemptuous of other religions and believers and can lead to religious bigotry and conflict. - All religions possess some level of truth; no religion has the whole truth or a monopoly on truth. Outline to the students that 'uniqueness' has a two-fold aspect, namely, the uniqueness of Jesus Christ as the one universal saviour (*"the way, the truth and the life"*: John 14:6) and Catholicism as the one revealed religion of God possessing the fullness of truth and the means of salvation. These beliefs are 'non-negotiable.' However, at the same time it is important to uphold such beliefs with charity and humility, recognising the elements of truth contained in other religions and the good will and human dignity of other believers. **Lesson Steps**	Kreeft, *Fundamentals of the Faith*, 74-80.
Recognise Jesus Christ as the unique mediator between God and humanity. Understand the necessity of belonging to the Catholic Church in God's plan of salvation.	15 mins	(i) What does the Catholic Church officially say about the uniqueness of Christ and the necessity of the Catholic Church for salvation? The best place to look is the *Catechism of the Catholic Church* (CCC). On a PowerPoint slide show the following: *"... the Council teaches that the Church, a pilgrim now on earth, is necessary for salvation: the one Christ is the mediator and the way of salvation; he ... affirmed ... the necessity of the Church ... Hence they could not be saved who, knowing that the Catholic Church was founded as necessary by God through Christ, would refuse either to enter it or to remain in it"* (Para. 846).	Kreeft & Tacelli, *Handbook of Christian Apologetics*, 353-360. Ratzinger, *Truth and Tolerance*, 162-182.

Open classroom discussion – Ask the students the following questions:

What are the two immediate implications arising from this paragraph?

Answers should include:
- Jesus Christ is the one "mediator" (way to God) and the "way of salvation."
- Jesus Christ founded the Catholic Church, and all should belong to it to be saved.

How might this be of concern to people who do not believe in Jesus Christ or who do not belong to the Catholic Church?

Answers may include:
- Some may find it narrow-minded, if not bigoted ("Aren't there many ways to God?").
- Non-Catholics may feel that they are not equal to, or inferior to Catholics ("Sounds arrogant, even racist!").
- Some may conclude that Catholics believe only Catholics go to heaven ("What about good people in other religions?").

How should Catholics respond to these concerns?

Answers should include (Show on a PowerPoint slide):
- Jesus Christ wishes for unity. He prayed that "all may be one" just as he and the Father are one (John 17:11).
- Jesus' 'unity prayer' can only be fulfilled by belonging to the Church he himself founded. This is "perfect communion."
- Baptised persons who do not realise that the Catholic Church is the Church Jesus Christ founded nevertheless possess an "imperfect communion" with her (CCC 838).
- Those who "through no fault of their own" do not know Christ or his Church but sincerely seek to do God's will "may achieve eternal salvation" (CCC 847).

Highlight how the Church in paras. 838 and 847 recognises that God does not 'condemn people' simply because they are not Catholic. God in his love and mercy acknowledges good will and sincerity. In turn, Catholics should always display charity and respect in their everyday dealings with those of other faiths.

Appreciate the importance of peaceful co-existence between Catholicism and other religions. Highlight examples of commonalities and instances where different religions can cooperate for the common good.	12 mins	(ii) Throughout history, conflict has plagued relations between various religions. Briefly mention some relevant examples (e.g., wars between Christianity and Islam; wars between Catholics and Protestants). Stress that for the sake of public order in modern-day multi-cultural/faith societies religious conflict can have no place. It also violates the Christian obligation to love our neighbours/enemies as ourselves. In multi-cultural/faith societies there is value in understanding what different religions have in common and how they may be able to cooperate in matters of common interest. This is called ecumenical and inter-faith cooperation. Exercise: Hand out Activity Sheet 31, *Commonalities and Common Good*. Ask the students to complete the two tables by answering the following questions: - *Besides our common humanity, what other matters, qualities, characteristics or practices do Catholics share with people of other faiths?* - *In what areas can different religions co-operate for the common good?* Answers for the first question may include: belief in a loving God; belief in a moral code (against murder, theft, lying, etc.); belief in human dignity; prayer; pilgrimage; fasting; almsgiving. Answers for the second question may include: cooperating to fight poverty; to fight injustices; to protect the environment; to protect religious freedoms; to campaign for pro-life issues, etc.	Costa, *The Catholic Church and the World Religions*, 34-105.
Acknowledge the limits of ecumenism and inter-faith cooperation.	10 mins	(iii) Tell the students that despite the many commonalities between major religions and areas where cooperation is possible, it is important to avoid a 'religious indifferentism' that regards all religions as fundamentally the same and dismisses differing religious teachings as unimportant. These differences are significant enough to place limits on ecumenical and inter-faith cooperation. Exercise: Hand out Activity Sheet 32, *The 'Non-Negotiables.'* Ask the students to list examples of important religious beliefs that cannot be 'watered down' for the sake of unity. Do this from a theistic, Christian and Catholic perspective. Some examples of 'not negotiable' beliefs are provided in each column as a starting point.	Braxton, "Catholic Education and the New Apologetics", 766-767. Spencer, "Islam and Catholicism", 36-40.

Value the importance of continuous ecumenical and inter-faith dialogue in the quest for ultimate unity under "one Lord and one shepherd."	10 Mins	(iv) Inform the students that in the face of many differences in belief between denominations/religions it may seem to some that ecumenical and inter-faith dialogue has little to no value, that it is a "waste of time" leading nowhere. Show the students the following YouTube video, *Insights: Ecumenism and Evangelism* by the Coming Home Network (3.46 minutes).  After viewing the video, invite the students to answer the following questions: - *Why is it important to have dialogue with non-Catholics?* - *Ecumenism works on what? Evangelism works on what?* - *How important is love in ecumenical/inter-faith dialogue?* - *What is the real "enemy" between people of different religions?* Allow 3 minutes for student answers. Finally, mention that ecumenical/inter-faith dialogue take place in the context of a journey where the participants walk together and charitably assist each other in their various material/ practical needs while concurrently discussing the religious differences in a journey towards truth. Without the desire to seek truth, dialogue will ultimately have no real benefit.		Bogle, "Grassroots Ecumenism."
	3 mins	**Lesson Closure:** Remind the students that for Catholics there is only one God and one Lord Jesus Christ, who established one church, namely, the Catholic Church. Religious divisions are human creations, while God wills religious unity under "one Lord and one shepherd." Catholics ought to engage in ecumenical and inter-faith activity as acts of charity and good will, while avoiding any element of religious indifferentism. Dialogue should always seek to discover similarities and discuss differences with the aim of ultimately embracing truth. **Transition:** Homework: Search the internet and write down the name of one agreement signed in recent decades resolving theological differences between Catholics and the Orthodox/or Protestants.		

Resources:
- Braxton, Edward. "Catholic Education and the New Apologetics." *Origins* 35 (2006): 766-767.
- D'Costa, Gavin. *The Catholic Church and the World Religions: A Theological and Phenomenological Account.* London: T&T Clark International, 2011, 34-105.
- Kreeft, Peter. *Fundamentals of the Faith: Essays in Christian Apologetics.* San Francisco: Ignatius Press, 1988, 74-80.
- Kreeft, Peter & Ronald K. Tacelli. *Handbook of Christian Apologetics: Hundreds of Answers to Crucial Questions.* Downers Grove: IVP Academic, 1994, 353-360.
- Ratzinger, Joseph. *Truth and Tolerance: Christian Belief and World Religions.* San Francisco: Ignatius Press, 2004, 162-182.
- Spencer, Robert. "Islam and Catholicism." *Catholic Answers* (Sept.-Oct. 2012): 36-40.
- *Catechism of the Catholic Church.* Libreria Editrice Vaticana: St Pauls, 1994, paras. 754, 839-848.
- YOUCAT (*Youth Catechism of the Catholic Church*). San Francisco, Ignatius Press, 2010, paras. 131, 136.
- Website: Bogle, Joanna. "Grassroots Ecumenism." https://www.catholic.com/magazine/print-edition/grassroots-ecumenism.
- YouTube: Coming Home Network. "Insight: Ecumenism and Evangelism." https://www.youtube.com/watch?v=XNO05G4Te0Q.

LESSON EVALUATION (to be completed AFTER the lesson)

Assessment of lesson objectives and suggestions for improvement:
Teacher self-reflection and self-evaluation:
[OFFICIAL USE ONLY] Comments by teacher supervisor:

"Always Be Prepared ..." – A 'New Apologetics' Course for Catholic Secondary Schools

Lesson 18: The Existence of Spirits – Angels and Demons

LESSON ORGANISATION

Year Level: Date: Time: Duration: Room:

Quote:
"Beside each believer stands an angel as protector and shepherd leading him to life" – St Basil the Great.

Prayer:
Come, Holy Spirit, fill the hearts of your faithful and enkindle in them the fire of your love.

V. Send forth your Spirit and they shall be created.
R. And you shall renew the face of the earth.

Let us pray.
O God, who by the light of the Holy Spirit, did instruct the hearts of the faithful, grant us in the same Spirit to be truly wise and ever to rejoice in his consolation.
Through Christ our Lord. Amen.

Lesson Outcomes:

As a result of this lesson, students will be able to:

- Recognise the existence of a spiritual world beyond human senses.
- Demonstrate that the existence of spirits is within reason.
- Refute arguments that belief in angels is absurd, superstitious or outdated.
- Provide examples of how human beings have personally engaged angels in everyday life.
- Relate the origin of demons, how they were originally created good and freely chose to rebel against God.

Activity Sheets:

Activity Sheet 33, *The 'Angel Gap.'*

LESSON DELIVERY

Outcome	Time	Motivation and Introduction:	Resources/ References
Recognise the existence of a spiritual world beyond human senses. Demonstrate that the existence of spirits is within reason.	7 mins	Welcome and settle the students. Prayer to the Holy Spirit (or other suitable prayer). Tell the students that today we will be seeking to defend belief in spirits, namely, angels and demons. Ask the students the following questions: *What do we know about angels and demons? From where did we get our information about them?* Take two-three responses. The students most probably know something about angels and demons and that most of what they know is derived from popular culture, particularly television shows, movies, etc. Consequently, they would not necessarily have an accurate understanding of these spiritual beings, possessing a degree of truth mixed with error, distortion or exaggeration. Remind the students that atheists and 'new atheists', as materialists, deny the existence of the spiritual; hence, they deny the existence of angels and demons. They generally view belief in such as absurd, superstitious or outdated. However, to argue for the existence of angels and demons it is not enough to simply quote passages from the Bible; one must argue for their existence from reason and logic. **Lesson Steps**	Flader, *The Creed: A Tour of the Catechism*, 78-79.
Recognise the existence of a spiritual world beyond human senses. Demonstrate that the existence of spirits is within reason.	15 mins	(i) Inform the students that to believe in angels/demons one must first prove the existence of a spiritual world beyond our observation. Ask the students, *Is this possible? Why/Why not?* Take two-three responses. Answers may include, *"It's in the Bible"; "I've personally had spiritual experiences"*, etc. Explain that answers such as these might have sway with believing Catholics or the credulous, but they will not impress materialists who demand reasonable and objective arguments/ evidence. However, it is difficult for believers to produce such arguments/evidence. Why? Because humans are not naturally equipped to perceive spiritual things. Provide the analogy of goldfish. They swim comfortably in their fishbowl and know no	Kreeft, *Angels and Demons*, 29-37.

		other world outside of it. Furthermore, they will never know any other world because they do not have the natural powers to perceive anything outside of the fishbowl. A similar thing can be said about humans and our limited ability to know what lies beyond the everyday world/universe we inhabit. Nevertheless, it is possible to prove the existence of the spiritual world through reason in the same way one can prove the existence of God, namely, via the *Five Ways of St Thomas Aquinas*. This was done in Lesson 2. If God exists, then he must dwell in some form of spiritual world. Conclude by declaring that, "Proving God = Proving Spiritual World." It follows that if there is a God inhabiting a spiritual world then the idea of angels also inhabiting that spiritual world is not unreasonable. Hand out Activity Sheet 33, *The 'Angel Gap.'* Ask the students to read through the argument set forth for the existence of angels. Invite them to affirm or critique this argument.	Sheehan, *Apologetics and Catholic Doctrine*, 335-336.
Refute arguments that belief in angels is absurd, superstitious or outdated.	10 mins	(ii) Classroom discussion: Having established that there is a reasonable argument for the existence of spirits (angels and demons), how should Catholics respond to the charge that to believe in the same is absurd, superstitious or outdated? On a PowerPoint slide, show the students the following (allow time for student questions/feedback): (a) Absurd? – To believe in something unseen is not by itself absurd. We cannot see love or hate, good or evil, but we can understand these things and experience them. We can also understand the idea of angels and many people have experienced encounters with them (see (iii) below). (b) Superstitious? – Superstition relates to assigning a creature greater power than it really has, e.g., believing that carrying around a rabbit's foot will provide good luck. If angels do not exist then attributing power to them is superstitious; but if reason says they can exist then it is only reasonable to believe that they would also possess various powers, etc. (c) Outdated? – It is claimed that advances in science, medicine and technology have made God and religion redundant, including angels. However, if belief in God and angels can be proved from reason, then belief in the same remains reasonable irrespective of scientific advances, etc.	Kreeft, *Angels and Demons*, 39, 104, 112.

Provide examples of how human beings have personally engaged angels in everyday life.	10 mins	(iii) Evidence for the existence of angels and demons can also derive from personal experience. The Catholic Church teaches that angels protect humans from dangers, suggest good thoughts, deliver messages; demons can tempt humans, appear as 'angels of light' to deceive, even possess human bodies. Show the students the following YouTube video, *Are Angels Real?* by Catholic Online (1.34 minutes). After viewing the video, ask students to answer the following questions: - *Relate two examples of encounters/experiences people in the video had with angels.* - *Provide one reason why God allows some people to experience angels.* - *Should we believe accounts of angel encounters without question? Why/Why not?* As a final point, mention that not all encounters with spirits are positive. There are innumerable accounts of Catholic priests engaging in exorcisms, delivering human victims from demonic possession. Many of these encounters are well documented (including film and voice recordings) and provide solid experiential proof of the existence of spiritual beings.	Kreeft, *Angels and Demons*, 114-115, 122. Sheehan, *Apologetics and Catholic Doctrine*, 328-331.
Relate the origin of demons, how they were originally created good and freely chose to rebel against God.	10 mins	(iv) Apologetics challenge: Ask the students to respond to the following argument: *Since God is love and goodness, he could not have created evil beings such as the Devil and demons. Therefore, the Devil and demons really do not exist.* Allow time for two-three student responses. After engaging student responses, provide the following on a PowerPoint slide: - The Devil was originally Lucifer ('Lightbearer'), the highest, beautiful and most powerful angel. - Lucifer and all the demons were originally good angels created outside the vision of God in grace and with free will. - Lucifer and all the angels were given a test to merit the vision of God. - Lucifer and many other angels failed this test, preferring their own wills over God's.	Kreeft & Tacelli, *Handbook of Christian Apologetics*, 115. Sheehan, *Apologetics and Catholic Doctrine*, 331-335.

	3 mins	- Lucifer and the rebellious angels were condemned to eternal punishment ("God did not spare the angels when they sinned but cast them into hell": 2 Pet. 2:4). - In hell, Lucifer and the demons continue forever in their rebellion against God, warring also against humanity. Conclusion: God did not 'create' the Devil or the demons, rather, like human beings they were free to accept or reject God's plan and they freely chose the path of rebellion and sin. **Lesson Closure**: Remind the students that even though we cannot see angels and demons belief in them is very reasonable and supported by many reliable personal experiences. If there exist strong arguments for the existence of God, then there likewise exist strong arguments for the existence of a spiritual world. If there exist bodies without spirits, then it is entirely reasonable to believe that there can exist spirits without bodies inhabiting the spiritual world. Any arguments that belief in angels and demons is absurd, superstitious, or outdated can also be challenged from reason. **Transition**: Homework: Direct the students to the 'Guardian Angel' prayer. Ask them to analyse the words of this prayer and write down what we ask our Guardian Angel to do for us. Encourage the students to afterwards recite this prayer.	
		Resources: - Flader, John. *The Creed: A Tour of the Catechism, Volume One.* Ballan, Victoria: Modotti Press, 2011, 78-79. - Kreeft, Peter. *Angels (and Demons): What Do We Really Know About Them?* San Francisco: Ignatius Press, 1995, 29-37, 39, 104, 112-115, 122. - Kreeft, Peter & Ronald K. Tacelli. *Handbook of Christian Apologetics: Hundreds of Answers to Crucial Questions.* Downers Grove: IVP Academic, 1994, 115. - Sheehan, Michael. *Apologetics and Catholic Doctrine*, rev. and ed. by Peter M. Joseph. London: Baronius Press, 2015, 328-336. - *Catechism of the Catholic Church.* Libreria Editrice Vaticana: St Pauls, 1994, paras. 328, 332-336, 391-395.	

		<ul><li>YOUCAT (*Youth Catechism of the Catholic Church*). San Francisco, Ignatius Press, 2010, para. 54-55.</li><li>Website: Stockhert, Hal. "Must we believe in Angels?" https://www.catholic.com/qa/must-we-believe-in-angels.</li><li>YouTube: Catholic Online. "Are Angels Real?" https://www.youtube.com/watch?v=y7j4TZjTU_0.</li></ul>

LESSON EVALUATION (to be completed AFTER the lesson)

Assessment of lesson objectives and suggestions for improvement:
Teacher self-reflection and self-evaluation:
[OFFICIAL USE ONLY] Comments by teacher supervisor:

Lesson 19: The Reality of Miracles

LESSON ORGANISATION

Year Level: Date: Time: Duration: Room:

Quote:
"Miracles are not in contradiction to nature. They are only in contradiction with what we know of nature" – St Augustine of Hippo.

Prayer:
Come, Holy Spirit, fill the hearts of your faithful and enkindle in them the fire of your love.

V. Send forth your Spirit and they shall be created.
R. And you shall renew the face of the earth.

Let us pray.
O God, who by the light of the Holy Spirit, did instruct the hearts of the faithful, grant us in the same Spirit to be truly wise and ever to rejoice in his consolation.
Through Christ our Lord. Amen.

Lesson Outcomes:

As a result of this lesson, students will be able to:

- Define the term 'miracle.'
- Illustrate that belief in miracles is not contrary to reason.
- Outline the purpose of miracles from a Catholic perspective.
- Explain why miracles occur rarely.
- Understand the criteria for discerning alleged medical miracles.
- Be familiar with one specific example of a modern miracle with supporting evidence for the same.

Activity Sheets:

Activity Sheet 34, *Miracles – Answering the Critics.*

"Always Be Prepared ..." – A 'New Apologetics' Course for Catholic Secondary Schools

LESSON DELIVERY

Outcome	Time	Motivation and Introduction:	Resources/ References
Define the term 'miracle.' Illustrate that belief in miracles is not contrary to reason.	7 mins	Welcome and settle the students. Prayer to the Holy Spirit (or other suitable prayer). Tell the students that today we will be learning about miracles and how belief in such is reasonable. Ask the students the following question: *What do you understand by the word 'miracle'?* Take two-three responses and then provide the following explanation: Back in the 18th century there was a philosopher by the name of David Hume. He defined a miracle as "a transgression of a law of nature by a particular volition of the Deity, or by the interposition of some visible agent." The key point for Hume was that miracles *contradicted nature*, which is why he did not believe in them. However, Hume's definition of miracles can be challenged. Provide the following on a PowerPoint slide: - Miracles are events which are perceived by human senses. - Miracles are beyond the power of natural causes. - Miracles are the result of the direct intervention of God. - Miracles do not *contradict* nature; God *suspends* the laws of nature when he works a miracle. Conclude by reinforcing that those who reject the possibility of miracles because they allegedly contradict nature are themselves unreasonable, as God can certainly override his own laws. To believe that God as the author of the laws of nature can suspend the same by his almighty power is entirely within reason. **Lesson Steps**	Duggan, *Beyond Reasonable Doubt*, 81-86. Ganssle, *A Reasonable God*, 25-30. Robinson, *The Realist Guide to Religion and Science*, 101-105.
Illustrate that belief in miracles is not contrary to reason.	12 mins	(i) Like David Hume, there are many today who deny the possibility of miracles. On a PowerPoint slide, outline the following as examples of their arguments: - "Modern science can today provide reasonable and natural explanations for alleged miracles."	Kreeft, *Fundamentals of the Faith*, 64-68.

			- "Belief in miracles contradicts the laws of nature and science which are fixed and unchangeable." - "Belief in miracles insults God by suggesting that he is an incompetent architect who after creating an ordered world needs to intervene in nature's regular workings." Hand out Activity Sheet 34, *Miracles – Answering the Critics.* Ask the students to match the arguments against miracles in Column A with the appropriate responses in Column B. The first one is done to help start off the students.	Kreeft & Tacelli, *Handbook of Christian Apologetics,* 109-114. Lewis, *Miracles,* 59-66.
Outline the purpose of miracles from a Catholic perspective. Explain why miracles occur rarely.	13 mins	(ii)	Classroom discussion: Ask the students to construct a 50-word response to the following question, *What is the purpose of miracles?* (Each student response should embody at least two purposes). Invite two-three students to read aloud their responses and allow the class to critique the same. Collate on the whiteboard any reasonable responses, adding some of your own. By the end of this discussion the students should have noted down (as a minimum) the following purposes: - To show forth God's glory. - To learn, know, understand something about God. - To display God's governance over nature. - To call people to conversion/faith. - To display God's love, care, mercy towards humanity. - To attest to someone's divine mission, authority, holiness. - To attest to the truth of Catholicism/Catholic beliefs. Afterwards, invite the students to relate any personal experiences with miracles. Most probably, only a few students will relate experiences. During this discussion the question may arise, *"Why are miracles so rare. Shouldn't a loving God do more miracles to help more people?"* Acknowledge this as a valuable question, one often asked by those who deny miracles. Provide the following answer: Miracles are rare because God highly respects his own creation and ordinarily wishes it to function predictably according to consistent laws. If God did miracles often, they would no longer be miracles but common events. There would also be no consistent laws of nature and so no science. God performs miracles exceptionally to remind us of his existence, lest we eventually fall into unbelief.	Robinson, *The Realist Guide to Religion and Science,* 104, 271.

Understand the criteria for discerning alleged medical miracles.	10 mins	(iii) Most alleged miracles relate to medical cures. An important question is, what, if any, is the test for verifying whether medical miracles are genuine or – as claimed by sceptics and unbelievers – concocted/fraudulent? On a PowerPoint slide, outline the following points under the heading, "The Lambertini Criteria": Lambertini was a Catholic Cardinal in the 18th century who later became Pope Benedict XIV. He decreed that for any medical cure to be recognised as a miracle by the Church the following five-point criteria needed to be satisfied:  - The original medical condition was permanent. - The alleged cure was instantaneous or exceedingly rapid. - The alleged cure is lasting. - The alleged cure is complete (not a partial cure). - There was no medical treatment/intervention involved. Ask the students to answer the following questions: - *Why do you think it is necessary to have a strict test for alleged medical miracles?* - *Which of the above criteria are negotiable, that is, can be dropped or not insisted upon?* - *Are there any other criteria you would add to strengthen the above test?* - *Do you think the above criteria – if satisfied – would satisfy sceptics/unbelievers? Why/Why not?*	Lay Witness, "The Church's Teaching on Miracles", 27-31.
Be familiar with one specific example of a modern miracle with supporting evidence for the same.	12 mins	(iv) Tell the students that there are countless thousands of miracles that have allegedly occurred in the history of the Catholic Church, miracles of all kinds. Of all these miracles, the most spectacular and most witnessed is the so-called 'Miracle of the Sun', which occurred in Fatima, Portugal, 13 October, 1917. Show the students the following YouTube video, *30,000 Witness Sun to Become UFO* by 'Strange Mysteries' (3.41 minutes). (Tell the students that this is a secular, not a Catholic video). 	Walsh, *Our Lady of Fatima*, 139-153.

		After viewing the video, ask the students to complete the following exercise:	
		Imagine you are an unbelieving journalist among the seventy thousand people who saw the 'Miracle of the Sun' at Fatima. You are asked by your newspaper to write a headline about what you saw. What will you write? (No more than ten words). Ask two-three students to read out and explain their headline.	
		Afterwards, discuss with the class the following questions:	
		What was most convincing about what happened at Fatima? *Is it possible to ignore the witness of so many people?*	
	3 mins	**Lesson Closure**:	
		Sum up for the students that belief in miracles is reasonable and there exists enough evidence to prove that they occur. If God is the author of the laws of nature, he can also suspend the same. Miracles are rare because God respects nature but occasionally he performs them out of mercy, or to strengthen faith, or to validate the Catholic faith, among other reasons. To be accepted as an official miracle, any claimed miracle needs to satisfy strict criteria. The 'Miracle of the Sun' is one example of a miracle witnessed by thousands and proven beyond all reasonable doubt.	
		Transition:	
		Homework: Search the internet or YouTube for 'miracles of Lourdes.' Write down the details of two approved miracles.	
		Resources: • Duggan, G. H. *Beyond Reasonable Doubt.* Boston, MA: St Paul Books & Media, 1987, 81-86. • Ganssle, Gregory E. *A Reasonable God: Engaging the New Face of Atheism.* Waco, Texas: Baylor University Press, 2009, 25-30. • Kreeft, Peter. *Fundamentals of the Faith: Essays in Christian Apologetics.* San Francisco: Ignatius Press, 1988, 64-68. • Kreeft, Peter & Ronald K. Tacelli. *Handbook of Christian Apologetics: Hundreds of Answers to Crucial Questions.* Downers Grove: IVP Academic, 1994, 109-114.	

		<ul><li>Lay Witness. "The Church's Teaching on Miracles." *Faith Facts: The Answers You Need* (March/April 2004): 27-31.</li><li>Lewis, C. S. *Miracles.* London: Fount Paperbacks, 1974, 59-66.</li><li>Robinson, Paul. *The Realist Guide to Religion and Science.* Leominster, United Kingdom: Gracewing, 2018, 101-105, 271.</li><li>Walsh, W. T. *Our Lady of Fatima.* New York: Macmillian Co., 1947, 139-153.</li><li>*Catechism of the Catholic Church.* Libreria Editrice Vaticana: St Pauls, 1994, paras. 547-549, 1335, 2003.</li><li>YOUCAT (*Youth Catechism of the Catholic Church*). San Francisco, Ignatius Press, 2010, paras. 90, 91.</li><li>Website: Brumley, Mark. "Why Miracles Can Happen." https://www.catholic.com/magazine/print-edition/why-miracles-can-happen.</li><li>YouTube: Strange Mysteries, "30,000 Witness Sun to Become UFO." https://www.bing.com/videos/search?q=fatima+miracle+of+the+sun+movie&&view=detail&mid=40961A130E2AFE37ED6C40961A130E2AFE37ED6C&&FORM=VDRVRV.</li></ul>

LESSON EVALUATION (to be completed AFTER the lesson)

Assessment of lesson objectives and suggestions for improvement:
Teacher self-reflection and self-evaluation:
[OFFICIAL USE ONLY] Comments by teacher supervisor:

Lesson 20: The Compatibility of Faith and Reason

LESSON ORGANISATION

Year Level:	Date:	Time:	Duration:	Room:

Quote:
"I would not believe if I did not realise that it is reasonable to believe" – St Thomas Aquinas.

Prayer:
Come, Holy Spirit, fill the hearts of your faithful and enkindle in them the fire of your love.

V. Send forth your Spirit and they shall be created.
R. And you shall renew the face of the earth.

Let us pray.
O God, who by the light of the Holy Spirit, did instruct the hearts of the faithful, grant us in the same Spirit to be truly wise and ever to rejoice in his consolation.
Through Christ our Lord. Amen.

Lesson Outcomes:

As a result of this lesson, students will be able to:

- Define faith and reason.
- Understand the claims of those who assert that faith is incompatible with reason.
- Articulate how faith and reason are inseparable and compatible 'wings' assisting humans in the contemplation of truth.
- Demonstrate that faith and reason work together and share the same goals.
- Provide examples of how the Catholic faith employs reason to support its beliefs, particularly those that are 'mysteries.'

Activity Sheets:

Activity Sheet 35, *The 'Two Wings' of Faith and Reason.*
Activity Sheet 36, *Faith Seeking Understanding.*

"Always Be Prepared ..." – A 'New Apologetics' Course for Catholic Secondary Schools

LESSON DELIVERY

Outcome	Time	Motivation and Introduction:	Resources/ References
Define faith and reason.	7 mins	Welcome and settle the students. Prayer to the Holy Spirit (or other suitable prayer). Tell the students that today we will be looking at faith and reason and responding to the allegation that they are incompatible. Before addressing this challenge, it is necessary to define both faith and reason. On a PowerPoint slide provide the following definitions: Faith: The act of believing in something on the authority of another. For Christians, it is the assent of the intellect moved by the will under the influence of grace to believe something God has revealed. The following is an example of a simple act of faith: *"O God, I believe in you and all that your Church teaches, because you have said it, and your word is true. Amen."* Reason: The process of the mind to search for, discover and embrace the truth. In its classical definition, reasoning involves three human acts: (a) discovering a truth; (b) understanding a truth; (c) proving a truth. In order to trust reason, one must believe that the human senses and intellect can reliably discover and understand truth. Conclude by asserting that humans can know truth through both faith and reason, that the truths known through faith and reason are compatible, and truths however known have their origin in God. **Lesson Steps**	Hardon, *Modern Catholic Dictionary*, 205 & 457. Kreeft & Tacelli, *Handbook of Christian Apologetics*, 27-33.
Understand the claims of those who assert that faith is incompatible with reason.	10 mins	(i) Show the students the following YouTube video, *Faith and Reason* by Catholic News Agency (2.50 minutes). After viewing this video, choose the quote from Galileo Galilee and ask the students what they think it means. (Answer: Faith and reason are compatible. The truths they know all come from God and they are not in contradiction).	Fisher & Ramsey, *Faith and Reason: Friends or Foes?*, xiv-xvi. Wiker, *The Catholic Church & Science*, 1-16.

		After taking two student answers, inform the class that there are many today who see faith and reason in opposition, even in conflict. This is the so-called 'warfare thesis.' This thesis has its beginnings in the clash between Galileo and the Catholic Church in the 17th century over his theory of 'heliocentrism' (i.e., that the sun, rather than the earth, is the centre of the solar system). Ever since, faith and science have supposedly been in irreconcilable conflict, with faith unable to provide any proof for its main teachings and retreating relentlessly in the face of science's advance.  Survey the students as to areas they think faith and reason could be in conflict. Examples may include: - The Creation account and the 'Big Bang' theory. - The age of the universe – young or old? - Adam and Eve and the existence of cave men. - The Trinity – how can one God supposedly be three Persons at the same time? Explain that the clash between religion and science/faith and reason is only *apparent*. The Catholic Church believes that reason is good and should be used to both defend faith and advance science. Examples of such will be looked at later in this lesson.	
Articulate how faith and reason are inseparable and compatible 'wings' assisting humans in the contemplation of truth.	12 mins	(ii) Hand out Activity Sheet 35, *The 'Two Wings' of Faith and Reason*. Invite the students to read the quote from Pope St John Paul II: *"Faith and reason are like two wings on which the human spirit rises to the contemplation of truth."* Ask them to then answer the following questions (Take student responses): - *Why do you think Pope St John Paul II chose to represent the relationship between faith and reason by two wings?* (Answer: Two wings are distinct. Faith and reason are distinct). - *How does the image of a bird with two wings symbolise the inseparability of faith and reason?* (Answer: The two wings are connected to the same body. The one body brings the two together into an inseparable bond).	Fisher & Ramsey, *Faith and Reason: Friends or Foes?*, xiv-xvi. Wiker, *The Catholic Church & Science*, 1-16.

		- *With two wings a bird flies with harmonious balance. What does this say about a person who lives by faith and reason?* (Answer: A person who lives by faith and reason will live a balanced and harmonious life in the fullness of truth). - *In what ways would a person's life be imbalanced if it had only one wing, that is, if it lived only by faith or only by reason?* (Answer: To live by faith alone is *fideism*. It denies reason and is open to the criticism of being 'blind faith.' To live by reason alone is *rationalism*. It denies the spiritual and is closed to the possibility of a world beyond our senses).	
Demonstrate that faith and reason work together and share the same goals.	12 mins	(iii) Hand out Activity Sheet 36, *Faith Seeking Understanding*. Invite the students to consider the following questions: - *What are St Augustine and St Anslem trying to say?* - *Are their thoughts in agreement or in contradiction?* Take two-three student responses. After the discussion, conclude that the two quotes appear at first to be in contradiction but really agree. For both saints, faith is a divine gift that comes first before understanding. St Augustine's point is that faith assists the believer to see the reasonableness of their beliefs. St Anselm's point is that Christians are not people of blind faith but people who engage their reason to understand their faith. On a PowerPoint slide show and explain the following points: (a) Faith is a divine gift; reason is our natural response to the world around us. (b) It is natural for humans to want to understand things. (c) Catholic/Christian beliefs should be supported or grounded in good thinking. (d) There are not two rival truths ('truths of faith' and 'truths of reason'). Truth is a unity that is arrived at through the two ways of faith and reason. (e) The two ways of faith and reason carry people to the truth in different ways. They each have different methods, authorities and standards but they ultimately have the same destination – the fullness of truth. (f) In conclusion, Catholics practise their faith supported by the natural power of reason. Faith and reason are not alternatives or in conflict. It is not one or the other but both.	Fisher & Ramsey, *Faith and Reason: Friends or Foes?*, xiv-xvi. Ganssle, *A Reasonable God: Engaging the New Face of Atheism*, 31-55.

Provide examples of how the Catholic faith employs reason to support its beliefs, particularly those that are 'mysteries.'	12 mins	(iv) Return to the discussion from earlier in the lesson where students identified possible areas of conflict between faith and reason. Two of the areas of possible conflict were the Genesis Creation account and the mystery of the Trinity. Guided discussion: Ask students to put their 'apologetics hats' on and think of points that could be employed in argument to defend the reasonableness of these beliefs. Invite the students to share their points with the rest of the class (they may also share points that question these beliefs). Collate on the whiteboard any reasonable responses, adding some of your own. By the end of this discussion the students should have noted down points similar to the following: Objection 1: The Genesis Creation account outlining that God created the world in six 24-hour days is contrary to everything we now know from science: Catholic response: - The six 'days' are not literally 24-hour days. - The Hebrew word for day – *Yom* – can mean a period of indeterminate length. - The light appearing before the creation of the sun on Day 4 corresponds to the first light appearing in the universe soon after the 'Big Bang', when the process of ionization began. This occurred billions of years before the creation of our sun. - The order of creation outlined in Genesis 1 corresponds to the order of creation and evolution espoused by science – the creation of the inanimate (earth, stars, sun, moon), followed by plants and animals, ending with the creation of humanity. - Genesis was never meant to be a scientific manual on creation; rather, it is a simple and symbolic account for ancient illiterate people that provides a general framework on how God created. Objection 2: Belief in the mystery of the Trinity is nonsense. How can God be three and one at the same time? This is a contradiction. (NB: This objection was dealt with in Lesson 13, God as Trinity).	Horn, *Hard Sayings*, 43-47. O'Neil & Black, *The Essential Moral Handbook: A Guide to Catholic Living*, 6-7.

		Catholic response: - God is one. - God is infinite and eternal. - God knows and loves himself from all eternity. - God's knowledge and love of himself are infinite and eternal – they are therefore not creatures. - God's infinite and eternal knowledge of himself is the Word, or second Person of the Trinity. - God's infinite and eternal love of himself (the mutual love between the Father and the Son) is the Holy Spirit, or Third Person of the Trinity. - The Trinity is, therefore, God knowing and loving himself.	
	3 mins	**Lesson Closure:** Remind the students that despite the centuries-old narrative, the two 'wings' of faith and reason are not in conflict but are friends and partners in the search for truth. Faith is a gift from God that enables us to believe divine things unseen, while reason is one of our natural powers that can be used to support faith. A Catholic faith is one that seeks understanding, so Catholics are not people of blind faith. At the same time, Catholics support reason's endeavour to advance science. Where certain Catholic/Christian beliefs appear to contradict reason/science, it is the role of the Catholic apologist to develop reasonable arguments in defence of these beliefs. All Catholic beliefs, including 'mysteries', can be so defended. **Transition:** Homework: Consider the following objection: "Science tells me that Holy Communion when tested is still just bread and wine, not anyone's body and blood. This is an example of another Catholic belief that is contrary to fact and reason." What is one thing you can say in response to this?	
		Resources: • Fisher, Anthony & Hayden Ramsey. *Faith and Reason: Friends or Foes in the New Millennium?* Hindmarsh, SA: ATF Press, 2004, xiv-xvi. • Ganssle, Gregory E. *A Reasonable God: Engaging the New Face of Atheism.* Waco, Texas: Baylor University Press, 2009, 31-55.	

- Hardon, John A. *Modern Catholic Dictionary.* New York: DoubleDay, 1980, 205 & 247.
- Horn, Trent. *Hard Sayings. A Catholic Approach to Answering Bible Difficulties.* San Diego: Catholic Answers Press, 2016, 43-47.
- Kreeft, Peter & Ronald K. Tacelli. *Handbook of Christian Apologetics: Hundreds of Answers to Crucial Questions.* Downers Grove: IVP Academic, 1994, 27-33.
- O'Neil, Kevin J. & Peter Black. *The Essential Moral Handbook: A Guide to Catholic Living.* Liguori, Missouri: Liguori, 2004, 6-7.
- Wiker, Benjamin. *The Catholic Church & Science: Answering the Questions, Exposing the Myths.* Charlotte, New Carolina: TAN Books and Publishers, 2011, 1-16.
- *Catechism of the Catholic Church.* Libreria Editrice Vaticana: St Pauls, 1994, paras. 153-159.
- YOUCAT (*Youth Catechism of the Catholic Church*). San Francisco, Ignatius Press, 2010, paras. 4-5, 21-23.
- Website: Hudson, Deal. "The Harmony of Faith and Reason." https://www.catholic.com/magazine/print-edition/the-harmony-of-faith-and-reason.
- YouTube: Catholic News Agency, "Faith and Reason." https://www.youtube.com/watch?v=seqtSQnBe2U.

LESSON EVALUATION (to be completed AFTER the lesson)

Assessment of lesson objectives and suggestions for improvement:
Teacher self-reflection and self-evaluation:
[OFFICIAL USE ONLY] Comments by teacher supervisor:

"Always Be Prepared …" – A 'New Apologetics' Course for Catholic Secondary Schools

Lesson 21:   The Existence and Knowability of Objective Truth

LESSON ORGANISATION

Year Level: Date: Time: Duration: Room:

Quote:
"We are moving toward a dictatorship of relativism which does not recognise anything as for certain and which has as its highest goal one's own ego and one's own desires" – Cardinal Joseph Ratzinger.

Prayer:
Come, Holy Spirit, fill the hearts of your faithful and enkindle in them the fire of your love.

V. Send forth your Spirit and they shall be created.
R. And you shall renew the face of the earth.

Let us pray.
O God, who by the light of the Holy Spirit, did instruct the hearts of the faithful, grant us in the same Spirit to be truly wise and ever to rejoice in his consolation.
Through Christ our Lord. Amen.

Lesson Outcomes:

As a result of this lesson, students will be able to:

- Understand and define relativism.
- Appreciate that objective truth exists, that it corresponds to reality and is true for all.
- Distinguish between objective and subjective statements of truth.
- Recognise that objective truth is capable of being perceived by the five senses and known and understood by the human intellect.
- Value the role of the Church to define, proclaim and defend objective truth.

Activity Sheets:

Activity Sheet 37, *Objective versus Subjective.*
Activity Sheet 38, *How Do We Know?*

LESSON DELIVERY

Outcome	Time	Motivation and Introduction:	Resources/ References
Understand and define relativism.	10 mins	Welcome and settle the students. Prayer to the Holy Spirit (or other suitable prayer). Tell the students that today we will be looking at the existence and knowability of objective truth. Explain that many people today believe and live as if there is no such thing as objective truth. Others believe that even if objective truth does exist, humans cannot know and understand it. Ask the students the following questions: *Has anyone heard of the term 'relativism'? What do you think it means?* Take two-three responses. On a PowerPoint slide outline and explain the following points under the heading, 'Slogans of Relativism': - "Truth does not exist." - "Truth is made rather than found." - "What's true for you is not necessarily true for me." - "All ideas are equally true." - "Truth is what works." - "Truth is what I feel." - "Truth is beyond human senses, beyond human intellect – it is unknowable." Question: *What does relativism ultimately mean for Christianity?* Answer: If there is no objective truth, then Catholicism/Christianity (like everything else) cannot be true. If it is not true, then what justification is there to proclaim, teach or defend it? This is why C. S. Lewis once call subjectivism "the most destructive belief we could possibly believe." **Lesson Steps**	Rice, *50 Questions on the Natural Law*, 75-76. Siniscalchi, "Rational Apologetics", 751-752. Toren, *Christian Apologetics as Cross-Cultural Dialogue*, 8-15.
Appreciate that objective truth exists, that it corresponds to reality and is true for all.	12 mins	(i) Show the students the following YouTube video, *Objective and Subjective Truth* by Neil deGrasse Tyson (3.18 minutes). After viewing this video, invite the students to answer the following questions (allow time for student feedback):	

| | | - *What is an objective truth?*
(Answer: A truth that exists outside of ourselves).
- *What is one example of an objective truth?*
(Answer: The earth has gravity).
- *What is one way to prove that there are objective truths?*
(Answer: They can be demonstrated through repeated scientific experiments).
- *Would there be a problem if I claimed that gravity did not exist, claiming the right to determine my own truth?*
(Answer: Yes, I would be living in my own fantasy world detached from reality).

On a PowerPoint slide provide and explain the following points under the heading, 'What Objective Truth Is/Is Not':

Objective Truth:
- Is independent (or outside) of the knower.
- Relates to what we know.
- Identifies and understands things as they really are.
- Is not an attitude.
- Is not determined by how we know.
- Is not dependent on how many believe or not.
- Is not dependent on being known or proved.

Sum up by stating that people who believe in objective truth are otherwise known as 'Realists.' Famous 'realist' philosophers include Aristotle and St Thomas Aquinas. To deny the existence or knowability of objective truth is to be a 'sceptic' who lives in a 'post-truth' world. | Kreeft & Tacelli, *Handbook of Christian Apologetics*, 362-364. |
| Distinguish between objective and subjective statements of truth. | 10 mins | (ii) Hand out Activity Sheet 37, *Objective versus Subjective*. Invite the students to consider the ten statements listed and categorise each by placing a cross (X) in one of the three columns, *Objective Truth, Subjective Truth, Subjective Non-Truth*. Discuss with the students the reasons for their decisions. (Reasons: A statement is objectively true if it corresponds to a reality or truth that is external [outside of] to the knower. A statement is subjectively true if it accurately expresses an internal emotion, opinion, preference or experience of an individual person. A statement is a subjective non-truth if it is the opinion of an individual that does not correspond to any reality or truth). | Kreeft & Tacelli, *Handbook of Christian Apologetics*, 362-364 & 372. |

Recognise that objective truth is capable of being known and understood by the five senses and the human intellect.	12 mins	(iii) Classroom discussion: Related to the question of objective truth is whether objective truth is knowable. It is argued by some that even if objective truth does exist it is still unknowable due to the unreliability of the five human senses and intellect. So, before debating whether objective truth exists it is necessary to discern whether humans have the proper 'knowing equipment.' Ask the students the question, *How do we know?* Take two-three responses and record any reasonable responses on the whiteboard. Hand out Activity Sheet 38, *How Do We Know?* Using the Word Bank, invite the students to fill the gaps relating to our knowing powers, where these powers are located in the human person, and what each of these powers can do. Conclude with discussion on the consequences of denying the same powers.	Robinson, *The Realist Guide to Religion and Science*, 4-15.
Value the role of the Church to define, proclaim and defend objective truth.	10 mins	(iv) Explain to the students that another source that enables human beings to know objective truth is *authority.* Humans need authority to believe in things they cannot know for themselves or immediately perceive with their senses. Ask the students to name something they believe in which they have not seen for themselves. Take two-three responses. One example is the number of planets in the solar system. Another is the existence of the continent of Antarctica. Probably all the students believe that Antarctica exists, not because they have seen it for themselves but because they trust in others who have been there, filmed it or written about it. Highlight how the Catholic Church is an authority on matters relating to faith and morals, namely, what we should believe and how we should live. The teaching authority of the Catholic Church and the Pope was examined earlier in Lesson 16. Here, we will revisit those verses in Scripture that evidence the teaching authority of the Church and how that teaching authority is preserved from error, enabling it to be a reliable definer, proclaimer and defender of objective truth. Show the following Scripture verses on a PowerPoint slide: The Church was founded by Jesus Christ: *"You are Peter, and on this rock I will build my church"* (Matt. 16:18).	Armstrong, *A Biblical Defense of Catholicism*, 247-257.

		The Church is concerned with truth: *"... the Church of the living God, the pillar and bulwark of the truth"* (1 Tim. 3:15). The Church is guided by the Holy Spirit to ensure that it will always be a faithful teacher of truth: *"And I will ask the Father, and he will give you another Counsellor, to be with you for ever"* (John 14:16). Classroom exercise: Work with the students to list at least three truths Catholics/Christians are called to believe in based solely on the teaching authority of the Church, truths we otherwise could not discover or know by ourselves. Examples include: - The number of books in the Bible. - The number of sacraments. - The number of persons and natures in Jesus. - The nature of Jesus' real presence in the Eucharist. - The day of the week Christians should keep holy. - Mary's Immaculate Conception. - Mary's assumption into heaven. Conclude by highlighting that humans cannot live functional lives unless they trust in various authorities to provide certainty in many areas of life. This is because humans, even though they possess reliable senses and intellect, do not have the time or means to know everything about everything. The teaching authority of the Catholic Church provides objective certainty (and hence peace of mind) about faith and morals in the midst of the many subjective and contradictory voices that are active in modern-day society.	
	3 mins	**Lesson Closure:** Remind the students that objective truth exists, that it is knowable via our senses and intellect, and that it is essential in order to function effectively as human beings. Our senses and intellect are trustworthy and made by God to know and understand things as they really are. The alternative to objective truth is a form of subjectivism that would disconnect individuals from reality, fragment society and lead to uncertainty, contradiction and chaos. God has also given humanity the Church as a teaching authority to assist in defining, knowing and defending objective truth.	

		Transition: Homework: Look up the meaning of 'self-evident.' How does this term relate to objective truth, our senses/intellect and the world around us?	
		Resources: • Armstrong, Dave. *A Biblical Defense of Catholicism.* Manchester, NH: Sophia Institute Press, 2003, 247-257. • Kreeft, Peter & Ronald K. Tacelli. *Handbook of Christian Apologetics: Hundreds of Answers to Crucial Questions.* Downers Grove: IVP Academic, 1994, 362-364 & 372. • Rice, Charles. *50 Questions on the Natural Law: What it is and Why We Need it.* San Francisco: Ignatius Press, 1993, 75-76. • Robinson, Paul. *The Realist Guide to Religion and Science.* Leominster, United Kingdom: Gracewing, 2018, 4-15. • Siniscalchi, Glenn B. "Postmodernism and the Need for Rational Apologetics in a Postconciliar Church." *Heythrop Journal* 52 (September 2011): 751-752. • Toren, Benno van den. *Christian Apologetics as Cross-Cultural Dialogue.* London: T&T Clark, 2011, 8-15. • *Catechism of the Catholic Church.* Libreria Editrice Vaticana: St Pauls, 1994, para. 2467. • YOUCAT (*Youth Catechism of the Catholic Church*). San Francisco, Ignatius Press, 2010, para. 32. • Website: Broussard, Karlo. "Is It True That There Is No Truth?" https://www.catholic.com/magazine/online-edition/is-it-true-that-there-is-no-truth. • YouTube: Tyson, Neil deGrasse. "Objective and Subjective Truth." https://www.youtube.com/watch?v=5K6dPq4Ad4k.	

LESSON EVALUATION (to be completed AFTER the lesson)

Assessment of lesson objectives and suggestions for improvement:
Teacher self-reflection and self-evaluation:
[OFFICIAL USE ONLY] Comments by teacher supervisor:

Lesson 22: The Existence and Need for Moral Absolutes

LESSON ORGANISATION

Year Level: Date: Time: Duration: Room:

Quote:
"Most people believe you have to have some moral absolutes if you want to hold back chaos" – Peter Kreeft.

Prayer:
Come, Holy Spirit, fill the hearts of your faithful and enkindle in them the fire of your love.

V. Send forth your Spirit and they shall be created.
R. And you shall renew the face of the earth.

Let us pray.
O God, who by the light of the Holy Spirit, did instruct the hearts of the faithful, grant us in the same Spirit to be truly wise and ever to rejoice in his consolation.
Through Christ our Lord. Amen.

Lesson Outcomes:

As a result of this lesson, students will be able to:

- Define and distinguish 'moral absolutes' and 'moral relativism.'
- Understand the arguments of those who oppose the existence of moral absolutes.
- Recognise how moral absolutes are written on the human heart.
- Appreciate why moral absolutes are unchangeable and incumbent upon all persons, times and places.
- Realise how moral absolutes liberate the human person and lead to comprehensive fulfilment in Christ.

Activity Sheets:

Activity Sheet 39, *Why We Need Moral Absolutes*.

LESSON DELIVERY

Outcome	Time	Motivation and Introduction:	Resources/ References
Define and distinguish 'moral absolutes' and 'moral relativism.'	10 mins	Welcome and settle the students. Prayer to the Holy Spirit (or other suitable prayer). Tell the students that today we will be looking at the existence and need for moral absolutes. Ask the students the following question: *What are moral absolutes?* Take two-three responses. Responses may include: - "Strong moral teachings." - "Things we have to believe in." - "Teachings that don't change." - "Unreasonable and inflexible rules." On a PowerPoint slide show and briefly explain the following definitions: - Moral absolutes: The belief that there are certain types of actions that are always morally bad ("intrinsically evil") no matter the intention, circumstance, or outcome. To believe in moral absolutes one must believe in an objective moral order. - Moral relativism: The belief that there are no objective moral standards or actions. Moral standards/actions are merely individual or social constructs that can vary from one person to another, one society to another, and from one period of history to another. Inform the students that there are Scripture quotes that support belief in moral absolutes. Show them the following two examples: *"Woe to those who call evil good and good evil, who put darkness for light and light for darkness, who put bitter for sweet and sweet for bitter!"* (Isaiah 5:20). *"Jesus Christ is the same yesterday and today and forever"* (Heb. 13:8). For Catholics, since Jesus does not change neither do his moral teachings, which like him are "the same yesterday and today and forever."	Hardon, *Modern Catholic Dictionary*, 361. May, *An Introduction to Moral Theology*, 108, 145-154.

		Lesson Steps	
Understand the arguments of those who oppose the existence of moral absolutes.	12 mins	(i) Tell the students that the existence of moral absolutes applicable to everyone might seem obvious but there is an increasing number of people in modern society who argue against such. On a PowerPoint slide provide the following three examples of such arguments: - "Morality is simply an opinion. There is no agreed test to determine what's right and what's wrong." - "Distinctions between 'good' and 'evil' are merely projections of human desires and aversions which change over time." - "Right and wrong are merely cultural conventions, words used by societies to describe what they approve or disapprove of." Ask the students the following question: *What is the underlying foundation for all these opinions?* Take 2-3 responses. (Answer: There is no God. Since there is no God there is no ultimate law-giver and no ultimate morality. Morality is left to the opinion of the individual. There can be nothing objective). Classroom discussion: Refer to the following quote from the philosopher Friedrich Nietzsche: *"A moral system valid for all is basically immoral."* Questions: *Why do you think Nietzsche would say such a thing? What type of moral system would he have preferred?*  (Answer: Nietzsche believed in no morals. People should be free to do whatever they want so long as they harm no one else. A universal moral system is immoral because it denies people the freedom to construct their own morality and live their own lives).	Hahn & Wiker, *Answering the New Atheism*, 102-103. Madrid & Hensley, *The Godless Delusion*, 55-66.
Recognise how moral absolutes are written on the human heart.	12 mins	(ii) Show the students the following YouTube video, *Atheists Can Know Objective Morality but Cannot Ground It* by Stand To Reason Videos (1.40 minutes). After  viewing this video, ask the students to answer the following questions: - *Which verse in the Bible says that people can know good and evil without believing in God?* (Answer: Romans 2).	Madrid & Hensley, *The Godless Delusion*, 60-61, 67.

		- *People can know good and evil because the moral law is written where?* (Answer: On our hearts). - *Can you believe in the contents of a book without believing that the book has an author?* (Answer: Yes, but it is not a well-grounded belief. Morality is written on the human heart [the book] but one should also acknowledge the author of this book [God]). Exercise: Invite the students to open a Bible and go to Romans chapter 2. Search for and copy the verse where St Paul speaks about how the (objective) law is written on the human heart. The passage reads as follows: *"They show that what the law requires is written on their hearts, while their conscience also bears witness and their conflicting thoughts accuse or perhaps excuse them …"* (Rom. 2:15). Conclude by highlighting that the word *"They"* in the above passage refers to all peoples – Gentile and Jew – and that every person has a mechanism (conscience) to know and judge whether they are faithful to the law written on the heart.	
Appreciate why moral absolutes are unchangeable and incumbent upon all persons, times and places.	10 mins	(iii) Hand out Activity Sheet 39, *Why We Need Moral Absolutes*. Invite the students to read through the list of actions outlined in Column A and place an X in either Column B or C stating whether the action is always and everywhere right or wrong. Afterwards, ask the students to write their opinion as to what societal consequences would follow if morality was changeable or its observance optional. Take two responses. (Answers may include: uncertainly, confusion, contradiction, fragmentation, chaos, dysfunction, breakdown, etc.)	May, *Moral Absolutes: Catholic Tradition, Current Trends, and the Truth*, 71-75.
Realise how moral absolutes liberate the human person and lead to comprehensive fulfilment in Christ.	10 mins	(iv) On a PowerPoint slide present the following two quotes from Pope St John Paul II about moral absolutes: *"These norms in fact represent the unshakable foundation and solid guarantee of a just and peaceful human coexistence and hence of genuine democracy …"* (*Veritatis Splendor* 96). *"The Crucified Christ – who gives to us the final answer why we must, if we are to be fully the beings God wants us to be, forbear doing the evil proscribed by absolute moral norms –*	May, *An Introduction to Moral Theology*, 148-149. Pope St John Paul II, *Veritatis Splendor*, 85 & 96.

reveals the authentic meaning of freedom: he lives it fully in the total gift of himself ..." (*Veritatis Splendor* 85).

Explain to the students that contemporary culture views moral norms as unreasonable constraints that inhibit people's free expression and takes away their enjoyment. (Allow two-three students to state whether they agree with this view or not).

Guided discussion: Looking at what Pope St John Paul II says above, what are the benefits of following moral absolutes? Write down on the whiteboard appropriate student responses under one of two headings, *Benefits for Society; Benefits for the Individual.* Answers may include:

Benefits for Society
- Establishes the same rules for everyone with no exceptions.
- Guarantees human rights and the dignity of persons.
- Facilitates peaceful coexistence and living in communion with others.
- Leads people to exercise responsible freedom.

Benefits for the Individual
- Helps to form a correct moral conscience.
- Enables people to live the liberating truth revealed by Jesus Christ.
- Educates people into unselfish and self-giving love.

Conclude by stating that moral absolutes enable people to love, and that it is by loving that we are truly human and truly free.

| | 3 mins | **Lesson Closure:**

Remind the students that belief in moral absolutes is not popular today but that they are vitally important for the proper functioning of society and human flourishing. The Church teaches moral absolutes and that they can be known by everyone, for they are based in God and written on the human heart. Moral absolutes safeguard human freedom and dignity and enable humans to live like Christ, unselfish and self-giving lives of love. Meanwhile, a world without moral absolutes would be a world characterised by division, confusion and selfishness, leading to the breakdown of society and human communion. | |

Transition:

Experiment: Suggest to the students to borrow something valuable from another family member. Then tell that family member that they will not get their item back. Note their reaction (then immediately return the item!). The reaction of the family member will confirm that all humans possess an instinctive sense of right and wrong, moral absolutes written on the human heart.

Resources:
- Hahn, Scott & Benjamin Wiker. *Answering the New Atheism: Dismantling Dawkins' Case Against God.* Steubenville, Ohio: Emmaus Road Publishing, 2008, 102-103.
- Hardon, John A. *Modern Catholic Dictionary.* New York: DoubleDay, 1980, 361.
- Madrid, Patrick & Kenneth Hensley. *The Godless Delusion: A Catholic Challenge to Modern Atheism.* Huntington, Indiana: Our Sunday Visitor Publishing, 2010, 55-67.
- May, William E. *Moral Absolutes: Catholic Tradition, Current Trends, and the Truth.* Milwaukee, Wisconsin: Marquette University Press, 1989, 71-75.
- May, William E. *An Introduction to Moral Theology.* Huntington, Indiana: Our Sunday Visitor Publishing, 1994, 108, 145-154.
- Pope St John Paul II. *Veritatis Splendor, On Certain Fundamental Questions of the Church's Moral Teaching.* Libreria Editrice Vaticana, 1993, 85 & 96.
- *Catechism of the Catholic Church.* Libreria Editrice Vaticana: St Pauls, 1994, paras. 1750-1754; 1950-1953.
- YOUCAT (*Youth Catechism of the Catholic Church*). San Francisco, Ignatius Press, 2010, para. 333.
- Website: Broussard, Karlo. "What to Say to Someone Who Doesn't Believe in Moral Absolutes." https://www.catholic.com/video/what-to-say-to-a-son-who-doesnt-believe-in-moral-absolutes.
- YouTube: STR Videos. "Atheists Can Know Objective Morality but Cannot Ground It." https://www.youtube.com/watch?v=aQeqYP3-KzQ.

LESSON EVALUATION (to be completed AFTER the lesson)

Assessment of lesson objectives and suggestions for improvement:
Teacher self-reflection and self-evaluation:
[OFFICIAL USE ONLY] Comments by teacher supervisor:

… "Always Be Prepared …" – A 'New Apologetics' Course for Catholic Secondary Schools

Lesson 23: <u>The Existence, Nature and Importance of Natural Law</u>

LESSON ORGANISATION

Year Level:	Date:	Time:	Duration:	Room:

Quote:
"The law is twofold – natural and written. The natural law is in the heart, the written law on tables. All men are under the natural law" – St Ambrose of Milan.

Prayer:
Come, Holy Spirit, fill the hearts of your faithful and enkindle in them the fire of your love.

V. Send forth your Spirit and they shall be created.
R. And you shall renew the face of the earth.

Let us pray.
O God, who by the light of the Holy Spirit, did instruct the hearts of the faithful, grant us in the same Spirit to be truly wise and ever to rejoice in his consolation.
Through Christ our Lord. Amen.

Lesson Outcomes:

As a result of this lesson, students will be able to:

- Define 'natural law' and understand contemporary objections.
- Distinguish between physical and moral natural laws.
- Recognise the most basic formulation of the moral natural law, namely, "do good and avoid evil."
- Demonstrate how humans can know and understand the moral natural law.
- Explain how natural law more than any other type of law respects human rights, achieves justice, and promotes the common good.

Activity Sheets:

Activity Sheet 40, *Physical and Moral Natural Laws*.

LESSON DELIVERY

Outcome	Time	Motivation and Introduction:	Resources/ References
Define 'natural law' and understand contemporary objections.	10 mins	Welcome and settle the students. Prayer to the Holy Spirit (or other suitable prayer). Tell the students that today we will be looking at the existence, nature and importance of natural law. Question: *What is natural law?* St Thomas Aquinas provided the following definition (display on a PowerPoint slide): *"The natural law is nothing else than the rational creature's participation in the eternal law."* Explain the above quote by stating that everything created has a certain nature. Everything must act in accord with their nature, including human beings. The laws that govern natures are 'natural laws.' These natural laws reflect the eternal law of God. The Catholic Church recognises the existence of natural law and says that it can be known instinctively and through experience. Natural law can be known by anyone, not just Catholics, as shown by the following quote from the first century BC Roman philosopher, Cicero (display on a PowerPoint slide): *"There is indeed a law, right reason, which is in accordance with nature; existing in all, unchangeable, eternal. Commanding us to do what is right, forbidding us to do what is wrong … No other law can be substituted for it, no part of it can be taken away … it is eternal and immutable for all nations and for all time"* (De Re Publica).  Cicero's quote is in line with what St Paul would soon after write to the Romans (display on a PowerPoint slide): *"They show that what the law requires is written on their hearts, while their conscience also bears witness and their conflicting thoughts accuse or perhaps excuse them …"* (Rom. 2:15). Conclude by noting that there are many contemporary objections to natural law, namely, that it is outdated, irrelevant or inferior to modern laws. For secularists/atheists, nature has no meaning, purpose or law, only pitiless indifference.	Levering, *Biblical Natural Law*, 224-234. Rice, *50 Questions on the Natural Law*, 43-45, 313.

		Lesson Steps	
Distinguish between physical and moral natural laws.	12 mins	(i) Reiterate that natural laws govern how a being/creature should act or behave. This in turn depends on what a being's nature and purpose is. For example, rocks have a 'mineral' nature. Unless acted upon, they just sit still, they do not nourish, grow or reproduce. Plants have a 'vegetative' nature. They can nourish, grow and reproduce. Fish have 'animal' nature which enables them, among other things, to swim under water. It would, therefore, be against the natural laws for rocks, plants and fish if rocks suddenly started growing, plants started swimming, and fish just stood still. Since the physical natures of rocks, plants and fish do not change, it follows that the natural laws governing rocks, plants and fish (and all creatures) do not change. Physical natural laws are, therefore, *immutable*. Human beings also have an unchangeable physical nature that enables them to sit, move, nourish, grow, etc. However, in addition to a physical nature humans have a spiritual nature that can do spiritual things, namely, know, understand, judge and love/hate. With these spiritual powers humans can freely make moral decisions, namely, chose between good and evil. The natural laws that govern humans are, therefore, both physical and moral. All human actions and laws should be consistent with natural laws. When humans freely act contrary to moral natural laws they commit *sin*. Hand out Activity Sheet 40, *Physical and Moral Natural Laws*. Invite the students to read through the left-hand column and designate with an X whether the listed human actions are governed by physical or moral natural laws. Provide explanatory feedback for each answer.	Feser, *The Last Superstition*, 133, 137, 148. Higgins, *Man as Man: The Science and Art of Ethics*, 118-120.
Recognise the most basic formulation of the moral natural law, namely, "do good and avoid evil."	10 mins	(ii) On a PowerPoint slide show the students the following sentence in over-sized lettering, *"Do good and avoid evil."* Explain that this is the most basic formulation of the natural law. Exercise: Invite the students to elaborate on the basic formulation of the natural law by listing examples of good actions that should be done and evils that should be avoided. The list may include, among other things, the following:	O'Neil & Black, *The Essential Moral Handbook: A Guide to Catholic Living*, 149-155.

Good actions that should be done	Evil actions that should be avoided
Love God. Love neighbour. Preserve life. Marry, have and educate children. Search for/adhere to/promote the truth. Live peacefully with others.	Worshipping other gods. Harming neighbour. Unjustly taking life. Adultery/Divorce. Abortion/Child abuse. Spreading falsehoods/heresies. Fomenting gossip, conflict, wars.

Conclude by highlighting that to "preserve life", "marry and educate children", "search for truth" and "to live peacefully" are known as the "four inclinations of the human heart and mind" and correspond with the Ten Commandments. *What does this say about the Ten Commandments?* (Answer: They are an elaboration of the moral natural law).

Demonstrate how humans can know and understand the moral natural law.	10 mins	(iii) Ask the students the following question, *How can we know and understand the moral natural law?* Take two-three student responses. Then show on a PowerPoint slide the following sentence in over-sized lettering, *"Written on the human heart."* Explain that this means we have an instinctive knowledge of what is right and wrong in-built into us by God from the moment of our creation. Theologians call this *synteresis*. St Thomas Aquinas put it this way (display on a PowerPoint slide): *"The natural law is nothing other than the light of understanding placed in us by God; through it we know what we must do and what we must avoid. God has given this light or law at the Creation"* (*On the Decalogue*).  Raise the following objection: *If the natural law is written on the human heart and can be known by all through reason then why is it not understood/followed by all?* Take two student responses. Provide the following answer: The weakness and disorder within human beings is due to original sin. Original sin clouds the intellect and weakens the will. To compensate, God comes to our assistance to clarify the natural law through revelation and gives grace to follow it. Question: *What revelation/ assistance has God given us to clarify the natural law?* Student responses may include:	Levering, *Biblical Natural Law*, 224 & 232. O'Neil & Black, *The Essential Moral Handbook: A Guide to Catholic Living*, 160-161.

		- The Ten Commandments (revealed through Moses). - The 'Golden Rule' – *"Do to others as you would have them do to you"* (revealed by Jesus Christ [Luke 6:31]). - The living teaching authority of the Church (Mark 16:15). Inform the students that the teaching authority of the Church (the 'Magisterium') has the role of reminding us who we truly are and what we should be before God and neighbour.	
Explain how natural law more than any other type of law respects human rights, achieves justice, and promotes the common good.	12 mins	(iv) Show the students the following YouTube video, *Positivist vs Naturalist* by Joshua Hales (2.42 minutes). After viewing this video, ask the students to answer the following questions: 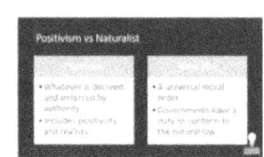 - *What is positivism?* (Answer: The belief that whatever is decreed and enforced by the legal authority is the law. "Because I said so, that's why!"). - *Naturalists believe that all human laws should conform to what?* (Answer: A universal moral order. Governments cannot make laws that do not conform to the natural law). - *What is one big problem with positivism?* (Answer: Unrestrained authorities can make their own laws and commit major atrocities, e.g., Hitler/Stalin/Mao). - *What is one example of an historic document based on the natural law?* (The American Declaration of Independence). - *What should citizens do when a government violates the natural law?* (Answer: Replace the government [if possible]). - *The narrator says there is a problem with natural law. What is that?* (Answer: Who decides what the natural law is?). *From what we know, what is the answer to this question?* (Answer: God/the Magisterium of the Church). Conclude by stating that the natural law is the best guarantor of human rights and justice as its core aim is to do good and avoid evil for each individual and society as a whole (the common good) and it is immutable (unchanging), while positive laws can be arbitrary, reflect solely the will of the law maker, can change from time to time, and can be subject to no restraints.	Finnis, *Natural Law and Natural Rights*, 23-25. Higgins, *Man as Man: The Science and Art of Ethics*, 127-128.

	3 mins	**Lesson Closure:** Remind the students that though natural law is no longer generally accepted as a source of law it is known instinctively by all persons, Catholic and non-Catholic, being "written on the human heart." In its most basic formulation, the natural law exhorts humans to "do good and avoid evil." Human beings, being physical and spiritual in nature, are subject to physical and moral natural laws. Since human nature does not change, the natural law for humans cannot change. All human (positive) laws should be consistent with the natural law, while to act contrary to the natural law is to commit sin. The unchangeability of natural law is the best guarantor of justice and human rights against arbitrary and dictatorial law makers. Revelation from God and the Magisterium of the Church help humans to have a clear view and understanding of the natural law. **Transition:** Homework: Looking at the "four inclinations of the human heart and mind" – preserve life, marry and educate children, search for truth, live peacefully – which of these would worshipping the true God fall under?	
		Resources: - Feser, Edward. *The Last Superstition.* South Bend, Indiana: St Augustine's Press, 2008, 133, 137, 148. - Finnis, John. *Natural Law and Natural Rights* (Second Edition). Oxford: Oxford University Press, 2011, 23-25. - Higgins, Thomas. *Man as Man: The Science and Art of Ethics.* Rockford, Illinois: TAN Books and Publishers, Inc., 1958, 118-120, 127-128. - Levering, Matthew. *Biblical Natural Law: A Theocentric and Teleological Approach.* Oxford: Oxford University Press, 2008, 224-234. - O'Neil, Kevin J. & Peter Black. *The Essential Moral Handbook: A Guide to Catholic Living.* Liguori, Missouri: Liguori, 2004, 149-155, 160-161. - Rice, Charles. *50 Questions on the Natural Law: What it is and Why We Need it.* San Francisco: Ignatius Press, 1993, 43-45, 313. - *Catechism of the Catholic Church.* Libreria Editrice Vaticana: St Pauls, 1994, paras. 1954-1960, 2036. - YOUCAT (*Youth Catechism of the Catholic Church*). San Francisco, Ignatius Press, 2010, paras. 45, 333.	

| | | <ul><li>Website: Broussard, Karlo. "The Natural Law: A Guide for How to be Human." https://www.catholic.com/magazine/online-edition/the-natural-law-a-guide-for-how-to-be-human.</li><li>YouTube: Hales, Joshua. "Positivist vs Naturalist." https://www.youtube.com/watch?v=0k1dtI1-zm8.</li></ul> |

LESSON EVALUATION (to be completed AFTER the lesson)

Assessment of lesson objectives and suggestions for improvement:
Teacher self-reflection and self-evaluation:
[OFFICIAL USE ONLY] Comments by teacher supervisor:

Lesson 24: The Relevance and Necessity of the Ten Commandments

LESSON ORGANISATION

Year Level:	Date:	Time:	Duration:	Room:

Quote:
"We must not see the Ten Commandments as limitations to liberty. No, they are not this, but we must see them as indications for liberty" – Pope Francis.

Prayer:
Come, Holy Spirit, fill the hearts of your faithful and enkindle in them the fire of your love.

V. Send forth your Spirit and they shall be created.
R. And you shall renew the face of the earth.

Let us pray.
O God, who by the light of the Holy Spirit, did instruct the hearts of the faithful, grant us in the same Spirit to be truly wise and ever to rejoice in his consolation.
Through Christ our Lord. Amen.

Lesson Outcomes:

As a result of this lesson, students will be able to:

- Recognise the divine origin of the Ten Commandments and contemporary objections.
- Appreciate that the Ten Commandments form a logical and organic unity governing all aspects of life.
- Understand the Ten Commandments as positive laws of life and love.
- Respond to the charge that the Ten Commandments are irrelevant, outdated and unreasonably restrict human freedom.
- Contend how humans can observe the Ten Commandments with the aid of God's grace.

Activity Sheets:

Activity Sheet 41, *The Ten Commandments – A Complete Way of Living.*
Activity Sheet 42, *The Ten Commandments – Laws of Liberty.*

LESSON DELIVERY

Outcome	Time	Motivation and Introduction:	Resources/ References
Recognise the divine origin of the Ten Commandments and contemporary objections.	10 mins	Welcome and settle the students. Prayer to the Holy Spirit (or other suitable prayer). Tell the students that today we will be looking at the relevance and necessity of the Ten Commandments. The Ten Commandments are otherwise known as the Decalogue, or 'ten words.' They were first given by God to Moses and the Israelites after escaping from Egypt nearly three thousand five hundred years ago. They formed the core of the covenant relationship between God and the Israelites. This is recorded in the Old Testament books of Exodus and Deuteronomy. Many today object to the Ten Commandments and wish to see them replaced or abolished. The following are examples of contemporary objections or criticisms (display on a PowerPoint slide): - "Modern humanity should not be bound by a random set of commandments constructed by crude, Bronze-Age barbarians." - "The Ten Commandments demand the impossible, especially by attempting to regulate our thoughts as well as actions." - "Jesus preached a gospel of love, not rules, regulations and commandments." - "Modern people can construct alternate and more relevant commandments for today relating to joy, wonder, freedom and non-judgementalism." For Catholics, the Ten Commandments remain relevant and necessary for salvation. Jesus reaffirmed the need to observe the Ten Commandments (*"If you wish to enter into life, keep the Commandments"*: Matt. 19:16) and St Paul gave us a better understanding of them as positive laws of love (Rom. 13:10). **Lesson Steps**	O'Neil & Black, *The Essential Moral Handbook: A Guide to Catholic Living*, 130. Vaghi, *The Commandments We Keep: A Catholic Guide to Living a Moral Life*, 14.
Appreciate that the Ten Commandments form a logical and organic unity governing all aspects of life.	10 mins	(i) Tell the students that rather than being a "random set of commandments" the Ten Commandments form a logical organic unity that govern all aspects of human life. Hand out Activity Sheet 41, *The Ten Commandments – A Complete Way*	O'Neil & Black, *The Essential Moral Handbook: A Guide to Catholic Living*, 130.

		of Living. Place the number of the Commandment in Column A with the aspect of human life it governs. Commandment 9 is done to help start the students off. Then invite the students to answer the question, *Which aspects of life are covered by multiple Commandments?* Highlight how the Ten Commandments cover our relationships with God, family and neighbour, protects life, marriage and the right to property, and regulates our actions, words and thoughts. *Can the students think of any aspect of life that the Ten Commandments do not cover?*	

Understand the Ten Commandments as positive laws of life and love.	12 mins	(ii) Ask the students the following question: *Is a life of love a life without rules or regulations?* Take two-three responses.
		Explain to the students that some reject the Ten Commandments because they view them as simply a collection of rules and regulations that seek to legalistically manage every aspect of our lives. For these same people, only one rule is necessary – the rule of love.
		
		Show the students the following YouTube video, *Pope Francis Explains How the Ten Commandments Are Fulfilled by Christ* by Rome Reports (2.31 minutes). After viewing  this video, ask the students to answer the following questions (Record appropriate student responses on the whiteboard):
		- *How does Pope Francis see the Ten Commandments?*
		  (Answer: Not as a series of rules but as a guide to an authentic human life).
		- *The Ten Commandments invite us into what?*
		  (Answer: A faithful and loving relationship with God the Father; a rejection of enslaving false idols).
		- *What are the characteristics of a redeemed life?*
		  (Answer: Fidelity, integrity, honesty towards our neighbour; authentic rest in the freedom of Christ and the Holy Spirit).
		
		Sum up for the students that it is wrong to view love and laws as incompatible opposites. The Ten Commandments outline the practical ways we can live out the laws of love towards God and neighbour. They are the basic rules of true love. Rather than being an opposite, love is the best way of fulfilling the law. As St Paul says, *"Love is the fulfilling of the law"* (Rom. 13:10).
			Cavarero & Scola, *Thou Shalt Not Kill: A Political and Theological Dialogue*, 18-22.
			
			Holden & Pinsent, *Apologia: Catholic Answers to Today's Questions*, 71.
			
			Vaghi, *The Commandments We Keep: A Catholic Guide to Living a Moral Life*, 11-12.

Respond to the charge that the Ten Commandments are irrelevant, outdated and unreasonably restrict human freedom.	10 mins	(iii) Guided discussion: *Is there a need for a new set of Ten Commandments?* Many today see the Ten Commandments as outdated and restrictive of human freedom, especially in the area of sexual behaviour. *Should the Ten Commandments be rewritten or scrapped altogether?* Hand out Activity Sheet 42, *The Ten Commandments – Laws of Liberty*. *What does Pope Francis say about the Ten Commandments and human liberty? Why do you think he says that the Ten Commandments free, rather than restrict, humanity?* (Answer: Because they purify the heart of the slavery of selfishness and direct us to love God and our neighbour as ourselves). Invite the students in the space provided to write down three new commandments they think are necessary for today. Challenge students to provide reasons for their suggested changes. (NB: Suggested changes should not contradict the current list of Commandments). 	O'Neil & Black, *The Essential Moral Handbook: A Guide to Catholic Living*, 31-40.
Contend how humans can observe the Ten Commandments with the aid of God's grace.	10 mins	(iv) On a PowerPoint slide show the students the following objection: *The Ten Commandments are too difficult to keep. They try to control how people act and how they should think. Not even Christians can obey them!* Invite the students to write a one-paragraph response to the above objection. Choose two students to read out their responses. Write appropriate points from these responses on the whiteboard. Explain to the students that the Ten Commandments are difficult to obey due to human pride, sensuality and selfishness and by ourselves we cannot obey them consistently. *That being the case, why should we bother having such laws?* In response, show and explain the following points: - The Church is not a society of the perfect but a hospital for sinners. - God is always willing and able to help us overcome any temptation (1 Cor. 10-13). - There are many helps God gives us through the Church – spiritual direction, good friendships, lives of saints, sacramental graces, especially the Eucharist and Reconciliation. Conclude by stating that when Jesus says *"Come, follow me"* (Matt. 4:19) he walks with us. We never walk alone.	Vaghi, *The Commandments We Keep: A Catholic Guide to Living a Moral Life*, 11-14.

| | 3 mins | **Lesson Closure**: Remind the students that the Ten Commandments, while reflecting the natural law ("Do good and avoid evil"), were originally given by God in written form to Moses and the Israelites over three thousand five hundred years ago and together govern all aspects of human life. Though originally Old Testament laws, both Jesus Christ and St Paul reaffirmed the Ten Commandments as positive laws of life and love for Christians and remain relevant as laws that liberate humanity from idolatry and excessive self-love. Ordinarily, the Ten Commandments are difficult to live out, but with the help of God's grace the *"commandments are not burdensome"* (1 John 5:3).

Transition:

Homework: Watch the YouTube video, *Did the Catholic Church Change the Ten Commandments?* by Tim Staples of Catholic Answers (https://www.youtube.com/watch?v=8l9NQSV8CzM) for an explanation as to why the Catholic listing of the Ten Commandments differs from the Protestant one. | |
| | | **Resources**:

- Cavarero, Adriana & Angelo Scola. *Thou Shalt Not Kill: A Political and Theological Dialogue.* Bologna, Italy: Fordham University Press, 2015, 18-22.
- Holden, Marcus & Andrew Pinsent. *Apologia: Catholic Answers to Today's Questions.* London: Catholic Truth Society, 2010, 71.
- O'Neil, Kevin J. & Peter Black. *The Essential Moral Handbook: A Guide to Catholic Living.* Liguori, Missouri: Liguori, 2004, 31-40, 130.
- Vaghi, Peter J. *The Commandments We Keep: A Catholic Guide to Living a Moral Life.* Notre Dame, IN: Ave Maria Press, 2011, 11-14.
- *Catechism of the Catholic Church.* Libreria Editrice Vaticana: St Pauls, 1994, paras. 2052-2074.
- YOUCAT (*Youth Catechism of the Catholic Church*). San Francisco, Ignatius Press, 2010, para. 349.
- Website: Wensing, Michael. "The True Ten Commandments." https://www.catholic.com/magazine/print-edition/the-true-ten-commandments.
- YouTube: Rome Reports. "Pope Francis Explains How the Ten Commandments Are Fulfilled by Christ." https://www.youtube.com/watch?v=4mEEKljapuY.
- YouTube: Staples, Tim. "Did the Catholic Church Change the Ten Commandments?" https://www.youtube.com/watch?v=8l9NQSV8CzM. | |

LESSON EVALUATION (to be completed AFTER the lesson)

Assessment of lesson objectives and suggestions for improvement:
Teacher self-reflection and self-evaluation:
[OFFICIAL USE ONLY] Comments by teacher supervisor:

Lesson 25: Law and Conscience

LESSON ORGANISATION

Year Level: Date: Time: Duration: Room:

Quote:
"Conscience is the aboriginal vicar of Christ" – St John Henry Newman.

Prayer:
Come, Holy Spirit, fill the hearts of your faithful and enkindle in them the fire of your love.

V. Send forth your Spirit and they shall be created.
R. And you shall renew the face of the earth.

Let us pray.
O God, who by the light of the Holy Spirit, did instruct the hearts of the faithful, grant us in the same Spirit to be truly wise and ever to rejoice in his consolation.
Through Christ our Lord. Amen.

Lesson Outcomes:

As a result of this lesson, students will be able to:

- Understand contemporary objections to the Catholic Church's teaching on law and conscience.
- Recognise conscience as the human person's 'secret core' calling us to do good and avoid evil.
- Appreciate the necessity of forming 'correct Catholic consciences.'
- Comprehend the difficulties associated with the 'primacy of conscience' position.
- Distinguish between the various types of conscience; respect the obligation not to compel others to act contrary to conscience.

Activity Sheets:

Activity Sheet 43, *Conscience – Our Most Secret Core*.

"Always Be Prepared …" – A 'New Apologetics' Course for Catholic Secondary Schools

LESSON DELIVERY

Outcome	Time	Motivation and Introduction:	Resources/ References
Understand contemporary objections to the Catholic Church's teaching on law and conscience.	8 mins	Welcome and settle the students. Prayer to the Holy Spirit (or other suitable prayer). Tell the students that today we will be looking at the Catholic Church's teaching on following one's conscience. Inform the students that this is a very highly contested area marked by much disagreement and confusion. One strong view advocated by many is the so-called 'primacy of conscience' position, which places following one's conscience over and above any objective law or Church teaching. Its main arguments can be summarised as follows (display on a PowerPoint slide): - "Each person is free to create and follow their own moral laws over and above any Church teaching." - "The Bible and the Church can contribute to moral discernment but ultimately conscience determines each person's actions." - "The Church can give people a guide-map on what to believe, how to live and how to vote but cannot tell them what to do. Conscience is the compass pointing which way to go." - "A Catholic can depart from known Church teaching on moral matters if they are satisfied they have a greater understanding of the facts or situation than the Church." Sum up by noting that conscience is something that must always be respected; however, there does exist an obligation on all persons to correctly form their consciences according to objective moral norms and Church teaching and to conform one's decisions and actions according to the same when known. **Lesson Steps**	O'Neil & Black, *The Essential Moral Handbook: A Guide to Catholic Living*, 77-82.
Recognise conscience as the human person's 'secret core' calling us to do good and avoid evil.	10 mins	(i) *What is conscience?* On a PowerPoint slide provide the following definition: *"Conscience is people's most secret core, and their sanctuary. There they are alone with God whose voice echoes in their depths"* (Vatican II, *Gaudium et Spes* 16).	Redemptorist Pastoral Publications, *The Essential Catholic Handbook*, 31-32.

Appreciate the necessity of forming 'correct Catholic consciences.'	12 mins	Hand out Activity Sheet 43, *Conscience – Our Most Secret Core*. Invite the students to read through the definition of conscience from *Gaudium et Spes* (a document from the Second Vatican Council) as well as the points outlining what conscience does. Then ask the students to answer the question, *Why do you think the voice of conscience is equivalent to the voice of God?* Take two student answers. (Answer: The voice of conscience calls us to "do good and avoid evil", i.e., to follow the objective moral natural law, the author of which is God).		
		(ii) Show the students the following YouTube video, *Conscience* by CGSE RE (3.07 minutes). The second half of the video touches on the need to inform, educate and develop the conscience as consciences are not inherently infallible. After viewing this video, list the ways we are to inform, etc., our consciences (Record appropriate student responses on the whiteboard). (Answers include: Listen to the reliable viewpoints of others; consult Church teachings; the Ten Commandments; Jesus' two great Commandments of loving God and neighbour). 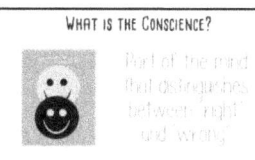 Classroom discussion: *Why should the personal conscience not be in opposition to the Church's teachings on moral issues?* Take two-three student responses. (Answer: The personal conscience is not infallible. The Catholic Church is by the will of Jesus Christ the teacher of truth. The Church's teachings are guided by the Holy Spirit). Sum up by stating that the word 'conscience' is always qualified by adjectives such as 'right', 'upright', 'correct', 'well-informed' or 'Christian' to avoid having confused, misled or deformed consciences.	Fisher, *Conscience and Authority*, 1-8. Rice, *50 Questions on the Natural Law*, 199-201.
Comprehend the difficulties associated with the 'primacy of conscience' position.	12 mins	(iii) Show the following quote from St John Henry Newman regarding conscience on a PowerPoint slide: *"I shall drink to the Pope, if you please, still, to conscience first, and to the Pope afterwards."* Exercise: Invite the students to write one paragraph outlining what they think Cardinal Newman meant by these words. Take two student responses. 	Flader, *Question Time: 150 Questions and Answers on the Catholic Faith*, 203-205.

		Raise the following point: It seems like Cardinal Newman is saying that while the teaching of the Pope should be respected, he prefers to put his own opinion first. Some see this quote as an expression of the 'primacy of conscience' view and claim that this view is official Church teaching. Classroom discussion: *Can anyone perceive a problem with the 'primacy of conscience' view?* After two minutes fielding student responses conclude with the following critique: 'Primacy of conscience' is problematic as it allows Catholics to feel justified in denying any Church teaching – substituting their own opinions in their place – while still claiming to be faithful Catholics. It seeks to use one alleged Church teaching to deny any and all others, resulting in the detachment of the conscience from objective truth. Cardinal Newman would later explain that he was referring not to the teachings of the Pope on faith and morals but to his non-infallible *"laws … commands … acts of state … administration … public policy."*	
Distinguish between the various types of conscience.	12 mins	(iv) Remind the students that while there is an obligation to form and follow one's conscience according to Catholic teaching this is not something that is quickly and easily done for many people. Most consciences are in various stages of development and require further formation, as well as respect and patience from others. On a PowerPoint slide display and explain the following different types of consciences: (a) *Correct conscience*: a conscience that judges as good that which is truly good and judges as evil that which is truly evil. (b) *Invincibly erroneous conscience*: a conscience that, after serious reflection, sincerely judges good that which is truly evil and judges as evil that which is truly good. (c) *Vincibly erroneous conscience*: a conscience that, without serious thought/effort to find out what is true, judges good that which is truly evil and judges as evil that which is truly good. (d) *Lax conscience:* a conscience that takes little trouble to find out whether an action is sinful or not, and easily judges wrong things as permissible or underrates their wrongfulness. (e) *Darkened conscience*: a conscience that has been made insensitive to evil through deliberate habitual malevolent acts. (f) *Doubtful conscience*: a conscience that is in doubt as to whether an action is good or evil.	Higgins, *Man as Man: The Science and Art of Ethics*, 134. O'Neil & Black, *The Essential Moral Handbook: A Guide to Catholic Living*, 78-81.

Respect the obligation not to compel others to act contrary to conscience.		Exercise: *In which of the above five scenarios can a person act without sin?* After a few moments considering student responses provide the following answers: In scenarios (a) and (b) due to the person's sincerity. However, in scenarios (c) and (d), the person is not without fault due to their negligence or refusal in finding out what is true. In scenario (e) the person is at fault for deliberately numbing their conscience to good and evil. In scenario (f) the person should not act if the action may be evil. Not to act at all is the safer course. Whatever the scenario, stress that a person with an erroneous or doubtful conscience should never be compelled to act against or be prevented from acting according to conscience, especially in religious matters. No person should be forced to assent to truth; they must freely adhere to the truth that they have themselves discovered. A person should also follow their own conscience even if it is objectively wrong, lest they condemn themselves (1 Cor. 8:7-11). However, once a person realises their error, they are obliged to adhere to the truth they have discovered, to avoid acting against their now correctly informed conscience.	O'Neil & Black, *The Essential Moral Handbook: A Guide to Catholic Living*, 77-78.
	3 mins	**Lesson Closure:** Remind the students that conscience is a person's "most secret core", wherein the voice of God speaks to each person to "do good and avoid evil." While each person is obliged to follow their conscience, the same is not infallible and requires formation according to objective moral principles and Church teaching. 'Primacy of conscience' is a popular concept among many but is not official Church teaching and cannot be relied upon to justify departure from or resistance to known Church teaching. No one should ever be compelled to act against conscience, though one should always seek the truth and embrace it once known. **Transition:** Homework: Watch the YouTube video, *"A Man for All Seasons – Trailer"* (https://www.youtube.com/watch?v=e2_foeO-z6o) for what St Thomas More says about conscience. Research the question of faith which St Thomas More would not compromise on.	

Resources:

- Flader, John. *Question Time: 150 Questions and Answers on the Catholic Faith.* Ballan, Vic.: Connor Court Publishing, 2008, 203-205.
- Higgins, Thomas. *Man as Man: The Science and Art of Ethics.* Rockford, Illinois: TAN Books and Publishers, Inc., 1958, 134.
- O'Neil, Kevin J. & Peter Black. *The Essential Moral Handbook: A Guide to Catholic Living.* Liguori, Missouri: Liguori, 2004, 77-82.
- Redemptorist Pastoral Publications. *The Essential Catholic Handbook: A Summary of Beliefs, Practices, and Prayers.* Liguori, Missouri: Liguori, 1997, 31-32.
- Rice, Charles. *50 Questions on the Natural Law: What it is and Why We Need it.* San Francisco: Ignatius Press, 1993, 199-201.
- *Catechism of the Catholic Church.* Libreria Editrice Vaticana: St Pauls, 1994, paras. 1782, 1790-1793, 2039.
- YOUCAT (*Youth Catechism of the Catholic Church*). San Francisco, Ignatius Press, 2010, paras. 295-298.
- Website: Fisher, Anthony. "Conscience and Authority — Struggling to Recover a Catholic Sense." A paper delivered to the Pontifical Academy for Life, Rome, 3 March 2007, 1-8.
http://www.zenit.org/english/visualizza.phtml?sid=103903.
- YouTube: CGSE RE. "Conscience." https://www.youtube.com/watch?v=lmx9b4aUIkw.
- YouTube: "A Man for All Seasons – Trailer." https://www.youtube.com/watch?v=e2_foeO-z6o.

LESSON EVALUATION (to be completed AFTER the lesson)

Assessment of lesson objectives and suggestions for improvement:

Teacher self-reflection and self-evaluation:

[OFFICIAL USE ONLY] Comments by teacher supervisor:

Lesson 26: The Origin and Importance of the Sacraments

LESSON ORGANISATION

Year Level: Date: Time: Duration: Room:

Quote:
"The sacraments are the salvation of those who use them rightly, and the damnation of those who misuse them" – St Augustine of Hippo.

Prayer:
Come, Holy Spirit, fill the hearts of your faithful and enkindle in them the fire of your love.

V. Send forth your Spirit and they shall be created.
R. And you shall renew the face of the earth.

Let us pray.
O God, who by the light of the Holy Spirit, did instruct the hearts of the faithful, grant us in the same Spirit to be truly wise and ever to rejoice in his consolation.
Through Christ our Lord. Amen.

Lesson Outcomes:

As a result of this lesson, students will be able to:

- Understand Protestant objections to the Catholic Church's belief in the seven sacraments.
- Identify all seven sacraments in the New Testament and how they continue the work of Jesus Christ in the world.
- Recognise the 'divine economy' in the distribution of the seven sacraments across all aspects of human life.
- Defend material objects as vehicles of spiritual grace as part of God's 'incarnational' way of relating to humanity.
- Respond to the charge that Catholic sacraments are more magic than mystery.

Activity Sheets:

Activity Sheet 44, *Sacraments in Scripture.*
Activity Sheet 45, *Sacraments for Life.*

LESSON DELIVERY

Outcome	Time	Motivation and Introduction:	Resources/ References
Understand Protestant objections to the Catholic Church's belief in the seven sacraments.	7 mins	Welcome and settle the students. Prayer to the Holy Spirit (or other suitable prayer). Tell the students that today we will be looking at the origin and importance of the sacraments. The word 'sacrament' comes from the Latin *sacramentum* (Greek: *mysterion*), which means "oath." Catholics believe that God has made an oath with his people to give them all the graces they need to faithfully travel the spiritual road towards heaven. God fulfils his oath through the seven sacraments, which span the length of a Christian's life. Most Protestant Christians, however, object to the Catholic 'sacramental system.' Their main objections can be summarised as follows (display on a PowerPoint slide and provide appropriate explanations): - "There are not seven sacraments. Only two are mentioned in the Bible, Baptism and the Lord's Supper." - "Sacraments get in the way of a relationship with God. We can get God's grace without the need for intermediaries." - "Material things such as water, oil, bread or wine cannot be vehicles of grace. Grace is something spiritual that can only be given by God." - "Sacraments are only symbols, signs of grace given by God. To believe that sacraments themselves give grace is to believe in magic." Begin a response to the above objections by examining what the Bible, principally the New Testament, says about sacraments. **Lesson Steps**	Kreeft, *Fundamentals of the Faith*, 282-286. Salza, *The Biblical Basis for the Catholic Faith*, 65.
Identify all seven sacraments in the New Testament and how they continue the work of Jesus Christ in the world.	17 mins	(i) Remind the students that the Catholic Church believes there are seven sacraments. List them on a PowerPoint slide as follows: Baptism, Confirmation, the Eucharist, Reconciliation, Anointing of the Sick, Holy Orders and Holy Matrimony. Hand out Activity Sheet 44, *Sacraments in Scripture*. Invite the students to read through the different quotes from the New Testament and in the spaces provided write which sacrament they think each quote relates to (Answers in order are: Holy Matrimony; the Eucharist; Baptism; Confirmation; Reconciliation; Anointing of the Sick; Holy Orders).	Clovis, *A Biblical Search for the Church Christ Founded*, 59-85. Gray, *Sacraments in Scripture: Salvation History Made Present*, 17-18.

		Afterwards, ask the students to write one paragraph as to what the following passage from the Old Testament book of Isaiah may mean and why it may relate to the sacraments: *"With joy you will draw water from the wells of salvation"* (Is. 12:3). (Answer: This verse is a prophecy relating to the future Messianic age [the Christian era]; the "wells of salvation" are the sacraments of the Church; the "water" is God's grace). Show the students the following YouTube video, *The Seven Sacraments* by ODB Films (2.37 minutes). Forty seconds into this video the narrator says, *"The sacraments are what Christ did on earth."* Ask the students, *What were some of the things Christ did on earth?* List appropriate student responses on the whiteboard. The list should eventually look as follows:  - He sent out his disciples to baptise (Baptism). - He sent the Holy Spirit upon his disciples at Pentecost (Confirmation). - He gave his disciples his Body and Blood to eat and drink (The Eucharist). - He forgave sins (Reconciliation). - He healed the sick (Anointing of the Sick). - He made his disciples priests at the Last Supper (Holy Orders). - He restored the sacredness of marriage (Holy Matrimony). Next to each point write the name of the sacrament that corresponds to the action. Highlight that this list shows that Christ (as Head) empowers the Church (his Body) through the sacraments to continue his work of sanctification and mission in the world.	
Recognise the 'divine economy' in the distribution of the seven sacraments across all aspects of human life.	10 mins	(ii) On a PowerPoint slide, show the students the following quote from Bishop Robert Barron: *"All the sacraments have a deifying purpose: Baptism introduces the Divine Life into us. Confession restores it when it's lost through sin. Confirmation strengthens it. Matrimony and Holy Orders give it vocational direction. Anointing of the Sick prepares us for the transition to our heavenly homeland. And the Eucharist is meant to Christify us."*  Classroom discussion: *What does the above quote tell us about the ordering of the sacraments?* Take two student responses. Afterwards, hand out Activity Sheet 45, *Sacraments for Life* and	Gray, *Sacraments in Scripture: Salvation History Made Present*, 29-30.

		invite the students to insert the name of the appropriate sacrament in Column B. Afterwards, ask the students to read the following: The sacraments are ordered to parallel the human life cycle and its spiritual journey towards the heavenly Kingdom. We are all born and there is a sacrament for spiritual birth (Baptism). We grow into adults and there is a sacrament of spiritual adulthood (Confirmation). We require daily food to live and there is a sacrament that provides daily heavenly food for the spiritual journey (the Eucharist). We fall sick from time to time and there is a sacrament that heals us when we fall spiritually sick (Reconciliation). As adults we make vocational choices and there are two sacraments of spiritual vocation (Holy Matrimony and Holy Orders). We all eventually pass from this world and there is a sacrament to assist believers to cross-over into the next life (Anointing of the Sick). This ordering reflects both God's wisdom and his care for the human family.	
Defend material objects as vehicles of spiritual grace as part of God's 'incarnational' way of relating to humanity.	10 mins	(iii) Show the word 'incarnational' in enlarged letters on a PowerPoint slide. Ask the students if any of them have heard of this word before. Some might respond that it could relate to 'incarnation', how Jesus took flesh and became one of us. Acknowledge the reasonableness of such an answer. Inform the students that with respect to the sacraments it refers to how God approaches and relates to humanity through things, persons, words and events that can be seen, heard or touched by our senses. Question: *What are some of the things used in the sacraments that are instruments of grace?* Answers should include water, oil, bread and wine. Jesus chose these items to be instruments of grace because they were commonly used in his time and they symbolise washing, healing, feeding and mission. However, not everyone believes that material items can confer spiritual grace. On a PowerPoint slide show the following quote by the famous anti-Catholic apologist, Loraine Boettner: *"The blessing is not inherent in the sacrament as such … but is bestowed directly by the Holy Spirit, and it is received by the one who exercises true faith"* (*Roman Catholicism*, 193). Invite the students to respond to Loraine Boettner. Give them the following two clues: Mark 5:25-34 and John 9:6-7. Take two	Gray, *Sacraments in Scripture: Salvation History Made Present*, 25-26. Kreeft, *Fundamentals of the Faith*, 282-286. Schreck, *Catholic and Christian*, 128-130.

		student responses. Student responses should note how Jesus healed people after someone simply touched his cloak or through applying mud mixed with spittle. Mark 5:25-34 and John 9:6-7 alone provide ample proof that material items (cloth, mud, spit, etc.) can be instruments of spiritual grace.	

Respond to the charge that Catholic sacraments are more magic than mystery.	10 mins	(iv) Show another quote from Loraine Boettner as follows: *"The Roman doctrine of the sacraments constitutes the most elaborate system of magic and ritual … ever invented"* (*Roman Catholicism*, 194).
		
		Question: *Is it fair to charge that the sacraments work like magic?* At first instance it may be. The Catholic definition of a sacrament is *"a visible sign instituted by Christ that both signifies and bestows the grace that it signifies."* It seems from this definition that the ritual itself creates and gives the grace. How can water, oil, bread, wine give grace unless through some form of magic?
		
		Show the students three words on a PowerPoint slide: *Mystery; Christ; Oath*.
		
		Highlight that these three words point to the reasons why the sacraments are not magical. Provide the students with the following explanations:
		   Mystery: The mystery is how Christ wishes to continue working in the world through his Church – the Catholic Church – and through the seven ritual sacraments of the Church.
		   Christ: Christ not only establishes each sacrament but 'stands behind' each one. He is the principal person at work in each sacrament. It is he who baptises, confirms, forgives, heals, etc. Everyone else involved in administering the sacraments are mere instruments in the hands of Christ.
		   Oath: Remember that the original word for sacrament – *sacramentum* – means oath, or promise. Christ promises to give sacramental grace when all the conditions (words, matter) are satisfied. Christ always keeps his promises.
		
		Conclude by emphasising that while it is Christ who makes the sacraments efficacious (effective), in the case of recipients with the use of reason they will only receive the grace signified if they partake of the sacraments worthily in faith.
			Gray, *Sacraments in Scripture: Salvation History Made Present*, 23.
			
			Kreeft, *Fundamentals of the Faith*, 282-286.

| | 3 mins | **Lesson Closure:**

Remind the students that all seven sacraments were given to the Church by Christ and are evident in the New Testament. The sacraments are visible signs that continue Christ's work of sanctification and mission in the world. The ordering of the sacraments parallels the human life cycle and illustrates God's wisdom and care for his people from cradle till grave. The material objects used in the sacraments were chosen by Christ and symbolise washing, healing, feeding and mission. The material objects and words recited do not in themselves have any power to bestow grace but they can do so because it is Christ himself who 'stands behind' each sacrament and acts through the ministers to baptise, confirm, forgive, etc. Recipients with the use of reason will only receive the grace signified if they partake of the sacraments worthily in faith.

Transition:

Homework: Choose three sacraments. Research and record what are the valid 'matter and form' for each one. 'Matter' relates to the material element that should be employed; 'form' to the words that should be said. (To assist the students, you may provide the following example: Baptism: Matter – water; Words – *"I baptise you in the name of the Father, and of the Son, and of the Holy Spirit. Amen."* | |
| | | **Resources:**

- Clovis, Linus F. *A Biblical Search for the Church Christ Founded.* Leominster, United Kingdom: Gracewing, 2012, 59-85.
- Gray, Timothy. *Sacraments in Scripture: Salvation History Made Present.* Steubenville, Ohio: Emmaus Road Publishing, 2001, 17-18 & 25-26.
- Kreeft, Peter. *Fundamentals of the Faith: Essays in Christian Apologetics.* San Francisco: Ignatius Press, 1988, 282-286.
- Salza, John. *The Biblical Basis for the Catholic Faith.* Huntingdon, Indiana: Our Sunday Visitor Publishing, 2005, 65.
- Schreck, Alan. *Catholic and Christian: An Explanation of Commonly Misunderstood Catholic Beliefs.* Cincinnati, Ohio: Servant Books, 2004, 128-130. | |

| | | <ul><li>*Catechism of the Catholic Church*. Libreria Editrice Vaticana: St Pauls, 1994, paras. 1091-1092, 1115, 1127-1128, 1210.</li><li>YOUCAT (*Youth Catechism of the Catholic Church*). San Francisco, Ignatius Press, 2010, paras. 172-178.</li><li>Website: Staples, Tim. "Did Jesus Institute All Seven Sacraments?" https://www.catholic.com/audio/caf/did-jesus-institute-the-seven-sacraments.</li><li>YouTube: ODB Films. "The Seven Sacraments." https://www.youtube.com/watch?v=qmfSwi3ZKH4.</li></ul> |

LESSON EVALUATION (to be completed AFTER the lesson)

Assessment of lesson objectives and suggestions for improvement:
Teacher self-reflection and self-evaluation:
[OFFICIAL USE ONLY] Comments by teacher supervisor:

Lesson 27: The Origin and Importance of the Mass

LESSON ORGANISATION

Year Level: _____ Date: _____ Time: _____ Duration: _____ Room: _____

Quote:
"If we only knew how God regards this sacrifice, we would risk our lives to be present at a single Mass" – St Padre Pio.

Prayer:
Come, Holy Spirit, fill the hearts of your faithful and enkindle in them the fire of your love.

V. Send forth your Spirit and they shall be created.
R. And you shall renew the face of the earth.

Let us pray.
O God, who by the light of the Holy Spirit, did instruct the hearts of the faithful, grant us in the same Spirit to be truly wise and ever to rejoice in his consolation.
Through Christ our Lord. Amen.

Lesson Outcomes:

As a result of this lesson, students will be able to:

- Understand traditional Protestant objections against the Mass.
- Recognise how the Mass has its origins in the Last Supper and has been celebrated continuously ever since.
- Realise how the Mass makes present Christ's 'once and for all' sacrifice on Mount Calvary in an unbloody form.
- Appreciate how the Catholic priesthood participates in Christ's priesthood.
- Comprehend how the Mass enables Christians to offer the infinite merits of Christ's sacrifice to the Father for their own personal intentions.

Activity Sheets:

Activity Sheet 46, *The Last Supper – A Sacrifice?*
Activity Sheet 47, *Participating in the Priesthood of Christ.*

LESSON DELIVERY

Outcome	Time	Motivation and Introduction:	Resources/ References
Understand traditional Protestant objections against the Mass.	8 mins	Welcome and settle the students. Prayer to the Holy Spirit (or other suitable prayer). Tell the students that today we will be looking at the origin and importance of the Mass. Inform the students that the Mass has been central in Catholic/Christian public worship for the past two millennia but the since the Reformation over five hundred years ago has been rejected by most Protestants. The main Protestant arguments against the Mass can be summarised as follows (display on a PowerPoint slide and provide appropriate explanations): - "The Last Supper was meant to be only a remembrance of what Christ did on the Cross. The idea of any sacrifice being involved is a medieval invention." - "The Mass is a re-crucifixion of Christ over and over again. Rome claims to continue what was completed once and for all two thousand years ago." - "There is only one priest, Jesus Christ. To have others claiming to be priests and offering sacrifices is usurping Christ's unique priesthood and implies that Christ's sacrifice on the Cross was inadequate. This is blasphemous." - "Christians only need to believe in Christ's sacrifice on the Cross to be forgiven for sin. Prayer is sufficient for all other intentions." Conclude by noting that most Catholics do not know or understand what the Mass is. A better understanding of the Mass would allow more Catholics to see its importance and spiritual value and, hopefully, lead to a greater number of the same attending, participating and receiving the Eucharist. **Lesson Steps**	Horn, *The Case for Catholicism*, 159-166. Keating, *Catholicism and Fundamentalism*, 246-258.
Recognise how the Mass has its origins in the Last Supper and has been celebrated continuously ever since.	12 mins	(i) Emphasise that any response to the above objections depends heavily on a proper understanding of the Last Supper. Was it a sacrifice or just a memorial meal? Question: *What is the best way to find out what the Last Supper really was?* Take two-three student responses. Responses may include reading and studying relevant parts of the Bible more closely or looking at what others have written about the Last Supper over the centuries, especially the early Christians. The answer is a blend	Horn, *The Case for Catholicism*, 166-169. Keating, *Catholicism and Fundamentalism*, 254-255.

		of both these approaches. Hand out Activity Sheet 46, *The Last Supper – A Sacrifice?* Invite the students to read through the three quotes from the Old and New Testaments and then the three quotes from the first/second-century early Church Fathers. Ask the students to write out those words/phrases which emphasise sacrifice. Answers include: "pure offering"; "given for you"; "poured out"; "altar"; "offer"; "sacrifice"; "offering"; "oblation"; "offers." Conclude by stressing that the Catholic Mass celebrated today is the same event celebrated by the first/second-century Christians in obedience to Christ's command at the Last Supper (*"Do this in memory of me"*) and is the fulfilment of the prophecy of the Old Testament prophet Malachi, both of which contain sacrificial language.	Schreck, *Catholic and Christian*, 140-143.
Realise how the Mass makes present Christ's 'once and for all' sacrifice on Mount Calvary in an unbloody form.	12 mins	(ii) Question: *If the Mass is a sacrifice, what is being sacrificed?* Answers may include: bread, wine, Christ's Body, Christ's Blood. Objection: *If bread and wine are being sacrificed, isn't this another sacrifice in addition to Christ's once and for all sacrifice on Mount Calvary? If it's Christ's Body and Blood, does this mean Christ is being re-sacrificed again and again? Either way, the Catholic Mass seems to deny the sufficiency of Christ's sacrifice on Mount Calvary, which is blasphemous.* Show the students the following YouTube video, *Do Catholics Re-Sacrifice Christ?* by Catholic Answers (5.41 minutes).  This is a long video in two parts and would be difficult for the students to understand by themselves. While showing the video briefly pause at various points and highlight the following aspects of Catholic teaching: - Only Christ's bloody sacrifice on the Cross on Mount Calvary takes away sin. - Christ's sacrifice on Mount Calvary replaced the Old Testament animal sacrifices. - The Mass makes present Christ's sacrifice in an unbloody manner (not 'represents'). - It is the glorified, not crucified, Christ who is made present. Conclude by referring the students to Hebrews 12:24. There we see Christ as the High Priest of the heavenly Temple offering his *"sprinkled blood"* to the Father. Christ continues to be priest in the heavenly Temple and perpetually offers the sacrifice of Mount Calvary to the Father on our behalf. It is this glorified Christ and this perpetual sacrifice that is made present among	Armstrong, *A Biblical Defense of Catholicism*, 95-97. Feingold, *The Eucharist*, 321-371. Sheehan, *Apologetics and Catholic Doctrine*, 531-534. Sungenis, *Not By Bread Alone*, 150-152.

		us and offered to the Father through the Mass. Hence, Jesus is not being re-crucified in the Mass.	
Appreciate how the Catholic priesthood participates in Christ's priesthood.	10 mins	(iii) The next objections relate to the Catholic priesthood. On a PowerPoint slide, show the following summary of these objections: - "Christ is the only mediator between God and man (1 Tim. 2:4) and hence the only priest." - "To have additional priests to Christ offering sacrifices is to either substitute for Christ's priesthood or insinuate that his priesthood is insufficient." - "Normal, sinful men cannot be worthy priests; only the sinless Christ can offer a pleasing sacrifice to God the Father." - "We are all priests (1 Pet. 2:5-9). There is no distinct ordained priesthood separate and apart from the laity." Hand out Activity Sheet 47, *Participating in the Priesthood of Christ*. Invite the students to read through the various quotes from the Old and New Testaments and construct an argument for an ordained ministerial priesthood endowed with various functions. Student feedback should identify prophecy, repeating the Last Supper, ordination, order, forgiving sins, anointing the sick. During student responses, emphasise how this ordained ministry was founded by Christ, is apostolic, is given to many, and continues Christ's saving work in the world.	Keating, *Catholicism and Fundamentalism*, 253-254. Sheehan, *Apologetics and Catholic Doctrine*, 531-534.
Comprehend how the Mass enables Christians to offer the infinite merits of Christ's sacrifice to the Father for their own personal intentions.	10 mins	(iv) There are many benefits for Christians who attend the Mass. Question: *If the Mass makes the glorified Christ and his sacrifice present how does this benefit Christians?* Classroom discussion: Explore with the students the concept of praying and sacrificing for our intentions. If we want or need something from God what do we normally do? Answers may include: - Recite our own prayers. - Fast or offer up other sacrifices. - Ask others to pray, fast or offer sacrifices for us, especially people who have a strong faith. It is a strong Catholic tradition to ask other 'holy people' to pray/fast/sacrifice for our own intentions. We do this because we believe that God more readily hears the prayers of such holy people (James 5:16). This is why prayers such as the Hail Mary/	Sheehan, *Apologetics and Catholic Doctrine*, 537-540.

		Rosary are so popular. What about asking Jesus himself to pray for our intentions? This is not a customary Catholic practice because Catholics normally view Christ as the one who answers our prayers, etc., rather than the one who prays for us. There is a popular Catholic practice, however, wherein someone may "offer up a Mass" for specific intentions, whether for our own or for others'. Ask the students if any of them have heard of this practice. What does such a practice involve? When a Catholic attends Mass, he/she can 'co-offer' the Eucharistic Sacrifice to God for themselves and for others. Why is this especially beneficial for Christians? Because Christ is the most holy of all and his sacrifice on the Cross (now made present and available to us through the Mass) was the most perfect act of worship/sacrifice ever made to God. Through the Mass, Christians can access and offer Christ's perfect and infinitely meritorious sacrifice to the Father for their own intentions. There is no more powerful prayer/sacrifice that any Christian could offer. Highlight that this is one, among many other reasons, why we should attend and participate in Mass.	
	3 mins	**Lesson Closure:** Remind the students that the Mass was given to us by Christ at the Last Supper, to be continually celebrated by the Church in obedience to his command, *"Do this in memory of me."* The early Church Fathers are unanimous in recognising the Mass as the fulfilment of the Old Testament prophecy of Malachi and that the Mass is the sacrifice of Christians. The Mass is not an additional or alternate sacrifice to Christ's on Mount Calvary but makes the glorified Christ and his perfect once and for all sacrifice present and available to all Christians in an unbloody manner. The ministerial priesthood, likewise, is not an alternate priesthood to Christ's but was established by him to perpetuate his work and mission in the world. Christians who attend the Mass can, among other things, 'offer up' Christ's perfect sacrifice for any and all their intentions as the most powerful prayer/sacrifice any Christian could offer. **Transition:** Homework: In the mid-second century there was a saint named Justin Martyr. He wrote to the Roman Emperors outlining what the Christians believed in and how they worshipped. He was the first to	

publicly write about the Mass as follows,

"And on the day called Sunday, all who live in the cities or in the country gather together to one place and the memoirs of the apostles or the writings of the prophets are read, as long as time permits; then, when the reader has ceased, the president verbally instructs, and exhorts to the imitation of these good things. Then we all rise together and pray, and, as we before said, when our prayer is ended bread and wine are brought, and the president in like manner offers prayers and thanksgivings, according to his ability, and the people assent, saying, Amen; and there is a distribution to each and a participation of that over which thanks have been given and to those who are absent a portion is sent by the deacons."

Look up the above quote on the Internet (*First Apology to the Emperor Antoninus Pius*, 67, inter AD 148-155) and after reading it identify the similarities between the Mass of the second century and today's Mass.

Resources:

- Armstrong, Dave. *A Biblical Defense of Catholicism.* Manchester, NH: Sophia Institute Press, 2003, 95-97.
- Feingold, Lawrence. *The Eucharist: Mystery of Presence, Sacrifice, and Communion.* Steubenville, Ohio: Emmaus Academic, 2018, 321-371.
- Horn, Trent. *The Case for Catholicism: Answers to Classic and Contemporary Protestant Objections.* San Francisco: Ignatius Press, 2017, 159-166.
- Keating, Karl. *Catholicism and Fundamentalism.* San Francisco: Ignatius Press, 1988, 246-258.
- Schreck, Alan. *Catholic and Christian: An Explanation of Commonly Misunderstood Catholic Beliefs.* Cincinnati, Ohio: Servant Books, 2004, 140-143.
- Sheehan, Michael. *Apologetics and Catholic Doctrine*, rev. and ed. Peter M. Joseph. London: Baronius Press, 2015, 531-540.
- Sungenis, Robert. *Not By Bread Alone.* Goleta, CA: Queenship Publishing Company, 2000, 150-152.
- *Catechism of the Catholic Church.* Libreria Editrice Vaticana: St Pauls, 1994, paras. 1330, 1345, 1362-1372.
- YOUCAT (*Youth Catechism of the Catholic Church*). San Francisco, Ignatius Press, 2010, paras. 212-217.

		<ul><li>Website: Evert, Jason. "Is the Mass a Sacrifice?" https://www.catholic.com/magazine/print-edition/is-the-mass-a-sacrifice.</li><li>YouTube: Catholic Answers. *Do Catholics Re-Sacrifice Christ?* https://www.youtube.com/watch?v=aM_H-VfRW44.</li></ul>

LESSON EVALUATION (to be completed AFTER the lesson)

Assessment of lesson objectives and suggestions for improvement:
Teacher self-reflection and self-evaluation:
[OFFICIAL USE ONLY] Comments by teacher supervisor:

Lesson 28: The Real Presence of Christ in the Eucharist

LESSON ORGANISATION

Year Level: Date: Time: Duration: Room:

Quote:
"There is nothing so great as the Eucharist. If God had something more precious, he would have given it to us" – St John Vianney.

Prayer:
Come, Holy Spirit, fill the hearts of your faithful and enkindle in them the fire of your love.

V. Send forth your Spirit and they shall be created.
R. And you shall renew the face of the earth.

Let us pray.
O God, who by the light of the Holy Spirit, did instruct the hearts of the faithful, grant us in the same Spirit to be truly wise and ever to rejoice in his consolation.
Through Christ our Lord. Amen.

Lesson Outcomes:

As a result of this lesson, students will be able to:

- Define the term 'transubstantiation' and understand Protestant objections against Catholic teaching.
- Identify foreshadowings of the Eucharist in the Old Testament.
- Offer an exegesis of the 'Bread of Life' discourse in John 6.
- Respond to various Protestant charges against transubstantiation and Eucharistic reception.
- Analyse quotes from the writings of pre-Nicene Church Fathers illustrating belief in the Real Presence.
- Appreciate examples of Eucharistic miracles supporting transubstantiation.

Activity Sheets:

Activity Sheet 48, *The 'Bread of Life' Discourse.*
Activity Sheet 49, *Fathers and Favours.*

LESSON DELIVERY

Outcome	Time	Motivation and Introduction:	Resources/ References
Define the term transubstantiation and understand Protestant objections against Catholic teaching.	8 mins	Welcome and settle the students. Prayer to the Holy Spirit (or other suitable prayer). Tell the students that today we will be looking at the Real Presence of Christ in the Eucharist. Catholics believe that when Jesus Christ said at the Last Supper, *"Take, eat, this is my Body"* and *"Drink of it, all of you; for this is my Blood"* (Matt. 26:26-28), the bread and wine were literally changed into the Body and Blood of Christ and given to his disciples as spiritual food and drink (the Eucharist). The presence of Christ in the Eucharist is called the "Real Presence" and this belief was defined by the Council of Trent in the 16th century as follows (show on a PowerPoint slide): *By the consecration of the bread and of the wine a conversion is made of the whole substance of the bread into the substance of the Body of Christ our Lord, and of the whole substance of the wine into the substance of his Blood; which conversion is by the holy Catholic Church suitably and properly called transubstantiation.* Protestants object to both the Real Presence of Christ in the Eucharist and the term 'transubstantiation.' Their main objections can be summarised as follows (display on a PowerPoint slide and provide appropriate explanations): - "The words 'This is my body' should not be taken literally. It is just another metaphor like 'I am the door' (John 10:7) or 'I am the vine' (John 15:5)." - "The words 'eat' and 'drink' in John 6:53-57 do not mean a literal eating and drinking. They are synonymous with believing or having faith." - "The Eucharist cannot be Jesus' physical body as he is currently seated at the right hand of the Father." - "Transubstantiation is a 'jumble of medieval superstition' that literally makes the sacrament a form of cannibalism." - "Scientists examining a consecrated host say that at the molecular level no change takes place, proving that transubstantiation is preposterous." A response to the above will involve understanding some basic philosophy, analysing various Old and New Testament passages, looking at a selection of writings from early Church Fathers and exploring various Eucharistic miracles.	Horn, *The Case for Catholicism*, 171-174. Keating, *Catholicism and Fundamentalism*, 240-241.

		Lesson Steps	
Identify foreshadowings of the Eucharist in the Old Testament.	10 mins	(i) Tell the students that the Eucharist is a gift from Christ given at the Last Supper, an event recorded in the New Testament. It was also foreshadowed by various 'types' (prefiguring images) in the Old Testament. On a PowerPoint slide show the following three 'types': - Melchizedek, *"king of Salem"* and *"priest of God Most High"* who offered to God a sacrifice of bread and wine (Gen. 14:18-20). - The Paschal Lamb sacrificed, drained of blood, and consumed as food to save the Hebrews from the Angel of death at the first 'passover' and enable them to escape from the bondage of Egypt (Exod. 12:5-11). - The manna, or bread that rained down from heaven, six days a week for forty years, sustaining the Hebrews in their journey from Egypt to the Promised Land (Exod. 16:4-35). Exercise: Invite the students to chose one of the above 'types' and outline in one paragraph how they think it prefigures Jesus Christ and the Eucharist. Chose one student response for each type. Lead student answers to identify the following: (a) Jesus Christ offered bread and wine at the Last Supper and is called a priest in the *"likeness of Melchizedek"* in Hebrews 7:15-17; (b) Jesus Christ is the Lamb of God (John 1:29 & 36) who is sacrificed, drained of blood on the Cross and eaten in the Eucharist to enable the Christian people to escape from the slavery of sin; and (c) the Eucharist is the 'new manna' or bread from heaven sent by the 'new Moses' (Jesus) to sustain the Christian people in their exodus journey from this world towards the heavenly Jerusalem.	Feingold, *The Eucharist*, 39-70. Gray, *Sacraments in Scripture: Salvation History Made Present*, 51-53. Ray, *Crossing the Tiber*, 192-200.
Offer an exegesis of the 'Bread of Life' discourse in John 6.	13 mins	(ii) Classroom discussion: One year before the Last Supper, Jesus had a very important conversation with his disciples and other followers which would later become known as the 'Bread of Life discourse.' This conversation would eventually be recorded by the Apostle John in his Gospel, chapter 6. Hand out Activity Sheet 48, *The 'Bread of Life' Discourse*. Invite selected students to read through the whole text and then lead them in a classroom discussion answering the following questions: - *What does Jesus promise in verse 27?* (Answer: Food for eternal life *"which the Son of man will give to you"* [note the future tense]).	Armstrong, *A Biblical Defense of Catholicism*, 83-92. Clovis, *A Biblical Search for the Church Christ Founded*, 68-71. Salza, *The Biblical Basis for the Catholic Faith*, 99-103.

		- *Jesus directly identifies the bread he promises with what?* (Answer: *"my flesh"* v. 51). - *What is a repeated promise associated with eating and drinking Jesus' flesh and blood?* (Answer: We *"will live forever"* v. 51; we will be raised up on the *"last day"* v. 54). - *Why do you think the Jews listening to Jesus were so disturbed?* (Answer: They understood him as meaning to cannibalise his flesh and blood, which was against the Law of Moses). - *In response to the concerns of the Jews, what does Jesus do?* (Answer: He reiterates the realism of his language. He does not correct himself or give an alternative symbolic meaning). - *Why do you think most of Jesus' listeners "no longer went about with him" (v. 66)?* (Answer: Because Jesus kept insisting on a realistic eating and drinking of his flesh and blood). - *Why can we call St Peter's response in vv. 68-69 a Catholic one?* (Answer: Because he believes what Jesus says on faith, even though he does not yet fully understand his meaning). - *When do you think Jesus gave "the food for eternal life" he promised in v. 27?* (Answer: At the Last Supper). Conclude by higlighting that since the Last Supper, the Mass and Eucharist have been central in the life of the Church and Christians, as evident in Acts 2:42 & 46 and 1 Cor. 10:16. In the latter verse, St Paul calls the Eucharist a *"participation in the blood of Christ … a participation in the body of Christ."*	
Respond to various Protestant charges against transubstantiation and Eucharistic reception.	12 mins	(iii) There are many Protestant objections against the Catholic belief in transubstantiation. Two common ones are as follows: - "If you examine a communion host under a microscope all you will see are molecules of bread; there will be no trace of flesh or blood." - "If Catholic communion is about eating and drinking Christ's Body and Blood then it is a form of cannibalism." Most young Catholics would find these arguments at first instance difficult to respond to, even persuasive. Inform the students that the first can be responded to from the very definition of transubstantiation originally coined by the Fourth Lateran Council in 1215: *"… his Body and Blood are truly present contained in the sacrament of the altar <u>under the forms of bread and wine</u> …"* This means that while the substance of	Flader, *Question Time: 150 Questions and Answers on the Catholic Faith*, 94-95. Keating, *Catholicism and Fundamentalism*, 251-252.

		the bread and wine changes into Christ's Body and Blood (and co-present are his Soul and Divinity) the appearances (i.e., 'accidents' – texture, colour, size, shape, etc.) remain the same. It should, therefore, be expected that a consecrated host still appear (and act in every other way) as bread when examined under a microscope. The charge of cannibalism is an ancient one, thrown at the early Christians during the days of the Roman Empire. Show the students the following YouTube video, *Are Catholics Cannibals?* by Deacon Dance Farrell (4.20 minutes). After viewing this video outline to the students that the essential elements of cannibalism are:  - The killing of the person about to be eaten. - The destruction of that person's body through eating. Ask the students the following question: *Is Jesus killed or destroyed when received in the Eucharist?* After taking two-three responses, invite the students to write down the following points: - Jesus is not killed or destroyed. He is received by us as spiritual food and we enter into *communion* with him. - While the 'accidents' of the bread and wine remain visible, Christ is present within us Body, Blood, Soul and Divinity, and during this time he is pouring sanctifying grace into our souls. - Once the 'accidents' of the bread and wine disappear, Christ's Real Presence within us also disappears and the period of Eucharistic communion with him ends. - Christ is not changed by us when we receive him; we are changed by him when he is received.	
Analyse quotes from the writings of pre-Nicene Church Fathers illustrating belief in the Real Presence. Appreciate examples of Eucharistic miracles supporting transubstantiation.	10 mins	(iv) Besides the Bible, there exist other 'external' forms of evidence that 'prove' the Real Presence of Christ in the Eucharist. The two most common are the writings of the early Church Fathers and Eucharistic miracles. There are numerous examples of writings and miracle accounts that can be cited. Hand out Activity Sheet 49, *Fathers and Favours*, which outlines two examples each of such writings and miracles. After asking selected students to read through the four paragraphs, invite them to consider the following two questions:	Feingold, *The Eucharist*, 129-175. Horn, *The Case for Catholicism*, 174-177. Sheehan, *Apologetics and Catholic Doctrine*, 507-511.

		- *What is the significance of writings testifying to the Real Presence of Christ in the Eucharist dating from the second century?* (Answer: The belief in the Real Presence of Christ in the Eucharist must be apostolic [from the Apostles]. It is not a medieval or later invention). - *Why do you think God grants Eucharistic miracles? What is he aiming to achieve?* (Answer: Eucharistic miracles are a grace [gift], a special favour to remove any doubt individuals may have about the Real Presence and to strengthen the overall faith of the Church in the same).	
	3 mins	**Lesson Closure:** Remind the students that the Eucharist is a gift from God given to the Church at the Last Supper and available to all Christians ever since through the Mass. The process by which the bread and wine during the Mass are transformed into the Body and Blood of Christ is called transubstantiation. As a heavenly spiritual food, the Eucharist is foreshadowed a number of times in the Old Testament and was announced in advance by Christ one year before the Last Supper in his 'Bread of Life discourse' (John 6). The Acts of the Apostles and St Paul evidence the centrality of the Mass and Eucharist in the life of the early Church. Protestant Christians still raise objections against belief in transubstantiation and the Real Presence, but these objections can all be accounted for. Further 'proofs' in support of belief in the Real Presence can be found in the writings of the early Church Fathers and numerous accounts of Eucharistic miracles, which are on the public record and available for anyone to study/examine. **Transition:** Homework: Go to 1 Cor. 11:27-30. Why is St Paul concerned about many of the Corinthians being *"weak and ill, and some have died"*? What does this tell us about the Eucharist and how we should prepare to receive it?	
		Resources: - Armstrong, Dave. *A Biblical Defense of Catholicism.* Manchester, NH: Sophia Institute Press, 2003, 83-92.	

| | | <ul><li>Clovis, Linus F. *A Biblical Search for the Church Christ Founded.* Leominster, United Kingdom: Gracewing, 2012, 68-71.</li><li>Feingold, Lawrence. *The Eucharist: Mystery of Presence, Sacrifice, and Communion.* Steubenville, Ohio: Emmaus Academic, 2018, 39-70, 129-175.</li><li>Flader, John. *Question Time: 150 Questions and Answers on the Catholic Faith.* Ballan, Vic.: Connor Court Publishing, 2008, 94-95.</li><li>Gray, Timothy. *Sacraments in Scripture: Salvation History Made Present.* Steubenville, Ohio: Emmaus Road Publishing, 2001, 51-53.</li><li>Horn, Trent. *The Case for Catholicism: Answers to Classic and Contemporary Protestant Objections.* San Francisco: Ignatius Press, 2017, 171-177.</li><li>Keating, Karl. *Catholicism and Fundamentalism.* San Francisco: Ignatius Press, 1988, 240-241 & 251-252.</li><li>Ray, Stephen K. *Crossing the Tiber: Evangelical Protestants Discover the Historic Church.* San Francisco: Ignatius Press, 1997, 192-200.</li><li>Salza, John. *The Biblical Basis for the Catholic Faith.* Huntingdon, Indiana: Our Sunday Visitor Publishing, 2005, 99-103.</li><li>Sheehan, Michael. *Apologetics and Catholic Doctrine*, rev. and ed. Peter M. Joseph. London: Baronius Press, 2015, 507-511.</li><li>*Catechism of the Catholic Church.* Libreria Editrice Vaticana: St Pauls, 1994, paras. 1335, 1341-1345, 1373-1376, 1436.</li><li>YOUCAT (*Youth Catechism of the Catholic Church*). San Francisco, Ignatius Press, 2010, paras. 208-223.</li><li>Website: Beaumont, Douglas M. "Is Transubstantiation Unbelievable?" https://www.catholic.com/magazine/online-edition/is-transubstantiation-unbelievable.</li><li>YouTube: Farrell, Deacon Dance. "Are Catholics Cannibals?" https://www.youtube.com/watch?v=bSxBJjWZDaE.</li></ul> |

LESSON EVALUATION (to be completed AFTER the lesson)

Assessment of lesson objectives and suggestions for improvement:
Teacher self-reflection and self-evaluation:
[OFFICIAL USE ONLY] Comments by teacher supervisor:

Lesson 29: Marriage, Divorce and Annulments

LESSON ORGANISATION

Year Level: Date: Time: Duration: Room:

Quote:
"Love that leads to marriage and family can also be a marvellous divine way, a vocation, a path for a complete dedication to God" – St Josemaria Escriva.

Prayer:
Come, Holy Spirit, fill the hearts of your faithful and enkindle in them the fire of your love.

V. Send forth your Spirit and they shall be created.
R. And you shall renew the face of the earth.

Let us pray.
O God, who by the light of the Holy Spirit, did instruct the hearts of the faithful, grant us in the same Spirit to be truly wise and ever to rejoice in his consolation.
Through Christ our Lord. Amen.

Lesson Outcomes:

As a result of this lesson, students will be able to:

- Define marriage according to the teaching of the Catholic Church.
- Explore how Jesus Christ restored the exclusivity and permanency of marriage and elevated it to a sacrament.
- Distinguish between divorce and annulments.
- Understand the reasons for limiting the definition of marriage to a union between one man and one woman.
- Appreciate the continued relevance of marriage as the basis for human happiness and societal flourishing.

Activity Sheets:

Activity Sheet 50, *Grounds for Annulments*.

"Always Be Prepared ..." – A 'New Apologetics' Course for Catholic Secondary Schools

LESSON DELIVERY

Outcome	Time	Motivation and Introduction:	Resources/ References
Define marriage according to the teaching of the Catholic Church.	10 mins	Welcome and settle the students. Prayer to the Holy Spirit (or other suitable prayer). Tell the students that today we will be looking at marriage, divorce and annulments. On a PowerPoint slide provide the following definition of Christian marriage and supporting points: - *"Marriage is an irrevocable covenant involving God, one man and one woman, instituted for the good of the spouses and ordained for the birth and education of children for God."* - Marriage was instituted by God when he created male and female (Adam and Eve), called them into a *"one flesh"* union and commanded them to *"be fruitful and multiply"* (Gen. 1:28; 2:24). - Jesus blessed marriage by his presence at the wedding at Cana where he performed his first miracle (John 2:1-11). - Jesus restored marriage to its original integrity and elevated it to a sacrament (Matt. 19:4-6). - The marriage between man and woman reflects the relationship between Christ and the Church (Eph. 5:23-32). Conclude by explaining that the topic of marriage is important as modern culture no longer supports the Christian understanding of chastity, relationships, matrimony, etc., resulting in most young people not maturing into adults capable of life-long, unselfish and sacrificial love. **Lesson Steps**	Gray, *Sacraments in Scripture: Salvation History Made Present*, 87-94. Horn, *Why We're Catholic: Our Reasons for Faith, Hope, and Love*, 180-183.
Explore how Jesus Christ restored the exclusivity and permanency of marriage and elevated it to a sacrament.	12 mins	(i) Ask the students the following question: *When people get married, how long do you think it should last for?* Take two-three student responses (make no comment or judgement on any response). Inform the students that Jesus was asked the same question and gave the following response (show on a PowerPoint slide): *"Have you not read that he who made them from the beginning made them male and female, and said, 'For this reason a man shall leave his father and mother and be joined to his wife, and the two shall become one*	Clovis, *A Biblical Search for the Church Christ Founded*, 84-85. Gray, *Sacraments in Scripture: Salvation History Made Present*, 90-93.

		flesh?' So they are no longer two but one flesh. What therefore God has joined together, let not man put asunder." They said to him, *"Why then did Moses command one to give a certificate of divorce, and to put her away?"* Jesus said to them, *"For your hardness of heart Moses allowed you to divorce your wives, but from the beginning it was not so"* (Matt. 19:4-8). Working with the students, identity the key elements Jesus associates with marriage. By the conclusion of this analysis, students should have noted down the following points: - *"… male and female."* - The two become *"one flesh."* - *"God has joined together …"* - *"… let no man put asunder."* The final point – *"let no man put asunder"* – was Jesus' way of abolishing divorce and restoring God's original plan of permanency for marriage. Inform the students that these words of Jesus shocked his audience, with some saying, *"If such is the case of a man with his wife, it is not expedient to marry"* (v. 10). Concede to the students that life-long marriage is difficult but not impossible. Since it is God who calls men and women to marry, God also helps the couple to faithfully and fruitfully live out their marriage vows. This he does principally through the sacrament of Holy Matrimony, which gives a baptised Christian couple sacramental grace to perfect their love and strengthen their unity. Classroom exercise: Revisit Matthew 19:4-8 and determine which of Jesus' words point to marriage being a sacrament. (Answer: *"What therefore God has joined together …"*). These words tell us that it is God who forms marriages. Marriage is a natural union created by God and when it occurs between two baptised persons it is raised to a supernatural union that is supported by sacramental graces.	Horn, *Why We're Catholic: Our Reasons for Faith, Hope, and Love,* 187-189.
Distinguish between divorce and annulments.	10 mins	(ii) While the Catholic Church opposes divorce and remarriage, one objection that is often raised relates to *annulments*. Whereas a valid sacramental marriage can only be dissolved by the death of one of the parties, an annulment is a declaration by the Church that, due to the absence of one or more necessary	Horn, *Why We're Catholic: Our Reasons for Faith, Hope, and Love,* 189-191.

		prerequisites, there *never existed a valid marriage in the first place*. It is sometimes alleged that annulments are just a form of 'Catholic divorce', allowing couples to separate and remarry on the shallowest of pretexts. Hand out Activity Sheet 50, *Grounds for Annulments*, and invite the students to look at each of the circumstances listed and place a tick against those that would provide grounds for an annulment and a cross against those that would not. (Clue: The grounds must have existed on the day of the wedding). Afterwards, again stress that annulments relate only to whether marriages were properly formed in the first place, not to the dissolution of validly formed marriages.		Salza, *The Biblical Basis for the Catholic Faith*, 111-112. Sheehan, *Apologetics and Catholic Doctrine*, 617-620.
Understand the reasons for limiting the definition of marriage to a union between one man and one woman.	12 mins	(iii) Remind the students that marriage, as an institution created by God, has always been regarded by the Judeo-Christian tradition as a mutual relationship between a man and a woman. Students would be well aware that in recent times most western societies have come to embrace 'same-sex marriage', yet the Catholic Church has not followed suit. Show the students the following YouTube video, *Why Doesn't the Catholic Church Allow Same-Sex Marriages?* by Deacon Harold Burke-Sivers (1.46 minutes).  Identify the four reasons given by Deacon Harold as to why marriage can only be between a man and a woman (Answers: [a] God created and hence defined marriage as a union between a man and a woman; [b] the culture can only be perpetuated through the union of a man and a woman; [c] we cannot simply change the definition of marriage to suit our own lifestyle choices; and [d] every child has a right to be raised by a mother and a father). Afterwards, invite the students to discuss the following statement: *"Marriage has one meaning or no meaning."* At the end of this discussion point out that changing the definition of marriage once opens up the possibility of other more radical changes. In the future, polygamous (a man marrying multiple women) or polyamorous (men and women marrying multiple male and female partners at the same time) marriages may also be accepted. Other future possibilities include incestuous (marrying a brother, sister, father or mother) or paedophilic (adults marrying underaged children) marriages. In some countries people have married themselves, animals, trees, etc. In the end, when marriage means whatever we want it to mean it will have no meaning at all.		O'Neil & Black, *The Essential Moral Handbook: A Guide to Catholic Living*, 221-250.

Appreciate the continued relevance of marriage as the basis for human happiness and societal flourishing.	10 mins	(iv) Inform the students that an increasing number of young people are choosing to either delay marriage or not marry at all. Large percentages of young adults are preferring to live together without making any permanent or exclusive commitment. Meanwhile, some of those who do marry are choosing not to have any children. Marriage for many of the young is no longer 'fashionable.' Question: *What does this ultimately mean for society and human flourishing?* Take two-three initial student responses. Afterwards, on a PowerPoint slide show and explain the following 'consequences' that generally result from the decline of marriage as a permanent and exclusive institution: - Higher rates of unstable relationships, separation, divorce, loneliness, unhappiness and depression. - Increased rates of single parenthood and poverty. - Higher rates of unwanted pregnancies and abortion. - Children raised in single parent homes are more prone to fall into crime, violence, imprisonment. - Declining birth-rates and aging population. - Economic stagnation. If young people are to become interested in marriage again, they need to see some form of benefit from it. Ask the students to note down three benefits they see in marriage. The benefits are many both in the material and spiritual dimensions. St Augustine of Hippo many centuries ago identified three 'goods' of marriage, namely, children, fidelity and sacrament. Discussion: *Are these three 'goods' really good things?* The answer is Yes x 3 – children are blessings from God; fidelity in marriage brings stability, security and certainty; marriage as a sacrament brings down God's graces to sanctify the couple and perfect their love. 	Horn, *Why We're Catholic: Our Reasons for Faith, Hope, and Love*, 187-188. Sheehan, *Apologetics and Catholic Doctrine*, 615-617.
	3 mins	**Lesson Closure:** Remind the students that marriage is an institution from God, who created male and female and commanded them to be fruitful and multiply. Jesus Christ blessed marriage and restored it to its original integrity as regards its exclusivity and permanence. Being a sacrament, God blesses marriage with graces to perfect the couple's love and strengthen their unity. Only the death of one of the spouses ends marriage, though a marriage can be declared null if any essential element was missing in its formation. Recent moves	

to redefine marriage beyond the traditional male-female union distort the meaning of marriage and expose it to future more radical redefinitions. The institution of marriage, though increasingly unpopular with the young, still provides great benefits to the couple – both material and spiritual – and to society overall.

Transition:

Homework: Read what St Paul says about marriage in Ephesians 5:23-32. *How does marriage reflect the union between Christ and the Church? What are the respective sacrifices the husband and wife should make to ensure a happy and holy marriage?*

Resources:

- Clovis, Linus F. *A Biblical Search for the Church Christ Founded.* Leominster, United Kingdom: Gracewing, 2012, 84-85.
- Gray, Timothy. *Sacraments in Scripture: Salvation History Made Present.* Steubenville, Ohio: Emmaus Road Publishing, 2001, 87-94.
- Horn, Trent. *Why We're Catholic: Our Reasons for Faith, Hope, and Love.* El Cajon: Catholic Answers Press, 2017, 180-183 & 187-191.
- O'Neil, Kevin J. & Peter Black. *The Essential Moral Handbook: A Guide to Catholic Living.* Liguori, Missouri: Liguori, 2004, 221-250.
- Salza, John. *The Biblical Basis for the Catholic Faith.* Huntingdon, Indiana: Our Sunday Visitor Publishing, 2005, 111-112.
- Sheehan, Michael. *Apologetics and Catholic Doctrine*, rev. and ed. Peter M. Joseph. London: Baronius Press, 2015, 615-620.
- *Catechism of the Catholic Church.* Libreria Editrice Vaticana: St Pauls, 1994, paras. 1601, 1604, 1613, 1617, 1638-1642, 1644-1645.
- YOUCAT (*Youth Catechism of the Catholic Church*). San Francisco, Ignatius Press, 2010, paras. 260-267.
- Website: Blackburn, Jim. "Why is Marriage a Sacrament?" https://www.catholic.com/qa/when-is-marriage-a-sacrament.
- YouTube: Burke-Sivers, Deacon Harold. "Why Doesn't the Catholic Church Allow Same-Sex Marriages?" https://www.youtube.com/watch?v=fvgnRYxRjWw.

LESSON EVALUATION (to be completed AFTER the lesson)

Assessment of lesson objectives and suggestions for improvement:
Teacher self-reflection and self-evaluation:
[OFFICIAL USE ONLY] Comments by teacher supervisor:

> "Always Be Prepared ..." – A 'New Apologetics' Course for Catholic Secondary Schools

Lesson 30: Beginnings of Life, Abortion, Contraception and Fertilisation Techniques

LESSON ORGANISATION

Year Level: Date: Time: Duration: Room:

Quote:
"Any country that accepts abortion, is not teaching its people to love, but to use any violence to get what it wants" – St Teresa of Calcutta.

Prayer:
Come, Holy Spirit, fill the hearts of your faithful and enkindle in them the fire of your love.

V. Send forth your Spirit and they shall be created.
R. And you shall renew the face of the earth.

Let us pray.
O God, who by the light of the Holy Spirit, did instruct the hearts of the faithful, grant us in the same Spirit to be truly wise and ever to rejoice in his consolation.
Through Christ our Lord. Amen.

Lesson Outcomes:

As a result of this lesson, students will be able to:

- Be familiar with the arguments and attitudes of those who advocate 'pro-choice' positions.
- Explore scientific and scriptural evidence supporting the ensoulment and full humanity of the pre-born from the moment of conception.
- Appreciate the right to life as the most fundamental of all human rights.
- Understand the moral distinction between artificial contraception and natural family planning.
- Comprehend the reasoning underpinning the Church's opposition to artificial reproductive technologies.

Activity Sheets:

Activity Sheet 51, *Human Life – When Does It Begin?*
Activity Sheet 52, *In-Vitro Fertilisation: Pro-Life or Problematic?*

LESSON DELIVERY

Outcome	Time	Motivation and Introduction:	Resources/ References
Be familiar with the arguments and attitudes of those who advocate 'pro-choice' positions.	10 mins	Welcome and settle the students. Prayer to the Holy Spirit (or other suitable prayer). Tell the students that today we will be looking at questions relating to the beginnings of life, abortion, artificial contraception and fertilisation techniques, etc. Inform the students that these questions are some of the most intensely debated issues in Western societies and have been debated for many decades between so-called 'pro-life' and 'pro-choice' groups. On a PowerPoint slide display the following arguments advanced by 'pro-choice' groups in support of abortion, birth control, etc.: - "Adults should be free to determine their own sexual and reproductive practices. Free and unlimited access to contraception, abortion and fertilisation techniques are rights that cannot be impinged upon by Church or State." - "No woman can call herself free who does not own and control her body." - "No one knows when life begins. It's a question that cannot be answered." - "A foetus is not a separate human being, it's a parasite." - "Allowing infertile couples to use in-vitro fertilisation, artificial insemination, surrogacy or cloning to have children is 'pro-life'." - "Natural family planning is Catholic sanctioned contraception, having the same intention to avoid having children." Sum up by emphasising that the Catholic 'pro-life' position is concerned with promoting a culture of life and love and respecting the rights of everyone – the mother, father and the unborn – and doing so with love and sensitivity towards all. **Lesson Steps**	O'Neil & Black, *The Essential Moral Handbook: A Guide to Catholic Living*, 247-248.
Explore scientific and scriptural evidence supporting the ensoulment and full humanity of the pre-born from the moment of conception.	12 mins	(i) Those who hold a 'pro-choice' position concerning abortion often claim that what is being terminated is merely a foetus, it does not yet know anything or feel any pain and, therefore, it is not yet a human being deserving of human rights, etc. Those who hold 'pro-life' views believe that life begins at conception,	Horn, *Why We're Catholic: Our Reasons for Faith, Hope, and Love*, 171-173.

		there exists a human life/soul from that moment onwards with the right to life and all other human rights, and that no one, including the mother, has the right to end that life. Hand out Activity Sheet 51, *Human Life – When Does It Begin?* Invite the students to consider the arguments from Scripture, reason and science concerning the beginning of human life and the status of the foetus and then compose a one-paragraph response to the following question, *"Isn't a foetus just a parasite?"* (Arguments against calling a foetus a parasite include: parasites are normally not the same species as the host being, while foetuses are the same species as the mother; dependency on the mother does not establish parasitical status, otherwise all human beings who depend on other humans in any way would be parasites).	Purcell, *From Big Bang to Big Mystery*, 305-308.
Appreciate the right to life as the most fundamental of all human rights.	12 mins	(ii) Explain to the students that human rights are a great concern to the Church, with modern Popes in particular (St John XXIII, St Paul VI, St John Paul II, Benedict XVI and Francis) speaking out regularly in defence of such. Classroom exercise: On a PowerPoint slide list the following three human rights: - To food, clothing, housing. - To marry and start a family. - To adequate employment and a just wage. Invite the students to suggest other rights that can be added to this list (e.g.: the right to freedom of expression and association; political participation; freedom of conscience; adequate health care; education; private property, etc.). Questions: *What is the foundational right that all other rights rest upon and why? Who has the right to take away this right?* Allow time for student feedback. Afterwards, explain that a 'foundational right' is one that comes before all others, without which we would have no other rights. We only have human rights because we have human life. Therefore, the right to life is the first, foundational and most important right. Since God is the author of human life, only he has the right to take it away, not governments, courts, doctors or even parents. This provides the justification to those who actively defend the right to life from conception till natural death, for they are defending the God-given rights of those who are the most vulnerable and defenceless.	O'Neil & Black, *The Essential Moral Handbook: A Guide to Catholic Living*, 259-261. Rice, *50 Questions on the Natural Law*, 286-294.

Understand the moral distinction between artificial contraception and natural family planning.	10 mins	(iii) The Catholic Church is well-known for its opposition to all forms of artificial contraception (the pill, condoms, intra-uterine devices, sterilisation, etc.) to prevent or regulate births. However, the Catholic Church does sanction 'natural family planning' (NFP) for the same, exposing itself to the criticism that NFP is just 'Catholic contraception.' At first glance such criticism seems reasonable, as couples using NFP are sometimes doing so for the same reasons as couples who use artificial methods. Show the students the following YouTube video, *How is NFP different from Contraception?* by Tim Staples of Catholic Answers (3.18 minutes). Afterwards, invite the students to answer the following questions:  - *What does NFP 'use' to regulate births?* (Answer: The natural cycle of fertility/infertility that women experience every month). - *What are some of the 'just reasons' that allow couples to use NFP?* (Answer: War, famine, disease, health of the mother, financial problems). - *When it comes to having children, what does God ask of couples?* (Answer: That they be open to life). - *Abstaining from sexual activity during the woman's fertile periods is akin to what?* (Answer: Fasting). - *When can NFP be used in a contraceptive/sinful way?* (Answer: Using it for an unjust reason, e.g., to never have children). NB: Sum up by noting that, unlike artificial contraception/ sterilisation, NFP works with nature and can be used only for just reasons, not against nature for any reason whatsoever.	Horn, *Why We're Catholic: Our Reasons for Faith, Hope, and Love*, 191-195. O'Neil & Black, *The Essential Moral Handbook: A Guide to Catholic Living*, 239-242.
Comprehend the reasoning underpinning the Church's opposition to artificial reproductive technologies.	10 mins	(iv) In recent decades, certain reproductive technologies have been developed to enable couples struggling with fertility to have children. At first instance, such technologies appear to be 'pro-life' and have brought joy to many families. To oppose such developments appears both unreasonable and anti-life. The Catholic Church supports the use of reproductive technologies provided that they do not lead to the separation of the 'unitive and procreative', meaning they assist but do not replace the natural way of conceiving children via sexual intercourse between the husband and wife. Reproductive technologies include in-vitro fertilisation, cloning, surrogacy or embryonic stem cell research. Hand out Activity Sheet 52, *In-Vitro*	O'Neil & Black, *The Essential Moral Handbook: A Guide to Catholic Living*, 207-212. Rice, *50 Questions on the Natural Law*, 258-263.

Fertilisation: Pro-Life or Problematic? Invite the students to note the various parts of the IVF process and write down reasons why each is morally problematic. Assist the students towards the following answers:
- *Collecting sperm from the husband* – involves the moral problem of masturbation.
- *Fertilising the egg with sperm in a petrie dish* – separates fertilisation from the natural sexual union of husband and wife.
- *Fertilising the wife's egg with sperm from someone other than the husband* – separates fertilisation from the natural sexual union of husband and wife and introduces a third party into the marriage, involving marital infidelity.
- *Fertilising multiple eggs and discarding the ones that are not required* – separates fertilisation from the natural sexual union of husband and wife and involves abortion.
- *Fertilising multiple eggs and freezing them indefinitely or experimenting on the ones that are not required* – separates fertilisation from the natural sexual union of husband and wife, offends the dignity of the fertilised embryo and involves abortion.
- *Removing and discarding unwanted fertilised eggs from the womb of the mother* – involves abortion.

Afterwards, re-affirm the need for couples to always work with nature when seeking to have children and if children are still not forthcoming to accept such as a spiritual cross and part of God's will for them. Other options for such couples may include fostering or adopting children or giving their lives in service to others.

Lesson Closure:

Remind the students that the Catholic Church is the defender of life, love and nature from conception till natural death. In opposition to the predominant culture, the Catholic Church opposes contraception and abortion as anti-life and contrary to the dignity of the human person. As an alternative to contraception, the Catholic Church approves the use of natural family planning where there are just reasons, which works with nature, not against. Scripture, reason and science affirm that human life begins at conception and that the foetus is a full human person, reinforcing its right to life, which ought to be firmly defended. Reproductive technologies can assist childless couples to create a family but the use of such is only morally acceptable if they do not separate the pro-creative from the unitive, that is, replace the natural way of conceiving children via sexual intercourse between the husband and wife. Childless couples should be counselled to accept their situation as a spiritual cross and be open to other possibilities, such as fostering or adopting children or giving their lives in service to others.

Transition:

Homework: Look up the encyclical *Humanae Vitae* by Pope St Paul VI. Read paragraph 14. What three things are condemned by the Pope in this paragraph? What are examples of *"well-grounded reasons"* that justify the use of natural family planning? (see paragraph 16).

Resources:

- Horn, Trent. *Why We're Catholic: Our Reasons for Faith, Hope, and Love.* El Cajon: Catholic Answers Press, 2017, 171-173 & 191-195.
- O'Neil, Kevin J. & Peter Black. *The Essential Moral Handbook: A Guide to Catholic Living.* Liguori, Missouri: Liguori, 2004, 207-212, 239-242, 247-248 & 259-261.
- Pope St Paul VI. *Humanae Vitae, On Human Life.* Libreria Editrice Vaticana, 1968, paras. 14 & 16.
- Purcell, Brendan. *From Big Bang to Big Mystery: Human Origins in the Light of Creation and Evolution.* Dublin, Ireland: Veritas Publications, 2011, 305-308.
- Rice, Charles. *50 Questions on the Natural Law: What it is and Why We Need it.* San Francisco: Ignatius Press, 1993, 258-263 & 286-294.
- *Catechism of the Catholic Church.* Libreria Editrice Vaticana: St Pauls, 1994, paras. 2271-2274, 2370-77, 2399.
- YOUCAT (*Youth Catechism of the Catholic Church*). San Francisco, Ignatius Press, 2010, paras. 383, 423.
- Website: Horn, Trent. "How to Prove Life begins at Conception." https://www.catholic.com/magazine/print-edition/how-to-prove-life-begins-at-conception.
- YouTube: Catholic Answers. "How is NFP different from Contraception?" https://www.youtube.com/watch?v=LaDtN_aiV_o.

LESSON EVALUATION (to be completed AFTER the lesson)

Assessment of lesson objectives and suggestions for improvement:
Teacher self-reflection and self-evaluation:
[OFFICIAL USE ONLY] Comments by teacher supervisor:

"Always Be Prepared ..." – A 'New Apologetics' Course for Catholic Secondary Schools

Lesson 31: "Thou Shalt Not Kill": Infanticide; Euthanasia; Capital Punishment; Just War

LESSON ORGANISATION

| Year Level: | Date: | Time: | Duration: | Room: |

Quote:
"The intrinsic value and personal dignity of every human being does not change depending on their circumstances" – Pope St John Paul II.

Prayer:
Come, Holy Spirit, fill the hearts of your faithful and enkindle in them the fire of your love.

V. Send forth your Spirit and they shall be created.
R. And you shall renew the face of the earth.

Let us pray.
O God, who by the light of the Holy Spirit, did instruct the hearts of the faithful, grant us in the same Spirit to be truly wise and ever to rejoice in his consolation.
Through Christ our Lord. Amen.

Lesson Outcomes:

As a result of this lesson, students will be able to:

- Understand current risks to life for the young and elderly.
- Appreciate the inherent dignity of each person and the sacredness of life from cradle to grave.
- Explore alternatives to euthanasia, namely, expert palliative care.
- Realise the practical non-necessity of capital punishment in the context of modern conditions.
- Identify the conditions necessary for self-defence and 'just war.'

Activity Sheets:

Activity Sheet 53, *The Death Penalty – For or Against?*

LESSON DELIVERY

Outcome	Time	Motivation and Introduction:	Resources/ References
Understand current risks to life for the young and elderly.	10 mins	Welcome and settle the students. Prayer to the Holy Spirit (or other suitable prayer). Tell the students that today we will be looking at questions relating to infanticide, euthanasia, capital punishment and 'just war theory.' The prevailing moral relativism in Western societies denies the inherent sacredness and dignity of human life, preferring to measure a person's worth against subjective values such as quality and enjoyment of life. The right to life from cradle to grave is no longer inviolable, leaving many of the sick, disabled, elderly and imprisoned vulnerable to having their lives taken away by others or the state without consent. Likewise, the right to self-defence for individuals and even nations is questioned. The following are illustrative of these various challenges (display on a PowerPoint slide): - "Parents may, with good reason, regret that a disabled child was ever born. Severe disability can be a reason for, rather than against, killing such a child." - "Killing someone who has not consented to being killed is legitimate when the motive for killing is the desire to prevent unbearable suffering on the part of the person killed." - "Christianity is a religion of mercy. Capital punishment, even when inflicted by the legitimate authority, is always and everywhere wrong." - "There is no just war. 'Just war theory' has been used too often to endorse rather than prevent war." Sum up by emphasising that the Catholic Church recognises the inherent dignity of all persons irrespective of their circumstances and at all times endeavours to practise charitable care, mercy, restorative justice and conflict avoidance/resolution. **Lesson Steps**	O'Neil & Black, *The Essential Moral Handbook: A Guide to Catholic Living*, 36-38, 212-218 & 272-273.
Appreciate the inherent dignity of each person and the sacredness of life from cradle to grave.	12 mins	(i) Ask the students the following questions: *What makes a human a person and can a human ever stop being a person?* Take two-three student responses and write appropriate answers on the whiteboard. Two student answers may include "human body" and "human soul." Highlight that with the soul humans have an	Feser, *The Last Superstition*, 203-204.

		intellect and a free will. Explain that it is the intellect and free will that makes a human a person in the image and likeness of God. This is the core of human dignity, a dignity that is given to us by God. Next question: *Are there other factors that increase or decrease human personhood?* Students may raise factors such as age, health, wealth, race, gender, etc. Explain that all these factors are *accidental* matters, none of which are essential to human personhood. That means that they can be part of someone's life, but they do not define whether or not someone is a person. This is important because factors such as age, health and wealth can change, and race and gender have variants; nevertheless, a human's personhood is not diminished or increased by such changes/variants. Classroom discussion: *What about children born deformed or people who are in a vegetative state because of brain damage, alzheimer's, dementia, etc?* Some argue that such people have no quality of life, their lives have no value, and they are often a burden on others. *Are people with these conditions any less human? Are their lives worth living? How should they be cared for?* After allowing a few moments for discussion, show on a PowerPoint slide the following quote from Pope St John Paul II (mention that he made this statement while in the last phases of Parkinson's disease): *"The loving gaze of God the Father continues to fall upon them, acknowledging them as his sons and daughters, especially in need of help … the value of a person's life cannot be made subordinate to any judgment of its quality expressed by others."*  Conclude by emphasising that every human person has a God-given dignity from birth till natural death irrespective of their circumstances or condition, as well as rights to love, life and care that must be respected by all. Failure to respect such rights is a failure to love. Infanticide and euthanasia are failures to love. Since God is the author of life, only he has the final say on how and when it should end. No one else has the right to 'play God.'	O'Neil & Black, *The Essential Moral Handbook: A Guide to Catholic Living*, 195-197.
Explore alternatives to euthanasia, namely, expert palliative care.	12 mins	(ii) Define euthanasia as "any act or omission intended to cause or lead to death with the purpose of eliminating all suffering." Those who support euthanasia often describe it in euphemistic	Rice, *50 Questions on the Natural Law*, 294-301.

		terms, such as "mercy killing", "self-delivery" or "dying with dignity." When voluntary, it is equivalent to suicide; when involuntary, it is equivalent to murder. Inform the students that more and more countries worldwide are legalising this practice, however, there are viable alternatives that both respect life and reduce suffering. Show the students the following YouTube video, *Be Not Afraid – The Gift of Palliative Care* by the Life, Marriage & Family Office, Melbourne  (4.14 minutes). Afterwards, invite the students to answer one of the following two questions: - *What does palliative care try to achieve?* (3 points). - *What Christian virtues are exercised through palliative care?* (3 points). As students feedback answers, record appropriate responses on the whiteboard. Eventually, the list should look something like the following: | Palliative Objectives	Christian Virtues
• Accompanying people in need. • Care for the person in their totality – physical, social-psycho, spiritual. • Provide comfort, pain control and relief. • Help patients feel loved, respected, wanted. • Care for surrounding family members.	• Love. • Sacrifice. • Unselfishness. • Compassion. • Empathy. • Patience.	 End this section by showing the students the following quote from Pope Francis: *"If the person feels love, the shadow of euthanasia disappears."*	O'Neil & Black, *The Essential Moral Handbook: A Guide to Catholic Living*, 212-218.
Realise the practical non-necessity of capital punishment in the context of modern conditions.	10 mins	(iii) Classroom debate: Hand out Activity Sheet 53, *The Death Penalty – For or Against?* Invite the students to write their opinions in one of the two columns provided. Take student responses and list them on the whiteboard under the headings 'For' and 'Against.' Arguments in favour of the death penalty may include: (a) It is necessary as a deterrence to serious crime and is a proportionate punishment for the worst of crimes; (b) It has support in the Bible, especially the Old Testament (Gen. 9:6; Exod. 21:17; Lev. 20:9); and (c) Great saints and doctors of the Church such as St Augustine of Hippo and St Thomas Aquinas, etc., have argued in favour of its morality. Arguments against include: (a) Jesus refraining from having the woman caught in	Flader, *Question Time: 150 Questions and Answers on the Catholic Faith*, 238-239.

		adultery being stoned to death (John 8:1-11); (b) Jesus rebuking the disciples who wished to call down fire from heaven to punish the inhospitable Samaritans (Luke 9:55); and (c) the death penalty seems to be more 'anti' than 'pro' life. Once students have concluded putting forward their arguments ask them to consider the following words of Pope St John Paul II and answer the two questions afterwards: *"This is the context in which to place the problem of the death penalty … The primary purpose of the punishment which society inflicts is to redress the disorder caused by the offence. Public authority must redress the violation of personal and social rights by imposing on the offender an adequate punishment for the crime … In this way authority also fulfils the purpose of defending public order and ensuring people's safety … It is clear that, for these purposes to be achieved, the nature and extent of the punishment must be carefully evaluated and decided upon, and ought not go to the extreme of executing the offender except in cases of absolute necessity: in other words, when it would not be possible otherwise to defend society. Today however, as a result of steady improvements in the organization of the penal system, such cases are very rare, if not practically non-existent"* (Evangelium Vitae, 56). *Do the above words of Pope St John Paul II make any sense? Do they change your thinking on the issue of the death penalty?* (Assist students to see the practical non-necessity of the death penalty when there exist viable alternatives that can achieve the same ends).	
Identify the conditions necessary for self-defence and 'just war.'	10 mins	(iv) Inform the students that self-defence is a natural right that everyone has. It is both instinctive and recognised by society as a whole. Besides defending oneself, a person can also defend their family, friends or private property. St Augustine of Hippo recognised that risking one's life to defend others is an act of selfless charity. Question: *Are there any preconditions or limitations to the right of self-defence?* Take two-three student responses. Responses may include: (a) the threat has to be real; (b) the threat has to be serious and imminent; (c) the act of self-defence has to be proportionate to the threat. Proportionality can sometimes be a difficult question, especially when split-second decisions need to be made in high pressure situations. An obvious example of disproportionality would be an adult shooting a child who only threw a rock at them. What about war? War is always an evil that results in great	O'Neil & Black, *The Essential Moral Handbook: A Guide to Catholic Living*, 273. Staples, "When and How Can Wars be Just?", 1-2.

death and destruction. It should always be avoided. There is an argument, however, that war is sometimes a necessary evil, while another argument says that war is always wrong no matter the situation. Challenge: Write a 50-word response to the claim, *"War is always wrong; it is against the commandment, 'Thou shalt not kill'."* Moderate an open discussion wherein students exchange their ideas. Afterwards, provide the students with what St Thomas Aquinas wrote concerning the pre-conditions for a so-called 'just war':

(a) The war must be prosecuted by the lawful authority;
(b) The war must be undertaken for a just cause;
(c) The war is undertaken with the right intention.

One can add that the war must always be one of proportionate self-defence against an unjust aggressor and not target non-combatants.

In an ideal world, war should never occur. However, in an imperfect world of hostile enemies and aggressors a defensive war is often the lessor of two evils and the only way to restore justice and peace.

As a final exercise, ask the students to label which of the following acts of war were just/unjust:

(a) The Japanese attack on Pearl Harbour (Answer: Unjust – a surprise offensive attack against a non-combatant country).
(b) The liberation of countries under Nazi occupation (Answer: Just – liberating victims of aggression and unjust occupation).
(c) The atomic bombings of Hiroshima and Nagasaki (Answer: Unjust – targeting non-combatants).

Lesson Closure:

Remind the students that life is sacred from conception till natural death and that each person has an inherent dignity irrespective of their condition or circumstances. The right to life is inviolable and cannot be arbitrarily taken away by others or the state. Persons suffering deformities, disabilities or in a vegetative state are no less persons and deserve constant special care. Infanticide and euthanasia are non-solutions and represent a failure to love. There are viable alternatives to euthanasia, particularly palliative care. The death penalty, though morally defensible, can in modern conditions be dispensed with in favour of non-lethal alternatives that achieve the same ends. Self-defence is always permissible but must be proportionate. Finally, war is always an evil but can be waged by the legitimate authority in proportionate self-defence against an unjust aggressor to restore justice and peace.

Transition:

Homework: Explore the sacrament of Anointing of the Sick and how it can benefit the terminally ill spiritually and physically.

Resources:

- Feser, Edward. *The Last Superstition.* South Bend, Indiana: St Augustine's Press, 2008, 203-204.
- Flader, John. *Question Time: 150 Questions and Answers on the Catholic Faith.* Ballan, Vic.: Connor Court Publishing, 2008, 238-239.
- O'Neil, Kevin J. & Peter Black. *The Essential Moral Handbook: A Guide to Catholic Living.* Liguori, Missouri: Liguori, 2004, 195-197 & 212-218.
- Rice, Charles. *50 Questions on the Natural Law: What it is and Why We Need it.* San Francisco: Ignatius Press, 1993, 294-301.
- *Catechism of the Catholic Church.* Libreria Editrice Vaticana: St Pauls, 1994, paras. 2263-2267, 2277-2279, & 2309.
- YOUCAT (*Youth Catechism of the Catholic Church*). San Francisco, Ignatius Press, 2010, paras. 379-382 & 398.
- Website: Staples, Tim. "When and How Can Wars be Just?" https://www.catholic.com/video/when-and-how-can-war-be-just.
- YouTube: Life, Marriage & Family Office, Melbourne. *"Be Not Afraid – The Gift of Palliative Care."* https://www.youtube.com/watch?v=G50Y_c3xUk8.

LESSON EVALUATION (to be completed AFTER the lesson)

Assessment of lesson objectives and suggestions for improvement:
Teacher self-reflection and self-evaluation:
[OFFICIAL USE ONLY] Comments by teacher supervisor:

Lesson 32: Marian Dogmas – Mary as Mother of God; The Immaculate Conception

LESSON ORGANISATION

Year Level: **Date:**   **Time:**   **Duration:**   **Room:**

Quote:
"Let us live as the Virgin Mary lived, loving God only, desiring God only, trying to please God only in all that we do" – St John Vianney.

Prayer:
Come, Holy Spirit, fill the hearts of your faithful and enkindle in them the fire of your love.

V. Send forth your Spirit and they shall be created.
R. And you shall renew the face of the earth.

Let us pray.
O God, who by the light of the Holy Spirit, did instruct the hearts of the faithful, grant us in the same Spirit to be truly wise and ever to rejoice in his consolation.
Through Christ our Lord. Amen.

Lesson Outcomes:

As a result of this lesson, students will be able to:
- Comprehend Protestant objections to Marian dogmas, namely, 'Mother of God' and the 'Immaculate Conception.'
- Appreciate that the Marian dogmas recognise what God did for Mary in light of her vocation as mother of Jesus Christ.
- Understand that in all things Mary is always subordinate to Jesus Christ.
- Grasp that the term 'Mother of God' (*Theotokos*) is a recognition of Christ's divinity, not an elevation of Mary to divinity.
- Recognise that through the Immaculate Conception God redeemed Mary and prepared an appropriate dwelling-place for himself on earth.

Activity Sheets:

Activity Sheet 54, *Comparing Jesus and Mary – Are They Equal?*
Activity Sheet 55, *Mary's Immaculate Conception – Answering the Objections.*

LESSON DELIVERY

Outcome	Time	Motivation and Introduction:	Resources/ References
Comprehend Protestant objections to Marian dogmas, namely, 'Mother of God' and the 'Immaculate Conception.'	8 mins	Welcome and settle the students. Prayer to the Holy Spirit (or other suitable prayer). Tell the students that today we will be looking at the Marian dogmas of 'Mother of God' and the 'Immaculate Conception.' Remind the students that a dogma is a solemn pronouncement by the Church that a particular belief has been revealed by God. It is the highest form of Church teaching. There are in total four Marian dogmas, each strongly opposed by most Protestants. Examples of Protestant arguments against the dogmas of 'Mother of God' and the 'Immaculate Conception' are as follows (show on a PowerPoint slide): - "In the Roman Church, Mary is to her worshippers what Christ is to Protestants … Mary did not give birth to God, nor to Jesus Christ as the eternal Son of God." - "The term 'Mother of God' may seem harmless but through its use Roman Catholics look upon Mary as equal to, if not stronger, more mature and more powerful than Christ." - "The doctrine of the Immaculate Conception of Mary places her on a plane equal to Jesus Christ so far as sinlessness is concerned." - "The Bible says that 'all have sinned and fallen short of the glory of God' (Rom. 3:23). Mary was a sinner requiring a saviour. She admitted the same when she declared 'my spirit rejoices in God *my saviour*' (Luke 1:47)." Sum up by noting that Protestants see the Marian dogmas as unbiblical pronouncements that elevate Mary well above the humble handmaid of Nazareth, while Catholics see them as recognising the totality of what God did for Mary in preparation and reward for her unique role as the mother of the Saviour. **Lesson Steps**	Mateo, *Refuting the Attack on Mary: A Defense of Marian Doctrines*, XI-XIII. Shea, *Mary Mother of the Son I: Modern Myths and Ancient Truth*, 15-72.
Appreciate that the Marian dogmas recognise what God did for Mary in light of her vocation as mother of Jesus Christ.	12 mins	(i) Most people who object to the Marian dogmas claim that they exaggerate Mary, making her into someone or something that she is not. Class exercise: *When we look at the Bible, what are we told about Mary?* Take four-five student responses and write appropriate responses on the whiteboard. The list should	Salza, *The Biblical Basis for the Catholic Faith*, 128-129.

include some of the following:
- She was a humble young woman.
- She was of the royal House of David.
- She was betrothed to St Joseph, a carpenter.
- Mary said "Yes" to the Angel Gabriel's invitation to be the mother of the Messiah.
- Mary conceived Jesus by the power of the Holy Spirit.
- Mary visited and stayed with her cousin St Elizabeth for three months to help her before the birth of John the Baptist.
- Mary gave birth to Jesus on the first Christmas day.
- Mary presented Jesus in the Temple when he was forty days old.
- Mary was told by the prophet Simeon that her son would be *"contradicted"* and her soul would be *"pierced."*
- Mary fled with the baby Jesus and St Joseph to Egypt to escape the plot of Herod the Great.
- Mary, Jesus and St Joseph returned from Egypt a few years later to live in Nazareth as ordinary poor people.
- Mary and St Joseph searched for and found Jesus in the Temple after being missing for three days.
- Mary urged Jesus to perform his first miracle at the wedding of Cana.
- Mary sometimes followed Jesus while he was publicly preaching.
- Mary, together with St John the Apostle and other holy women, were at the foot of the Cross at Jesus' crucifixion.
- Mary was with the infant Church and praying when the Holy Spirit descended on Pentecost Day.

Note that Catholics and Protestants agree on all the above when it comes to Mary, but Protestants point out that nowhere does the Bible call Mary 'Mother of God' (*Theotokos*) or 'immaculate', among other things. They claim these are dangerous exaggerations that make the 'Catholic Mary' someone different than the 'Biblical Mary.'

A Catholic response to the above begins with Mary's own words. Show the students the following quote from Luke 1:48: *"For behold, henceforth all generations will call me blessed."* Highlight that the *"all generations"* are all faithful Christians until the end of time, especially Catholics. Christians are meant to praise Mary in recognition for her "Yes" to God's plan as well

Schreck, *Catholic and Christian*, 170-177.

Understand that in all things Mary is always subordinate to Jesus Christ.		as for her fidelity and holiness, for which God is responsible. If Mary is worth praising it is because of the great things God did to her, which were done to prepare her for her unique role as mother of the Messiah. This started with enabling Mary to be conceived without original sin (the 'immaculate conception') so she would be a worthy vessel to house the God-man (Jesus Christ), that is, to be the 'Mother of God.' Later in this lesson we will explore the Scripture texts that provide justification for calling Mary 'Mother of God' and 'immaculate.'	
	10 mins	(ii) *"Are Catholics trying to make Mary equal to Jesus?"* Emphasise that this is an allegation that is often made against Catholics. Catholics are said to equate Mary with Jesus and then worship her ('Mariolatry'). Hand out Activity Sheet 54, *Comparing Jesus and Mary – Are They Equal?* Ask the students to look at the two columns under the respective headings of "Jesus" and "Mary." Point out that the contents look the same but then query, *Are they really the same?* Focus on two of Mary's qualities – "Mother of God" and "Conceived without sin." Acknowledge how they appear to be very similar to the corresponding entries in the Jesus column ("God" and "Sinless") and then invite the students to write down how as Catholics they would argue that they are nevertheless very different. (Answers: Jesus is a divine person, Mary is a human person. Calling Mary 'Mother of God' does not make her a divine person, it simply acknowledges Jesus' divinity; Jesus is sinless by nature, Mary is preserved from original sin by God and remains sinless all her life. Being sinless does not make Mary a divine person; it makes her equivalent to Eve (and Adam) who were also initially created sinless.

Conclude by noting that it is a matter of celebration that Mary is similar to Jesus in so many ways. This does not mean that Mary is equal to Jesus or in any sense divine. It is the Christian vocation to imitate Jesus and Mary is the greatest of all Christians. Every privilege Mary possesses was given to her by God and at all times she remains the faithful and obedient *"handmaid of the Lord"* (Luke 1:38). | Armstrong, *A Biblical Defense of Catholicism*, 167-171.

Schreck, *Catholic and Christian*, 181-185. |
| Grasp that the term 'Mother of God' (*Theotokos*) is a recognition of Christ's divinity, not an elevation of Mary to divinity. | 12 mins | (iii) Show on a PowerPoint slide in enlarged letters the term 'Mother of God.' Ask the students the following two questions:
- *What do you think Catholics mean by this term?*
- *How could this term be misunderstood?* | Bauer, *The Essential Mary Handbook*, 7-13. |

		After listening to student responses, outline to the students that many Protestants have very serious objections to this term. Firstly, they say that it is not in the Bible, so it should never be used with respect to Mary. Secondly, the term is blasphemous because God, being eternal and infinite, cannot have a beginning, cannot have a mother. If Mary is God's mother, then she must have existed before God and gave God existence when she gave birth to him. She would then be greater than God and herself be God. This is blasphemy added to blasphemy.	Mateo, *Refuting the Attack on Mary: A Defense of Marian Doctrines*, 3-6. Shea, *Mary Mother of the Son II: First Guardian of the Faith*, 17-54.

Question: *Is there any Biblical support for the term 'Mother of God'?* Pause for any student responses. Then show the students the following passage from Luke 1:43:

"And why is this granted me, that the mother of my Lord should come to me?"

These are the words of St Elizabeth (the mother of John the Baptist) directed to Mary after she came to visit her at her home in Ein Karem. Which words of St Elizabeth support the term 'Mother of God'? Answer: *"mother of my Lord."* Explain that as a Jewish woman, St Elizabeth would have had only one Lord, namely God. In effect, St Elizabeth was saying to Mary that she was *"the mother of my God"*, which is equivalent to saying, "Mother of God."

Show the students the following YouTube video, *Is Mary the Mother of God?* by Trent Horn of Catholic Answers (3.00 minutes). Afterwards, invite the students to answer the following two questions:

- *What is one reason why it is legitimate to call Mary, 'Mother of God'?*
- *What does the term 'Mother of God' reinforce?*

After listening to student responses, conclude by emphasising that the term 'Mother of God' is essentially a defence of Jesus' divinity, that Mary in bearing and giving birth to Jesus was bearing and giving birth to God, and that Jesus was not simply a man who later became the Son of God at his baptism, etc.

Recognise that through the Immaculate Conception God redeemed Mary and prepared an appropriate dwelling-place for himself on earth.	10 mins	(iv) Classroom discussion: Revisit Protestant objections to the Immaculate Conception of Mary as outlined in the beginning of the lesson. Summarise that in believing that Mary was sinless, Catholics allegedly elevate her to the same level of Jesus, exempt her from needing a saviour, and contradict St Paul who says that *"all have sinned*, etc." Furthermore, another objection can be raised, namely, that even St Thomas Aquinas, the greatest Catholic philosopher and theologian, did not believe in the Immaculate Conception! Hand out Activity Sheet 55, *Mary's Immaculate Conception – Answering the Objections*. Together with the students read through the various objections and explain the Catholic responses to each. (a) *"Believing that Mary was sinless makes her divine like Jesus"*: Answer – Mary was not the first human to be created without sin. Adam and Eve were so created before they sinned. By believing in Mary's sinlessness, Catholics believe she was the 'New Eve', not divine like Jesus. (b) *"Not even St Thomas Aquinas, the greatest Catholic theologian and philosopher, believed in the Immaculate Conception!"*: Answer – St Thomas' objections to the Immaculate Conception of Mary were more biological than theological. He believed that the human soul was infused *some time after conception*, not at the moment of conception. Consequently, as Mary had yet no soul, she could not have received sanctifying grace at conception (hence, no immaculate conception). St Thomas, nevertheless, believed that Mary was born free of all sin and remained sinless all her life. (c) *"The Immaculate Conception of Mary has no support in Scripture"*: Answer – Note the following two verses: *"I will put enmity between you and the woman, and between your seed and her seed; he shall bruise your head, and you shall bruise his heel"* (Gen. 3:15). *"And he came to her and said, 'Hail, full of grace, the Lord is with you!'"* (Luke 1:28). Mary fulfilled these two verses. How? She is the *"woman"* ('New Eve') in Gen. 3 that will be at *"enmity"* with the Devil. The enmity God places between the two is sanctifying grace, which frees Mary from sin and the dominion of the Devil. How do we know God did this for Mary? We know from the	Keating, *Catholicism and Fundamentalism*, 268-272. Mateo, *Refuting the Attack on Mary: A Defense of Marian Doctrines*, 19-26. Shea, *Mary Mother of the Son II: First Guardian of the Faith*, 103-154.

words of the Angel Gabriel in Luke 1, who greets Mary as *"full of grace."* God must have placed Mary fully in grace from the moment of her conception so to be always at enmity with the Devil.

(d) *"The Immaculate Conception makes Mary exempt from needing a Redeemer"*: Answer – Being a daughter of Adam, Mary needed redemption. Mary's Immaculate Conception, far from exempting her from needing a redeemer, was how God redeemed her. It was an application of the merits of Jesus Christ applied to her in advance, namely, *redemption by pre-emption*. One can be cured of a disease after having contracted it or one can be spared of that same disease by being inoculated against it in advance. Mary's redemption was affected in this latter manner, sparing her from ever being under the dominion of the Devil.

(e) *"St Paul in Romans 3 says 'All have sinned and fallen short of the glory of God.' Mary is one of the 'all'."* Answer – St Paul's words in Romans 3 do not refer to *individuals* being in sin but to all *races* and specifically mentions the Jews and Greeks. While races may be estranged from God, God can sanctify individuals within those races as exceptions. For example, the prophets Jeremiah (Jer. 1:5) and John the Baptist (Luke 1:41) were purified of sin in their mother's wombs. Mary was another and more perfect exception.

Conclude by highlighting than Mary's Immaculate Conception was not something that was *necessary*, it was something that was *appropriate*, appropriate for Mary as the Mother of God, and appropriate for Jesus who, as King of kings, should dwell in an earthly house free from the dominion of the Devil.

| | 3 mins | **Lesson Closure:**

Remind the students that there are four Marian dogmas and together they recognise the special gifts and privileges given to Mary by God in light of her unique vocation as the mother of the Messiah, Jesus Christ. Protestants generally reject these dogmas as unbiblical and allege that they elevate Mary to the same divine level as Jesus. The first of these dogmas, 'Mother of God', is the most controversial and misunderstood dogma, but from the Catholic perspective it simply recognises Mary's principal vocation and the divinity of her Son, Jesus. The dogma of the 'Immaculate Conception' recognises how God created an appropriate dwelling | |

place for himself on earth, one completely free from the dominion or influence of the Devil. It was also the means by which God redeemed Mary through the future merits of Jesus Christ. Both these dogmas have material support in Scripture and, understood properly, illustrate Mary's elevated but subordinated status as the faithful *"handmaid of the Lord."*

Transition:

Homework: Research the *Litany of Loreto*. This is a litany that both honours Mary and invokes her prayerful intercession under fifty titles. The second of these titles is "Mother of God." There are four other titles that either refer to or support belief in Mary's sinlessness. Read through all fifty titles and write down in full these specific four titles. (Answers: *Mother most pure, Mother inviolate, Mother undefiled,* and *Queen conceived without original sin*). Then conclude by prayerfully reciting the whole litany.

Resources:

- Armstrong, Dave. *A Biblical Defense of Catholicism.* Manchester, NH: Sophia Institute Press, 2003, 167-171.
- Bauer, Judith A. *The Essential Mary Handbook.* Liguori, Missouri: Liguori Publications, 1999, 7-13.
- Keating, Karl. *Catholicism and Fundamentalism.* San Francisco: Ignatius Press, 1988, 268-272.
- Mateo, Father. *Refuting the Attack on Mary: A Defense of Marian Doctrines.* San Diego: Catholic Answers, 1999, XI-XIII & 3-6.
- Salza, John. *The Biblical Basis for the Catholic Faith.* Huntingdon, Indiana: Our Sunday Visitor Publishing, 2005, 128-129.
- Schreck, Alan. *Catholic and Christian: An Explanation of Commonly Misunderstood Catholic Beliefs.* Cincinnati, Ohio: Servant Books, 2004, 176-177.
- Shea, Mark. *Mary Mother of the Son I: Modern Myths and Ancient Truth.* San Diego: Catholic Answers, 2009, 15-72.
- Shea, Mark. *Mary Mother of the Son II: First Guardian of the Faith.* San Diego: Catholic Answers, 2009, 17-54 & 103-154.
- *Catechism of the Catholic Church.* Libreria Editrice Vaticana: St Pauls, 1994, paras. 411, 466, 490-493, 495 509.
- YOUCAT (*Youth Catechism of the Catholic Church*). San Francisco, Ignatius Press, 2010, paras. 82-84.

		<ul><li>Website: Akin, Jimmy. "How to Defend the Immaculate Conception." https://www.catholic.com/magazine/online-edition/how-to-defend-the-immaculate-conception.</li><li>YouTube: Horn, Trent. "Is Mary the Mother of God." https://www.youtube.com/watch?v=n88xsp57cZY.</li></ul>

LESSON EVALUATION (to be completed AFTER the lesson

Assessment of lesson objectives and suggestions for improvement:
Teacher self-reflection and self-evaluation:
[OFFICIAL USE ONLY] Comments by teacher supervisor:

"Always Be Prepared ..." – A 'New Apologetics' Course for Catholic Secondary Schools

Lesson 33: Marian Dogmas – Perpetual Virginity; Assumption Into Heaven

LESSON ORGANISATION

Year Level:	Date:	Time:	Duration:	Room:

Quote:
"The Assumption reminds us that Mary's life, like that of every Christian, is a journey of following, following Jesus, a journey that has a very precise destination" – Pope Benedict XVI.

Prayer:
Come, Holy Spirit, fill the hearts of your faithful and enkindle in them the fire of your love.

V. Send forth your Spirit and they shall be created.
R. And you shall renew the face of the earth.

Let us pray.
O God, who by the light of the Holy Spirit, did instruct the hearts of the faithful, grant us in the same Spirit to be truly wise and ever to rejoice in his consolation.
Through Christ our Lord. Amen.

Lesson Outcomes:

As a result of this lesson, students will be able to:

- Comprehend Protestant objections to Marian dogmas, namely, Mary's perpetual virginity and assumption into heaven.
- Identify the 'brothers' of Jesus as the children of the Mary married to Clopas.
- Appreciate how the Catholic Church greatly esteems both virginity and marriage.
- Demonstrate how Mary's assumption into heaven has support in Scripture and Tradition.
- Understand the assumption as Mary's ultimate reward for her fidelity and a foreshadowing of the reward for all faithful Christians.

Activity Sheets:

Activity Sheet 56, *The Brothers of Jesus – Who Are They?*

LESSON DELIVERY

Outcome	Time	Motivation and Introduction:	Resources/ References
Comprehend Protestant objections to Marian dogmas, namely, Mary's perpetual virginity and assumption into heaven.	10 mins	Welcome and settle the students. Prayer to the Holy Spirit (or other suitable prayer). Tell the students that today we will be looking at the Marian dogmas of 'perpetual virginity' and 'assumption into heaven.' The Catholic Church solemnly believes that Mary was a virgin before, during and perpetually after giving birth to Jesus Christ and after completing her life on earth was assumed body and soul into heavenly glory. Like the dogmas of 'Mother of God' and 'Immaculate Conception', most Protestants strongly oppose these dogmas and advance the following arguments for doing so (show on a PowerPoint slide): - "Matthew 1:25 implies Mary had sexual relations with Joseph after Jesus was born, Jesus is called Mary's *'first born'* (Luke 2:7), Matthew 13:55 lists the names of Jesus' four *'brothers'*, and Paul in Galatians 1:25 calls James *'the Lord's brother'*." - "Insisting on Mary's perpetual virginity implies that sexuality within marriage is somehow defiling. It was invented to justify celibacy of priests and nuns." - "The doctrine of Mary's assumption is meant to parallel Christ's resurrection and ascension. It has no Scripture support whatsoever." - "The Bible equates death and corruption with all human beings except Christ. Why should Mary be another exception?" Sum up by stating that while there are strong biblically-based responses to all the above objections, we cannot address all of them in the limits of this lesson. Priority will be given to identifying who the 'brothers' of Jesus actually were, how the Catholic Church highly esteems both virginity and marriage, and the scriptural support for belief in Mary's assumption. **Lesson Steps**	Horn, *The Case for Catholicism*, 331-332. Mateo, *Refuting the Attack on Mary: A Defense of Marian Doctrines*, 7-17 & 27-35.
Identify the 'brothers' of Jesus as the children of Mary married to Clopas.	15 mins	(i) Inform the students that there are many challenges based on various passages in Scripture that question Mary's perpetual virginity. One of the most significant passages is Matthew 13:54-57, which reads as follows (show on a PowerPoint slide):	Keating, *Catholicism and Fundamentalism*, 268-272.

		"Where did this man get this wisdom and these mighty works? Is not this the carpenter's son? Is not his mother called Mary? And are not his brethren James and Joseph and Simon and Judas? And are not all his sisters with us? Where then did this man get all this?' And they took offence at him." Ask the students the following questions: - *Who is this passage speaking of and how do we know this?* (Answers: Jesus; son of a carpenter; mother's name is Mary). - *What are "brethren"?* (Answer: Brothers). - *How many brethren does Jesus purportedly have?* (Answer: Four brothers plus an unknown number of sisters). - *What are the names of Jesus' four 'brothers'?* (Answer: James, Joseph, Judas and Simon). - *What is the implication here about Mary?* These brethren and sisters are children of Mary and St Joseph, Mary had other children besides Jesus and, therefore, she did not remain a virgin all her life and the Catholic dogma of her perpetual virginity is false. Is there a possible response to the above? Hand out Activity Sheet 56, *The Brothers of Jesus – Who Are They?* Ask the students to compare the 'Catholic Holy Family' in Column A with the 'Protestant Holy Family' in Column B and then from the data provided in the various Scripture passages, etc., construct another family in Column C under the heading 'The Family of Mary and Clopas.' By the end of this exercise it should be apparent that the *"brethren"* mentioned in Matt. 13:54-57 are in fact the children of Mary and Clopas, not Mary and Joseph, and that they are Jesus' first cousins, not brothers. It is a case of how in the ancient world the word *"brethren"* (or *"brothers"*) also meant first cousin.	Mateo, *Refuting the Attack on Mary: A Defense of Marian Doctrines,* 7-17. Newman, *Mary,* 145-151. Staples, *Behold Your Mother,* 131-192.
Appreciate how the Catholic Church greatly esteems both virginity and marriage.	10 mins	(ii) On a PowerPoint slide show the following quote by the Australian anti-Catholic apologist, Ray Galea: *"Insisting on Mary's perpetual virginity implies that sexuality within marriage is somehow unspiritual or defiling, sullying Mary in some way"* (Nothing In My Hand I Bring, 88).	Mateo, *Refuting the Attack on Mary: A Defense of Marian Doctrines,* 8-10.

		Invite the students to respond to Ray Galea's accusations. (In three points). Assist the students with some prompts. After taking two-three responses, show and explain the following on a PowerPoint slide: - The Catholic Church highly esteems marriage as a holy and life-long bond and recognises it as a sacrament (Matt. 19:6). - The Catholic Church compares the marital bond between a man and a woman to the bond between Christ and his Church (Eph. 5). - Mary was not the only Biblical figure believed to be a perpetual virgin. Elijah, Elisha, John the Baptist, Jesus, and St Paul were virgins all their lives. - Jesus Christ highly praises celibacy and speaks of the reward awaiting those who freely embrace it for God's Kingdom (Matt. 19:11-12 and Luke 18:29-30). - St Paul expressly states that celibacy is a higher state than the state of marriage (1 Cor. 7:38). - In the book of Revelation 14:4, those who *"follow the Lamb wherever he goes"* are all virgins. Conclude by noting that Mary's perpetual virginity signified her total consecration to God. Its value lies in sacrificing something supremely good and holy, not something unspiritual or defiling.	Shea, *Mary Mother of the Son II: First Guardian of the Faith*, 83-86.
Demonstrate how Mary's assumption into heaven has support in Scripture and Tradition.	10 mins	(iii) Moving onto the dogma of the assumption of Mary body and soul into heaven, again this is rejected by most Protestants as unbiblical and another Catholic attempt to unduly equate Mary with Jesus and his ascension into heaven. As the argument goes, if Mary was really assumed into heaven, the Bible should have something to say about it. Since it says nothing, it can only be assumed that Mary died like any other Christian, with her body being buried and decaying like any other person's. Biblical exegesis: On a PowerPoint slide show the following text from the Book of Revelation 12:1-5: *"And a great portent appeared in heaven, a woman clothed with the sun, with the moon under her feet, and on her head a crown of twelve stars; she was with child and she cried out in her pangs of birth, in anguish for delivery. And another portent appeared in heaven; behold, a great red dragon, with seven heads and ten horns, and seven diadems upon his heads … And the dragon stood before the woman who was about to bear a child, that he might devour her child when she brought it forth;*	Mateo, *Refuting the Attack on Mary: A Defense of Marian Doctrines*, 27-35. Staples, *Behold Your Mother*, 197-210.

she brought forth a male child, one who is to rule all the nations with a rod of iron …"

Invite the students to read through this passage and together as a class discuss and answer the following questions (guide the students towards the answers in brackets):

- *Where is this event taking place?* (Answer: heaven).
- *What is the "great portent" that appears in heaven?* (Answer: A *"woman clothed with the sun"*).
- *Fully describe this woman.* (Answer: Clothed with the sun; has the moon under her feet; wears a crown of twelve stars).
- *What is the significance of the crown?* (Answer: She is a Queen – Queen of Heaven).
- *How do we know this figure is Mary?* (Answer: She bears a *"male child"* who is to *"rule all the nations."* This child can only be Jesus Christ).
- *What evidence indicates Mary is in heaven <u>body and soul</u>?* (Answer: The language describing Mary is very 'bodily' – *"clothed", "feet", "head", "with child."* She is not referred to as just a "soul" or "spirit" as others in heaven are [Heb. 12:23 and Rev. 6:9]).

Furthermore, there are other precedents in Scripture of people being taken up into heaven body and soul, e.g., Enoch (Gen. 5:21-24) and Elijah (2 Kings 2:11). Considering these precedents, it is not unreasonable to believe that God would bestow upon Mary an even more sublime privilege in reward for fulfilling her proportionately greater vocation as Mother of God.

Conclude by highlighting another very important argument from tradition, namely, the ancient Christian practice of shrines and pilgrimages. While the remains of Apostles, martyrs and saints have been carefully preserved and venerated over the centuries, no Christian centre has ever claimed to possess the bodily remains of Mary. No doubt her bodily remains would have been preserved and enshrined as a focal point for pilgrimage if they had remained on earth.

Understand the assumption as Mary's ultimate reward for her fidelity and a foreshadowing of the reward for all faithful Christians.	10 mins	(iv) Show the students the following YouTube video, *Mary: The Assumption* by Dr Edward Sri (4.52 minutes). Afterwards, invite the students to answer the following three questions: - *By being assumed into heaven, what does Mary share in?* 	Mateo, *Refuting the Attack on Mary: A Defense of Marian Doctrines,* 27-28.

| | | (Answer: Christ's glorious death and resurrection).
- *What God does for Mary as a faithful disciple is a foreshadowing of what?* (Answer: What God will do for the rest of his people).
- *What does Mary's assumption remind us of?* (Answer: Our destiny, sharing in Christ's bodily resurrection at the end of time if we remain faithful to the end).
In conclusion, stress that while Mary's assumption appears to be a unique privilege, it is a reminder of what God originally intended for all humanity before sin and death entered the world, and through the merits of Christ, is a gift restored and now available to all his disciples, of which Mary was the first. | Salza, *The Biblical Basis for the Catholic Faith*, 141-142. |
| | 3 mins | **Lesson Closure**:

Remind the students that the dogma of Mary's perpetual virginity recognises her unique status as the consecrated Mother of God and spouse of the Holy Spirit. The many challenges to this dogma can all be responded to, especially the identity of Jesus' *"brothers"* mentioned in Matthew 13:54-57. The Catholic Church simultaneously esteems consecrated virginity and matrimony as two sacred callings that serve God in different ways. Meanwhile, the dogma of Mary's assumption into heaven recognises how God rewarded her for a life of total fidelity. There are precedents in the examples of Enoch and Elijah who were also taken from the world body and soul and scriptural support in the *"woman"* of Revelation 12. The assumption of Mary is a sign and foretaste of what lies ahead for all Christians who remain faithful till the end.

Transition:

Homework: Open a Bible to Ezekiel 44:1-2 which reads as follows: *"Then he brought me back to the outer gate of the sanctuary, which faces east; and it was shut. And he said to me, 'This gate shall remain shut; it shall not be opened, and no one shall enter by it; for the Lord, the God of Israel, has entered by it; therefore it shall remain shut'."* Consider how this passage may refer to Mary's perpetual virginity. (Answer: The *"sanctuary"* is Mary's body. The *"gate"* is the entry to Mary's womb. The Lord who *"has entered by it"* is the Holy Spirit who conceived Jesus in Mary's womb. *"No one shall enter by it"* refers to how Mary will not know any man after the Holy Spirit has impregnated her). | |

		Resources: - Horn, Trent. *The Case for Catholicism: Answers to Classic and Contemporary Protestant Objections.* San Francisco: Ignatius Press, 2017, 331-332. - Keating, Karl. *Catholicism and Fundamentalism.* San Francisco: Ignatius Press, 1988, 282-289. - Mateo, Father. *Refuting the Attack on Mary: A Defense of Marian Doctrines.* San Diego: Catholic Answers, 1999, 7-17 & 27-35. - Newman, Kiran. "Mary." In *Answering the Anti-Catholic Challenge: A Response to Ray Galea*, ed. Robert M. Haddad. Ballan, Victoria: Modotti Press, 2012, 145-151. - Staples, Tim. *Behold Your Mother.* San Diego: Catholic Answers Press, 2014, 131-192 & 197-210. - Salza, John. *The Biblical Basis for the Catholic Faith.* Huntingdon, Indiana: Our Sunday Visitor Publishing, 2005, 141-142. - Shea, Mark. *Mary Mother of the Son II: First Guardian of the Faith.* San Diego: Catholic Answers, 2009, 83-86. - *Catechism of the Catholic Church.* Libreria Editrice Vaticana: St Pauls, 1994, paras. 496-498, 502-507 & 966. - YOUCAT (*Youth Catechism of the Catholic Church*). San Francisco, Ignatius Press, 2010, paras. 80-81. - Website: Staples, Tim. "The Case For Mary's Perpetual Virginity." https://www.catholic.com/magazine/print-edition/the-case-for-marys-perpetual-virginity. - YouTube: Sri, Dr Edward. "Mary: The Assumption." https://www.youtube.com/watch?v=ayz15mdkh5o&t=214s.

LESSON EVALUATION (to be completed AFTER the lesson)

Assessment of lesson objectives and suggestions for improvement:
Teacher self-reflection and self-evaluation:
[OFFICIAL USE ONLY] Comments by teacher supervisor:

Lesson 34: The Communion of Saints

LESSON ORGANISATION

Year Level: Date: Time: Duration: Room:

Quote:
"What is the Church if not the assembly of all the saints?" – St Nicetas of Remesiana.

Prayer:
Come, Holy Spirit, fill the hearts of your faithful and enkindle in them the fire of your love.

V. Send forth your Spirit and they shall be created.
R. And you shall renew the face of the earth.

Let us pray.
O God, who by the light of the Holy Spirit, did instruct the hearts of the faithful, grant us in the same Spirit to be truly wise and ever to rejoice in his consolation.
Through Christ our Lord. Amen.

Lesson Outcomes:

As a result of this lesson, students will be able to:

- Understand the various Protestant objections against the teaching and practices relating to the 'communion of saints.'
- Recognise the Church as a spiritual unity in Jesus Christ of all believers on earth, in heaven and in purgatory.
- Demonstrate from Scripture how the departed in Christ are a living "cloud of witnesses" who can intercede on behalf of the Church on earth.
- Distinguish veneration from adoration and how prayers to the saints have their final end in God.
- Reconcile belief in the communion of saints with Jesus Christ's unique role as sole Mediator.

Activity Sheets:

Activity Sheet 57, *Are the Dead Really Dead?*

LESSON DELIVERY

Outcome	Time	Motivation and Introduction:	Resources/ References
Understand the various Protestant objections against the teaching and practices relating to the communion of saints.	8 mins	Welcome and settle the students. Prayer to the Holy Spirit (or other suitable prayer). Tell the students that today we will be looking at the teaching and practices relating to the 'communion of saints.' Catholics who attend Mass would be familiar with this term, hearing it each time the Apostles' or Nicene Creed is recited. Essentially, it means that all the believers in Christ whether on earth, in heaven or in purgatory form one family ("body of Christ") who are spiritually united in their experiences, joys, sufferings, etc. Protestantism generally rejects this doctrine, citing the following concerns (show on a PowerPoint slide): - "There is no point invoking the dead saints for they are dead. They cannot hear our prayers. Nor can one saint hear the simultaneous prayers of thousands." - Invoking the dead saints is the same as necromancy – trying to contact the dead – which is forbidden in Scripture (Deut. 18:9-12)." - "Invoking the saints is idolatry. Prayer should be directed to God alone." - "Invoking the saints is an insult to Christ who is the one and only mediator between God and humanity (1 Tim. 2:5)." Sum up by noting that there exists another reason why the doctrine of the communion of saints needs to be properly understood and practised by Catholics, namely, to counter the modern-day influence of individualism that now permeates much of society, a mindset that has entered Christian circles under the guise of 'Jesus and me Christianity.' **Lesson Steps**	Claudel, *I Believe in God: A Meditation on the Apostles' Creed*, 222-239. Horn, *The Case for Catholicism*, 283-288. Madrid, *Any Friend of God is a Friend of Mine*, 13-39.
Recognise the Church as a spiritual unity in Jesus Christ of all believers on earth, in heaven and in purgatory.	12 mins	(i) Ask the students the following question: *What is the Church and where do we find it?* Take two-three student responses. Student answers may include: - The local parish. - The worldwide Catholic Church. - Wherever two or three people are gathered together praying in the name of Jesus. - Wherever I myself may be praying, e.g., my bedroom.	Madrid, *Any Friend of God is a Friend of Mine*, 9-12. Schreck, *Catholic and Christian*, 163-166.

Explain to the students that all the above answers are partially correct, however, the Church is much bigger than we may at first think. This is because God is the God of all his people, past and present, alive or dead. Jesus himself hinted at this when he said the following: *" … have you not read in the book of Moses … how God said to him, 'I am the God of Abraham, the God of Isaac, and the God of Jacob.' He is not the God of the dead, but of the living"* (Mark 12:26-27). It follows that the Church is the body of believers wherever they exist – on earth, in heaven and even in purgatory. St Paul calls this the *"body of Christ"*, which is so spiritually bound that *"If one member suffers, all suffer together"* (1 Cor. 12:26). Consequently, the Church is a communion of believers rather than a collection of separate individuals, Christians travel together in their spiritual journey towards heaven, and Christians wherever they are can assist each other along this journey.

Classroom exercise: On a PowerPoint slide show the following quote from the Second Vatican Council:
"The union of the living with their brethren who have fallen asleep in Christ is not broken; the Church has rather believed through the ages that it gains strength from the sharing of spiritual benefits" (*Sacrosanctum Concilium* 5).
Question: *What are some examples of "spiritual benefits" believers "living" and "asleep in Christ" can share to assist each other?* List these in three columns under the headings, "Living Assisting the Living"; "Living Assisting the Dead"; and "Dead Assisting the Living." As students feedback answers, record appropriate responses on the whiteboard. Eventually, the list should look something like the following:

Living Assisting the Living	Living Assisting the Dead	Dead Assisting the Living
• Perform acts of charity for each other. • Pray for each other. • Offer fasts and penances for each other. • Offer Mass for each other. • Provide spiritual advice/counsel to each other. • Support the grieving. • Visit the sick, lonely and imprisoned.	• Pray for the dead. • Offer fasting and other penitential sacrifices for the dead. • Offer Masses for the dead. • Obtain a plenary indulgence for the dead.	• Intercessory prayer for the living. • Obtain from God favours or miracles for the living when invoked. • Occasionally appear to the living with messages, etc.

Demonstrate from Scripture how the departed in Christ are a living "cloud of witnesses" who can intercede on behalf of the Church on earth.	12 mins	(ii) On a PowerPoint slide show the students Psalm 115:17, which reads as follows: *"The dead do not praise the Lord, nor do any that go down into silence."* Explain that some Protestants use this verse to claim the following: "The dead are dead. They do not know what is happening on earth. They do not hear our prayers and they cannot pray for us. In any case, how can one saint respond to the petitions of thousands of different people at the same time?" Hand out Activity Sheet 57, *Are the Dead Really Dead?* Invite the students to read Matthew 17:1-3, Hebrews 12:1 and Revelation 6:9-11 and construct an argument for why the dead in Christ are still alive, know what is happening on earth, and can pray for us. (Answer: Christ is speaking to Moses and Elijah, two men who had been dead or departed for centuries; the faithful dead are described as a *"cloud of witnesses"*; the martyrs in heaven are depicted praying to God to avenge their deaths. Together, these verses tell us that the faithful dead are alive in the next world, are witnesses to what is happening on earth, and can pray to God in heaven). After taking two student responses, explain how saints can hear multiple petitions at the same time and why praying to them is not the same as necromancy. (Answers: God grants the saints supernatural knowledge of all the petitions directed to them, that is, he makes them 'multiscient.' Also, praying to the saints does not amount to necromancy, as the latter involves using magic or the occult to directly contact or 'conjure up' the dead for information).	Armstrong, *A Biblical Defense of Catholicism*, 106-117. Horn, *The Case for Catholicism*, 283-291. Keating, *Catholicism and Fundamentalism*, 264-266.
Distinguish veneration from adoration and how prayers to the saints have their final end in God.	10 mins	(iii) The next objection Protestants have against praying to the saints is that such a practice violates the first commandment, which commands that worship be given to God alone. As the argument goes, prayer is central to worship, so prayer should only be directed to God. To direct prayer to saints, who are only creatures, is therefore idolatry, which is the worship of any creature in the place of God. Show on a PowerPoint slide the following words: - Veneration, or *Dulia*. - Adoration, or *Latria*. Mention that veneration/dulia is a form of honour that can be given to anyone. It can be given to parents, the elderly, judges,	Salza, *The Biblical Basis for the Catholic Faith*, 151-153. Schreck, *Catholic and Christian*, 167-169.

| | | Kings/Queens, Prime Ministers, Presidents, the Pope, famous people, etc. The term derives from the Greek word *doulos*, meaning servant or slave. It was the form of service/respect given by a servant/slave to their employer or master. Catholics give dulia to saints and 'hyper-dulia' to the Virgin Mary as she is the greatest of all the saints. In contrast, latria, or the worship of adoration, can only be given to God for he alone is the infinite, eternal Being, creator of all things, etc. To give any saint the worship of latria would certainly be idolatrous. However, there is no risk of idolatry when we simply ask a saint to pray or intercede for us.

Show the students the following YouTube video, *Why Praying to Saints is Not Like Praying to Other Gods* by Catholic Answers (4.01 minutes).  Afterwards, invite the students to answer the following two questions:
- *What is the original meaning of the word 'pray'?* (Answer: 'To ask').
- *What are we asking the saints to do for us?* (Answer: To be our prayer partners and pray to God for us).

Conclude by emphasising that our prayers to the saints do not have their final end with them for their prayers rise up to God, as seen by St John the Apostle in his vision of the heavenly Elders who held *"golden bowls full of incense, which are the prayers of the saints"* (Rev. 5:8). | |
| Reconcile belief in the communion of saints with Jesus Christ's unique role as sole Mediator. | 10 mins | (iv) The final objection Protestants have against invoking the saints claims that such a practice insults Jesus Christ who, according to Scripture, is the *"one mediator"* between God and humanity (1 Tim. 2:5). To invoke a saint or saints is to have more than one mediator, diluting the uniqueness of Christ.
Show on a PowerPoint slide the following two words:
Mediator; Intercessor
Ask the students to look up and record the meaning of these words in their notebooks. Take two-three student responses. Student responses should closely correspond to the following:
- *Mediator:* "A person who attempts to reconcile parties/ persons who are in conflict."
- *Intercessor:* "A person who intervenes, pleads or prays on behalf of another." | Horn, *The Case for Catholicism*, 288-291.

Salza, *The Biblical Basis for the Catholic Faith*, 144-146. |

		Question: *Having regard to the above definitions, how would you respectively classify Jesus Christ and the saints and why?*	
		Answer: Jesus Christ is a mediator for his sacrifice on the Cross reconciles an estranged humanity back into friendship with God. The saints are intercessors for they pray to God on behalf of those who invoke their assistance.	
		Conclude by emphasising that the intercessory function of the saints in heaven works with, not against Christ's unique mediatorship. All prayer, whether the prayers of Mary, or of the other saints in heaven, or of the saints alive on earth, is directed to God the Father through Jesus Christ, the one God-man, saviour and mediator.	
	3 mins	**Lesson Closure:**	
		Remind the students that no Christian is an individual who walks the pilgrimage of life alone. All Christians belong to the 'communion of saints', which is the spiritual union of all believers on earth, in heaven and in purgatory. As members of one communion, all Christians can spiritually assist each other through prayers, sacrifices, Masses, etc. Though physically dead, the saints in heaven are still alive in their spirits and are witnesses to what is happening on earth and can pray for those who invoke them, etc. Invoking the saints is not idolatry nor is it necromancy; rather, the saints are venerated and their prayerful assistance is sought without directly contacting or 'conjuring them up', while adoration is given to God alone. As prayer intercessors, the saints pray to the Father in heaven and always do so through Jesus Christ, the one mediator between God and humanity.	
		Transition:	
		Homework: Turn to the second book of Maccabees in the Old Testament. Read the following passages: 2 Maccabees 15:11-16 and 2 Maccabees 12:46. In the first of these passages, which two deceased Israelites are revealed praying for the people of Judah? In the second passage, what does it say about praying for the dead? Write out these passages in full in your notebooks.	

| | | **Resources:**

- Armstrong, Dave. *A Biblical Defense of Catholicism.* Manchester, NH: Sophia Institute Press, 2003, 106-117.
- Claudel, Paul. *I Believe in God: A Meditation on the Apostles' Creed.* San Francisco: Ignatius Press, 2002, 222-239.
- Horn, Trent. *The Case for Catholicism: Answers to Classic and Contemporary Protestant Objections.* San Francisco: Ignatius Press, 2017, 283-292.
- Keating, Karl. *Catholicism and Fundamentalism.* San Francisco: Ignatius Press, 1988, 262-266.
- Madrid, Patrick. *Any Friend of God is a Friend of Mine: A Biblical and Historical Explanation of the Catholic Doctrine of the Communion of Saints.* San Diego: Basilica Press, 1996, 9-39.
- Schreck, Alan. *Catholic and Christian: An Explanation of Commonly Misunderstood Catholic Beliefs.* Cincinnati, Ohio: Servant Books, 2004, 163-169.
- Salza, John. *The Biblical Basis for the Catholic Faith.* Huntingdon, Indiana: Our Sunday Visitor Publishing, 2005, 144-146 & 151-153.
- *Catechism of the Catholic Church.* Libreria Editrice Vaticana: St Pauls, 1994, paras. 946-962.
- YOUCAT (*Youth Catechism of the Catholic Church*). San Francisco, Ignatius Press, 2010, para. 146.
- Website: Madrid, Patrick. "Any Friend of God is a Friend of Mine." https://www.catholic.com/magazine/print-edition/any-friend-of-god-is-a-friend-of-mine.
- YouTube: Catholic Answers. "Why Praying to Saints is Not Like Praying to Other Gods." https://www.youtube.com/watch?v=oh7gDmjX-XU. |

LESSON EVALUATION (to be completed AFTER the lesson)

Assessment of lesson objectives and suggestions for improvement:

Teacher self-reflection and self-evaluation:

[OFFICIAL USE ONLY] Comments by teacher supervisor:

Lesson 35: Eternal Life with God

LESSON ORGANISATION

Year Level: Date: Time: Duration: Room:

Quote:
"How insignificant earth seems to me when I consider heaven" – St Ignatius of Loyola.

Prayer:
Come, Holy Spirit, fill the hearts of your faithful and enkindle in them the fire of your love.

V. Send forth your Spirit and they shall be created.
R. And you shall renew the face of the earth.

Let us pray.
O God, who by the light of the Holy Spirit, did instruct the hearts of the faithful, grant us in the same Spirit to be truly wise and ever to rejoice in his consolation.
Through Christ our Lord. Amen.

Lesson Outcomes:

As a result of this lesson, students will be able to:

- Understand the various objections against the Christian vision of heaven and eternal life.
- Provide reasonable arguments in favour of life after death.
- Outline how Jesus Christ, St Paul and others spoke about eternal life in heaven, namely the vision of God, as the reward for those who live out faithful lives in love.
- Contend that not everyone will be rewarded with eternal life in heaven.
- Prove the existence of purgatory where souls are perfected for entry into the heavenly afterlife.

Activity Sheets:

Activity Sheet 58, *Proving Purgatory*.

LESSON DELIVERY

Outcome	Time	Motivation and Introduction:	Resources/ References
Understand the various objections against the Christian vision of heaven and eternal life.	7 mins	Welcome and settle the students. Prayer to the Holy Spirit (or other suitable prayer). Tell the students that today we will be looking at belief in the afterlife, more specifically about eternal life in heaven with God. This is a fundamental Christian belief and is embedded at the end of all Catholic Creeds in the words *"life everlasting."* Briefly point out that there are many contemporary challenges to the traditional Christian view of heaven arising from a wide variety of sources. Respectively, heaven is either a delusion (atheism), an excuse not to improve our current material condition (secularism), a material and sensual paradise (Islam), a privileged place reserved only for a select few (Jehovah's Witnesses), or the final destiny for everyone (universalism). Sum up by noting that all the above positions either do not accurately portray traditional Christian beliefs or embody one of a variety of extreme views. For Catholicism, heaven is the ultimate reward for those who loved God *and* neighbour on earth, it consists of the vision of God face to face. God wills that all be saved and enter heaven, but ultimately not all are saved because of the decisions humans themselves freely choose to make. **Lesson Steps**	Horn, *Why We're Catholic: Our Reasons for Faith, Hope, and Love*, 204-210. Kreeft, *Fundamentals of the Faith*, 69-73. Schreck, *Catholic and Christian*, 205-207.
Provide reasonable arguments in favour of life after death.	10 mins	(i) Inform the students that when it comes to convincing atheists/secularists about the existence of the afterlife it is not sufficient to simply quote verses from the Bible. This is because they have no regard for the Bible as a sacred or authoritative text. What are we left, then, to prove the existence of the afterlife? Remind the students that we partly considered this question in Lessons 8 and 18 when we looked at the human person as a union of body and spiritual soul and the existence of angels/demons. What is the significance of humans having a *spiritual* soul? Take two-three student responses. Afterwards, on a PowerPoint slide display and explain the following sequence of arguments:	Kreeft & Tacelli, *Handbook of Christian Apologetics*, 242-243.

Outline how Jesus Christ, St Paul and others spoke about eternal life in heaven, namely the vision of God, as the reward for those who live out faithful lives in love.	15 mins	(a) The human person is a union of body and spiritual soul. (b) The body is made up of component parts; the spiritual soul is *simple*, meaning it has no component parts. (c) After death, the body decomposes, breaking up into its component parts. (d) The human soul, however, having no component parts cannot decompose. The human soul lives on. (e) If the human soul lives on after death, then there must be an afterlife. (f) Reason can also prove that God exists (The 'Five Ways' of St Thomas Aquinas) and where God exists that is where the heavenly afterlife must be. (g) For the rest of the picture, that is, what the afterlife is like and whether all souls end up in heaven or not, we need the help of revelation. (ii) *What is heaven like?* Take two-three student responses. We can only imagine. Some (e.g., Islam) teach that it is a place of physical, material and sensual delights, a place of great joy and pleasure but without the vision of God. Christian thinkers have written much about heaven. Display the following quote from St Augustine of Hippo: *"You have made us for yourself, O Lord, and our heart is restless until it rests in you."* For St Augustine, the ultimate fulfilment for the human person is to be with God. This is heaven. Next display the following words of St Paul describing heaven as follows: *"… no eye has seen, nor ear heard, nor the heart of man conceived what God has prepared for those who love him"* (1 Cor. 2:9). For St Paul, heaven is beyond the imagination, something God has prepared for those who love him. It will also be the place where the faithful will see God *"face to face"* (1 Cor. 13:12). Finally, display the following words of Jesus himself who said: *"In my Father's house there are many rooms … I go to prepare a place for you … that where I am you may be also"* (John 14:2-3). For Jesus, heaven is to dwell forever in the Father's house together with him.	Horn, *Why We're Catholic: Our Reasons for Faith, Hope, and Love*, 204-205. Sheed, *Theology and Sanity*, 244-253.

		Next show the students the following YouTube video, *What Will Heaven Be Like?* by Christ the King Productions (6.27 minutes). Afterwards, invite the students to answer the following three questions (Take three student responses): - *What are two things we will do in heaven?* - *What is the most attractive thing about heaven?* - *Why do you think heaven should be nothing less than the possession of God?* As for the last question, round off student feedback by emphasising that nothing less than God can satisfy humans for all eternity. If heaven just provided creaturely delights, we would eventually exhaust the satisfaction we get from these. However, because God is infinite, it is impossible to exhaust the joy and satisfaction we will get from seeing him face to face.	
Contend that not everyone will be rewarded with eternal life in heaven.	10 mins	(iii) Ask the students the question, *Who wants to get to heaven?* Most students will probably answer with a definite, *"Yes!"* Introduce the term *universalism*. This is the name of the view that teaches that ultimately everyone gets to heaven. Nevertheless, as much as we would like to see everyone make it to heaven, Scripture indicates that this will not be the case. Scripture exegesis: Refer the students to the text from the Gospel of Matthew 25:34-46 known as the "Judgement of the Nations", which reads as follows: *"When the Son of man comes in his glory, and all the angels with him, then he will sit on his glorious throne … Then the King will say to those at his right hand, 'Come, O blessed of my Father, inherit the kingdom prepared for you from the foundation of the world; for I was hungry and you gave me food, I was thirsty and you gave me drink, I was a stranger and you welcomed me, I was naked and you clothed me, I was sick and you visited me, I was in prison and you came to me' … Then he will say to those at his left hand, 'Depart from me, you cursed, into the eternal fire prepared for the devil and his angels; for I was hungry and you gave me no food, I was thirsty and you gave me no drink, I was a stranger and you did not welcome me, naked and you did not clothe me, sick and in prison and you did not visit me'."*	Flader, *Question Time: 150 Questions and Answers on the Catholic Faith*, 55-57. Keating, *What Catholics Really Believe – Setting the Record Straight*, 85-86.

		Inform the students that this is just one of a number of New Testament verses that indicate not everyone will get to heaven (cf., Matt. 7:14 & 22:14; Luke 13:24). Looking closer at Matthew 25:34-46, ask the students to answer the following questions: - *Who is the King enthroned judging the nations?* (Answer: The *"Son of man"*, or Jesus Christ). - *How are those on the right- and left-hand sides of the King respectively judged?* (Answer: Those on the right *"inherit the Kingdom"*; those on the left are sent to *"eternal fire"*). - *What are the criteria used by the King to determine whether one "inherits the kingdom" or goes to "eternal fire"?* (Answer: Whether one fed the hungry and thirsty, welcomed the stranger, clothed the naked, visited the sick and imprisoned). Conclude by stressing that the answer to the last question is doubly important because it rebuts the secular accusation that belief in heaven is used as an excuse not to work for social justice in the world. Those condemned to *"eternal fire"* are so condemned because they had no concern for the plight of their disadvantaged neighbours.	
Prove the existence of purgatory where souls are perfected for entry into the heavenly afterlife.	10 mins	(iv) The Catholic Church teaches that the afterlife for many may also involve spending some time in a place called purgatory. On a PowerPoint slide show the students the word 'purgatory' together with the following points: - 'Purgatory' comes from the word 'purge', or to cleanse. - God sends certain souls to purgatory to complete temporal punishment still owing for sins forgiven and/or to receive the final purification necessary to enter heaven. - Those in purgatory can be assisted by the prayers, sacrifices and Masses offered up by the faithful on earth. - All those who go to purgatory eventually end up in heaven. Inform the students that not everyone believes in purgatory. Most Protestants reject purgatory on the ground that it is not mentioned in the Bible. Hand out Activity Sheet 58, *Proving Purgatory*. Invite the students to read the various quotes from Scripture and identify with a tick or cross which ones do/do not provide proof for the existence of a place in the afterlife where people go to complete temporal punishment or receive final purification. [Ticks should be placed next to quotes (a), (c), (d), (f), & (g)]. Ask them to circle the words in each quote which influenced their decision.	Flader, *Question Time: 150 Questions and Answers on the Catholic Faith*, 49-52. Keating, *What Catholics Really Believe – Setting the Record Straight*, 86-88. Salza, *The Biblical Basis for the Catholic Faith*, 26-27.

| | 3 mins | **Lesson Closure**:

Remind the students that there is an afterlife following death, which can be proved from both reason and revelation. For the good, this is an eternal life in heaven, possessing and enjoying the vision of God face to face. Only God can satisfy all the desires of the human heart for eternity. According to Jesus, each person will have a special 'room' prepared for them in the Father's house. Though we would like to believe that everyone goes to heaven, this will only be the case for those who lived lives of faith, hope and love, loving God and neighbour in Christ. Purgatory exists and can be adduced from various passages in Scripture. It is the place of final temporal punishment and/or purification for those who die in friendship with Christ, so that each soul can be perfected for the eternal vision of God.

Transition:

Homework: Look up Revelation 21:27 which reads as follows: *"But nothing unclean shall enter it, nor anyone who practises abomination or falsehood, but only those who are written in the Lamb's book of life."* This verse says "nothing unclean" can enter heaven. How do you think this passage may relate to purgatory? | |
| | | **Resources**:

- Horn, Trent. *Why We're Catholic: Our Reasons for Faith, Hope, and Love.* El Cajon: Catholic Answers Press, 2017, 204-210.
- Flader, John. *Question Time: 150 Questions and Answers on the Catholic Faith.* Ballan, Vic.: Connor Court Publishing, 2008, 55-57.
- Keating, Karl. *What Catholics Really Believe – Setting the Record Straight.* San Francisco: Ignatius Press, 1992, 85-86.
- Kreeft, Peter. *Fundamentals of the Faith: Essays in Christian Apologetics.* San Francisco: Ignatius Press, 1988, 69-73.
- Kreeft, Peter & Ronald K. Tacelli. *Handbook of Christian Apologetics: Hundreds of Answers to Crucial Questions.* Downers Grove: IVP Academic, 1994, 242-243.
- Salza, John. *The Biblical Basis for the Catholic Faith.* Huntingdon, Indiana: Our Sunday Visitor Publishing, 2005, 222-227.
- Schreck, Alan. *Catholic and Christian: An Explanation of Commonly Misunderstood Catholic Beliefs.* Cincinnati, Ohio: Servant Books, 2004, 205-207. | |

		<ul><li>Sheed, Frank J. *Theology and Sanity.* London: Sheed & Ward, 1973, 244-253.</li><li>*Catechism of the Catholic Church.* Libreria Editrice Vaticana: St Pauls, 1994, paras. 163, 1023-1028, 2519.</li><li>YOUCAT (*Youth Catechism of the Catholic Church*). San Francisco, Ignatius Press, 2010, paras. 52, 158-160.</li><li>Website: Staples, Tim. "What is Heaven?" https://www.catholic.com/magazine/online-edition/what-is-heaven.</li><li>YouTube: Christ the King Productions. "What Will Heaven Be Like?" https://www.youtube.com/watch?v=Yl7TZ8kECO0.</li></ul>

LESSON EVALUATION (to be completed AFTER the lesson)

Assessment of lesson objectives and suggestions for improvement:
Teacher self-reflection and self-evaluation:
[OFFICIAL USE ONLY] Comments by teacher supervisor:

Lesson 36: Eternal Separation from God

LESSON ORGANISATION

Year Level: Date: Time: Duration: Room:

Quote:
"The pains of hell are not the greatest part of hell; the loss of heaven is the weightiest woe of hell" – St John Chrysostom.

Prayer:
Come, Holy Spirit, fill the hearts of your faithful and enkindle in them the fire of your love.

V. Send forth your Spirit and they shall be created.
R. And you shall renew the face of the earth.

Let us pray.
O God, who by the light of the Holy Spirit, did instruct the hearts of the faithful, grant us in the same Spirit to be truly wise and ever to rejoice in his consolation.
Through Christ our Lord. Amen.

Lesson Outcomes:

As a result of this lesson, students will be able to:

- Comprehend the diverse objections against the Christian belief in hell and eternal damnation.
- Cite verses in the New Testament where Jesus Christ speaks of hell and its eternity.
- Explain how and why, despite the love and mercy of God, any soul would ultimately end up in hell.
- Describe the nature of hell and its various punishments.
- Outline the negative consequences that would result if there were no eternal hell.

Activity Sheets:

Activity Sheet 59, *Hell: What Jesus Taught*.

"Always Be Prepared …" – A 'New Apologetics' Course for Catholic Secondary Schools

LESSON DELIVERY

Outcome	Time	Motivation and Introduction:	Resources/ References
Comprehend the diverse objections against the Christian belief in hell and eternal damnation.	8 mins	Welcome and settle the students. Prayer to the Holy Spirit (or other suitable prayer). Tell the students that today we will be looking at belief in hell and eternal damnation. Emphasise that this is not a pleasant topic and the idea of hell, etc., is not a popular one in many circles both inside and outside the Catholic Church. On a PowerPoint slide, outline and briefly explain the following challenges to the traditional Christian belief in hell: - "The doctrine of hell is unscriptural, unreasonable, contrary to God's love and mercy, and repugnant to justice." - "The images of tormenting fires and demons are medieval exaggerations, the figments of superstitious minds." - "If there is a hell it is only temporary. All those within it will eventually be purified and cleansed. In the end, God will become 'all in all'." - "There is no eternal punishment. The souls of the wicked are annihilated at death. With the death of the body their journey is finished." Sum up by highlighting that, ironically, it is the loving and merciful Jesus who gives us the most detailed teachings on the existence and nature of hell. We will now examine various examples of what Jesus taught about hell. **Lesson Steps**	Flader, *The Creed: A Tour of the Catechism*, 232-234. Schreck, *Catholic and Christian*, 207-208.
Cite verses in the New Testament where Jesus Christ speaks of hell and its eternity.	10 mins	(i) In response to the claim that belief in an eternal hell is contrary to the spirit and teachings of Jesus, it is best to simply refer to what he himself taught on the topic. Hand out Activity Sheet 59, *Hell: What Jesus Taught*. Invite the students to read the four quotes from Jesus – one from each of the Gospels – and then circle or highlight the words that refer to hell's eternity or the nature of its punishments. Conclude by noting that Jesus spoke on numerous other occasions about hell in addition to these four examples: Matt. 3:10-12; 5:22; 7:19; 8:11-12; 10:28; 18:7-9; 22:11-13; 25:41ff. To ignore the teachings of Jesus on hell is to ignore the main reason why he came and died on the Cross – to deliver us from sin and its consequences.	Horn, *Why We're Catholic: Our Reasons for Faith, Hope, and Love*, 198-199. Redemptorist Pastoral Publications, *The Essential Catholic Handbook*, 43-44.

Explain how and why, despite the love and mercy of God, any soul would ultimately end up in hell.	12 mins	(ii) Classroom debate: Invite the students to choose a side to debate the following question: *How could a loving and merciful God send any soul to suffer in hell for all eternity?* Over the next 7-8 minutes take as many student responses as possible and list them on the whiteboard under one of the following two headings, *Possible, Not Possible*. Eventually, the list should look something like the following: | Possible	Not Possible
• God is a God of justice as well as mercy. • Jesus taught it, so it must be true. • It says so in Scripture, both Old and New Testaments. • People end up in heaven or hell according to their own lifestyle choices. • God made us free and does not interfere with or alter our choices.	• God is a God of mercy. • God could not be so cruel and sadistic. • To be punished forever is not fair. He does send some people to hell but eventually everyone gets to heaven. • It is more merciful that God simply extinguish the souls of the bad at death rather than make them suffer forever.

Conclude by emphasising God's total respect for human freedom and our own choices. God does not send any one to heaven or hell; he simply confirms the choices we ourselves make. Those who freely choose to love and obey God during their lifetimes get God as their permanent reward; those who freely choose to reject and live without God during their lifetimes get that same choice confirmed for eternity. | Horn, *Why We're Catholic: Our Reasons for Faith, Hope, and Love*, 200-202.

Kreeft & Tacelli, *Handbook of Christian Apologetics*, 290-291.

Nichols, *Death and Afterlife*, 177-178. |
| Describe the nature of hell and its various punishments. | 12 mins | (iii) When one thinks about hell, one normally thinks about the Devil and never-ending fire. The four quotes outlined in Activity Sheet 59 all mentioned fire or flame. Is fire the sole or main punishment of hell? Show the students the following YouTube video, *The Four Sufferings of Hell According to St Catherine of Siena* by Ken Yasinski of Catholic Minute (5.17 minutes). Afterwards, invite the students to answer the following three questions (Take three student responses): 
- *List the four sufferings of hell?* (Answer: Loss of God; agony of regret; vision of the demons; spiritual fire).
- *What is the main suffering of hell and why?* (Answer: The loss of the vision of God. We are made to be in relationship with God and see him in heaven). | Nichols, *Death and Afterlife*, 176-178.

Schreck, *Catholic and Christian*, 208-209.

Sheed, *Theology and Sanity*, 246-247. |

Outline the negative consequences that would result if there were no eternal hell.	10 mins	- *Who is responsible for the eternal loss of God?* (Answer: Those in hell, who chose their own selfish desires over the glory of God). Round up the discussion by reminding the students that we talk about hell for one main reason, namely, to remind ourselves of our true destination – heaven – and what we must do to get there. (iv) Discussion question: *If hell was only temporary or the bad were simply annihilated at death, what would be the consequences?* Moderate this last discussion as an open forum. Students need not take down any notes, except for the concluding point. Some light-hearted observations in response to the above question may include: - "Great! Let's just eat, drink and be merry, for tomorrow we die." - "I could probably cope with some temporary punishment in hell, so long as I eventually get out." - "I'm relieved. I'd rather disappear than suffer for ever." More serious observations in response to the above question may include: - "Free will and our choices in the end don't really matter if we all end up in heaven." - "Likewise, morality and the difference between good and evil would disappear if we all end up in heaven." - "What incentive would there be to live unselfish, sacrificial, and heroic lives?" - "What deterrence would exist to prevent future great atrocities like those committed by Hitler, Stalin and Mao?" - "It would be highly unjust if everyone gets to heaven, for the unbeliever, lazy and corrupt would receive the same reward as saints, martyrs and heroes." - "If there is no eternal hell, then why bother evangelise and bring the unbaptised to Christ and the baptised to holiness?" - "If there is no eternal hell, then Jesus cannot be a saviour, for what did he save us from?" Conclusion: Without an eternal hell, the whole purpose of the Christian life and Christ's mission would be altered. There would be no absolute incentive to do good or evil, live lives of service and charity, strive for heroism and greatness and proclaim Christ and conversion to the world.	Kreeft & Tacelli, *Handbook of Christian Apologetics*, 282-287. Nichols, *Death and Afterlife*, 179-181.

| | 3 mins | **Lesson Closure:**

Remind the students that the idea of hell is not a pleasant one, something most people prefer not to think about. Nevertheless, Jesus Christ taught about hell on numerous occasions, its nature and how we should live to avoid it. The Christian life is not a negative one focused on how to avoid hell, but a positive one striving to reach heaven through the living out of faith, hope and love. God does not condemn any person to hell but allows people to make their own free choices for or against a life with him. There are multiple punishments associated with hell, with the most severe being the loss of the vision of God. If there were no eternal hell, there would be no need to practise unselfishness, sacrifice, heroism or greatness, no need for evangelisation or conversion, and no need for Jesus Christ as saviour.

Transition:

Homework: The great moral theologian St Alphonsus Liguori once said, *"If you pray, you will be certainly saved; if you do not pray, you will be certainly damned."* Spend some time contemplating these words and then make a resolution as to how you will better live out your Catholic life. | |
| | | **Resources:**

- Horn, Trent. *Why We're Catholic: Our Reasons for Faith, Hope, and Love.* El Cajon: Catholic Answers Press, 2017, 198-202.
- Flader, John. *The Creed: A Tour of the Catechism, Volume One.* Ballan, Victoria: Modotti Press, 2011, 232-234.
- Kreeft, Peter & Ronald K. Tacelli. *Handbook of Christian Apologetics: Hundreds of Answers to Crucial Questions.* Downers Grove: IVP Academic, 1994, 284-291.
- Nichols, Terence. *Death and Afterlife: A Theological Introduction.* Grand Rapids: Brazos Press, 2010, 176-181.
- Redemptorist Pastoral Publications. *The Essential Catholic Handbook: A Summary of Beliefs, Practices, and Prayers.* Liguori, Missouri: Liguori, 1997, 43-44.
- Schreck, Alan. *Catholic and Christian: An Explanation of Commonly Misunderstood Catholic Beliefs.* Cincinnati, Ohio: Servant Books, 2004, 208-209. | |

		<ul><li>Sheed, Frank J. *Theology and Sanity.* London: Sheed & Ward, 1973, 246-247.</li><li>*Catechism of the Catholic Church.* Libreria Editrice Vaticana: St Pauls, 1994, paras. 1033-1037.</li><li>YOUCAT (*Youth Catechism of the Catholic Church*). San Francisco, Ignatius Press, 2010, paras. 161-162.</li><li>Website: Horn, Trent. "Yes, Hell is Real and it is Eternal." https://www.catholic.com/magazine/online-edition/yes-hell-is-real-and-eternal.</li><li>YouTube: Yasinski, Ken. "The Four Sufferings of Hell According to St Catherine of Siena." https://www.youtube.com/watch?v=hfa4ddKq1q8.</li></ul>

LESSON EVALUATION (to be completed AFTER the lesson)

Assessment of lesson objectives and suggestions for improvement:
Teacher self-reflection and self-evaluation:
[OFFICIAL USE ONLY] Comments by teacher supervisor:

Assessment Schedule

Students will be required to complete three tasks for this course as follows:

Item No.	Assessment Type & Description	Weighting %	Due Date
Item 1	Exam Lessons 1-12	30	End of Week 4
Item 2	Open Book Exam Lessons 13-24	30	End of Week 8
Item 3	Assignment Lessons 25-36	40	End of Week 12

- Item 1 will comprise thirty (30) multiple choice questions drawn from Lessons 1-12.
- Item 2 will comprise twenty-four (24) short answer questions drawn from Lessons 13-24 (Open Book Exam).
- Item 3 will be a one thousand (1000) word response defending the Catholic position from Scripture on one of the following topics:
    - The Ten Commandments
    - Conscience
    - The Seven Sacraments
    - The Mass
    - The Real Presence of Christ in the Eucharist
    - Divorce and Remarriage
    - Contraception
    - Abortion
    - Euthanasia
    - Mary as Mother of God
    - Mary's Assumption into Heaven
    - The Communion of Saints
    - The Eternity of Hell

END OF PART I

Always Be Prepared

'New Apologetics' Activity Sheets for Catholic Secondary Students

ACTIVITY SHEETS
INDEX

Activity Sheet 1	History of Heresies	iii
Activity Sheet 2	The 'Four Horsemen' of the Anti-Apocalypse	iv
Activity Sheet 3	The 'Five Ways' of St Thomas Aquinas	v
Activity Sheet 4	The 'Five Ways' – Filling the Gaps	vi
Activity Sheet 5	The 'God' of Richard Dawkins	vii
Activity Sheet 6	The Human Face of God	viii
Activity Sheet 7	Types of Evil and Suffering	ix
Activity Sheet 8	The Sufferings of Job	x
Activity Sheet 9	Saints and Scholars	xi
Activity Sheet 10	Great Beauty and Service	xii
Activity Sheet 11	Pope Says Sorry for Sins of Church	xiii
Activity Sheet 12	Fr George Lemaître and the 'Big Bang'	xiv
Activity Sheet 13	The Anthropic Principle	xv
Activity Sheet 14	The 'Cambrian Explosion'	xvi
Activity Sheet 15	'African Adam' and 'Mitrochondrial Eve'	xvii
Activity Sheet 16	Adam and Eve: Evolved or Specially Created?	xviii
Activity Sheet 17	The Human Person: Material, Spiritual, or Both?	xix
Activity Sheet 18	Revealed Religion	xx
Activity Sheet 19	God's Plan of Loving Goodness	xxi
Activity Sheet 20	Abraham, Moses and Jesus – Did They Exist?	xxii
Activity Sheet 21	Manuscript Evidence in Support of the Bible	xxiii
Activity Sheet 22	Debating Boettner	xxiv
Activity Sheet 23	Paradise Lost and Regained	xxv
Activity Sheet 24	Comparing the Narratives	xxvi
Activity Sheet 25	Understanding the Trinity	xxvii
Activity Sheet 26	Comparing the Creeds	xxviii
Activity Sheet 27	Jesus: God, Man, or Both?	xxix
Activity Sheet 28	Who Saw Jesus Christ Risen?	xxx
Activity Sheet 29	Theories Denying the Resurrection of Jesus	xxxi
Activity Sheet 30	'Infallibility' – What it Does and Does Not Mean	xxxii
Activity Sheet 31	Commonalities and Common Good	xxxiii
Activity Sheet 32	The 'Non-Negotiables'	xxxiv
Activity Sheet 33	The 'Angel Gap'	xxxv
Activity Sheet 34	Miracles – Answering the Critics	xxxvi

Activity Sheet 35	The 'Two Wings' of Faith and Reason	xxxvii
Activity Sheet 36	Faith Seeking Understanding	xxxviii
Activity Sheet 37	Objective versus Subjective	xxxix
Activity Sheet 38	How Do We Know?	xl
Activity Sheet 39	Why We Need Moral Absolutes	xli
Activity Sheet 40	Physical and Moral Natural Laws	xlii
Activity Sheet 41	The Ten Commandments – A Complete Way of Living	xliii
Activity Sheet 42	The Ten Commandments – Laws of Liberty	xliv
Activity Sheet 43	Conscience – Our Most Secret Core	xlv
Activity Sheet 44	Sacraments in Scripture	xlvi
Activity Sheet 45	Sacraments for Life	xlvii
Activity Sheet 46	The Last Supper – A Sacrifice?	xlviii
Activity Sheet 47	Participating in the Priesthood of Christ	xlix
Activity Sheet 48	The 'Bread of Life' Discourse	l
Activity Sheet 49	Fathers and Favours	li
Activity Sheet 50	Grounds for Annulments	lii
Activity Sheet 51	Human Life – When Does It Begin?	liii
Activity Sheet 52	In-Vitro Fertilisation – Pro-Life or Problematic?	liv
Activity Sheet 53	The Death Penalty – For or Against?	lv
Activity Sheet 54	Comparing Jesus and Mary – Are They Equal?	lvi
Activity Sheet 55	Mary's Immaculate Conception – Answering the Objections	lvii
Activity Sheet 56	The Brothers of Jesus – Who Are They?	lviii
Activity Sheet 57	Are the Dead Really Dead?	lix
Activity Sheet 58	Proving Purgatory	lx
Activity Sheet 59	Hell: What Jesus Taught	lxi

LESSON 1
Activity Sheet 1

HISTORY OF HERESIES

HERESY	NAME OF FOUNDER(S)	YEAR OF FOUNDATION	CHALLENGES	CATHOLIC APOLOGISTS WHO OPPOSED THIS HERESY	NATURAL, CHRISTIAN OR CATHOLIC APOLOGETICS?
DOCETISM	Julius Cassianus	Late 1st century	Denied Jesus Christ came in the flesh	St John the Apostle St Ignatius of Antioch	
ARIANISM	Arius of Alexandria	Early 4th century	Denied the divinity of Christ	St Athanasius of Alexandria	
NESTORIANISM	Nestorius of Constantinople	c. AD 431	Denied that Mary was the 'Mother of God'	St Cyril of Alexandria	
ISLAM	Mohammad	AD 610	Denies the Trinity, the divinity of Christ and his resurrection	St John Damascene St Thomas Aquinas	
PROTESTANTISM	Martin Luther Ulrich Zwingli John Calvin Thomas Cranmer	First half of 16th century	Denies the authority of the Pope, the need for good works for salvation, free will	St Robert Bellarmine	
JEHOVAH'S WITNESSES	Charles Taze Russell	1872	Denies the Trinity, divinity of Christ, immortality of the soul, eternity of Hell	Rev. L. Rumble, Rev. John F. Coffey Louise D'Angelo	
NEW ATHEISM	Richard Dawkins Christopher Hitchens Daniel Dennett Sam Harris	Late 20th, early 21st century	Denies the existence of God and the rationality of all religion	Edward Feser Scott Hahn Trent Horn	

Students complete the final column designating each heresy under one of the following categories – Natural Apologetics, Christian Apologetics or Catholic Apologetics.

LESSON 2
Activity Sheet 2

THE 'FOUR HORSEMEN' OF THE ANTI-APOCALYPSE

HITCHENS

DENNETT

You pray for me.
I'll think of you.

HARRIS

DAWKINS

LESSON 2
Activity Sheet 3

THE 'FIVE WAYS' OF ST THOMAS AQUINAS

THE FIRST 'WAY'
Argument from Motion

1. Our senses tell us that things are in motion.
2. If something moves it is because it has been put into motion by something else.
3. The thing causing the motion in another thing likewise has been moved by another.
4. The sequence of motion extends backward; however, it cannot extend backwards forever for then there would be no beginning.
5. Therefore, the first motion must have been caused by a first mover who cannot and has never been moved.
6. We call this first 'unmoved mover' God.

THE THIRD 'WAY'
Argument from Necessity

1. Our senses tell us that all things come into existence and then go out of existence. These things are called 'contingent' (non-necessary) things.
2. If it is possible that everything at one point in the future could go out of existence, then it is possible at some point in the past that everything could have ceased to exist.
3. If there were ever a time in the past when everything ceased to exist, then there would exist nothing now.
4. Since it is absurd to say that nothing exists now, then something must have always existed.
5. Since no creature can exist for all time, there must be a non-creature which of necessity has existed for all time.
6. We call this necessary non-creature God.

THE FOURTH 'WAY'
Argument from Perfection

1. Our senses tell us that there exist different degrees of perfection in creatures.
2. When we speak of different degrees of perfection it must be in reference to an ultimate model of perfection.
3. The perfect model in a species must be the source and cause of all perfection in that species.
4. Therefore, there must exist an infinitely perfect being which is the source and cause of all perfections in all beings.
5. We call this infinitely perfect being God.

THE SECOND 'WAY'
Argument from Cause

1. Our senses tell us that things exist in the world.
2. Nothing can cause itself to exist out of nothing.
3. If something exists, it must have been caused by a pre-existing other thing.
4. The sequence of causes extends backwards; however, it cannot extend backwards forever for then there would be no beginning.
5. Therefore, the first thing caused must have been caused by a first cause who cannot and has never been caused.
6. We call this first 'uncaused cause' God.

THE FIFTH 'WAY'
Argument from Order

1. Our senses tell us that all things work towards a certain goal.
2. However, most things do not possess intelligence and will to move themselves to that goal.
3. Non-intelligent things working towards a certain goal must do so because they are directed by some intelligence.
4. Some intelligent being, therefore, must exist by whom all non-intelligent beings are directed to their goal.
5. We call this intelligent being God.

LESSON 2
Activity Sheet 4

THE 'FIVE WAYS' – FILLING THE GAPS

WAY

First Way

Second Way

Third Way

Fourth Way

Fifth Way

EFFECT

Proof from _____

Proof from _____

Proof from Necessity

Proof from grades of perfection

Proof from _____

CAUSE

First Unmoved _____

First _____ cause

First _____ Being

First _____ Being

Supreme _____

WORD BANK

Perfect   Intelligence   Order   Mover

Motion   Cause   Necessary   Uncaused

LESSON 3
Activity Sheet 5

THE 'GOD' OF RICHARD DAWKINS
(FROM 'THE GOD DELUSION', P.31)

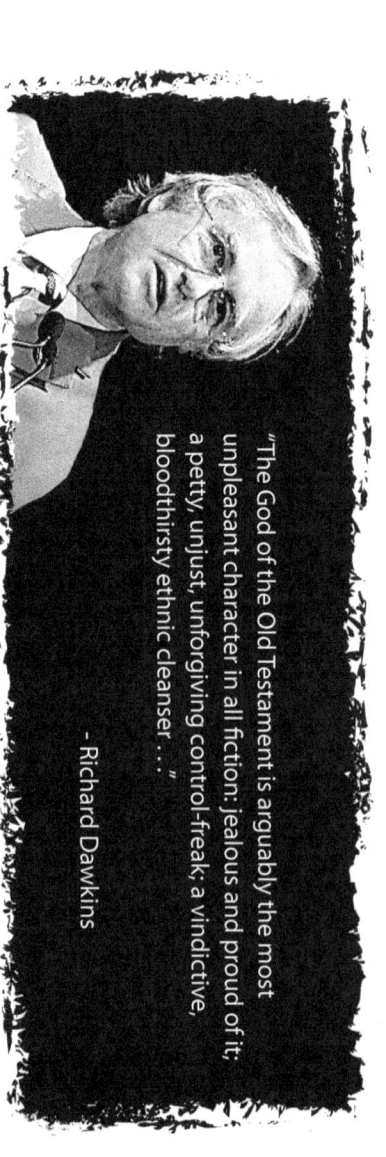

"The God of the Old Testament is arguably the most unpleasant character in all fiction: jealous and proud of it; a petty, unjust, unforgiving control-freak; a vindictive, bloodthirsty ethnic cleanser..."

- Richard Dawkins

In the space below, write a one-paragraph response to Richard Dawkins. Do you think this is a fair portrayal of God?

Can the same things be said about the God of the New Testament?

_____
_____
_____
_____
_____
_____
_____
_____
_____
_____
_____

LESSON 3
Activity Sheet 6

THE HUMAN FACE OF GOD

THE PARABLE OF THE PRODIGAL SON

"There was a man who had two sons; and the younger of them said to his father, 'Father, give me the share of property that falls to me.' And he divided his living between them. Not many days later, the younger son gathered all he had and took his journey into a far country, and there he squandered his property in loose living. And when he had spent everything, a great famine arose in that country, and he began to be in want. So he went and joined himself to one of the citizens of that country, who sent him into his fields to feed swine. And he would gladly have fed on the pods that the swine ate; and no one gave him anything. But when he came to himself he said, 'How many of my father's hired servants have bread enough and to spare, but I perish here with hunger! I will arise and go to my father, and I will say to him, "Father, I have sinned against heaven and before you; I am no longer worthy to be called your son; treat me as one of your hired servants."' And he arose and came to his father. But while he was yet at a distance, his father saw him and had compassion, and ran and embraced him and kissed him. And the son said to him, 'Father, I have sinned against heaven and before you; I am no longer worthy to be called your son.' But the father said to his servants, 'Bring quickly the best robe, and put it on him; and put a ring on his hand, and shoes on his feet; and bring the fatted calf and kill it, and let us eat and make merry; for this my son was dead, and is alive again; he was lost, and is found'" (Luke 15:11-24).

1. Which person in this parable represents God?

   _____

2. What does this parable tell us about the type of relationship God wishes to have with us?

   _____

3. How do we know from this parable that God is always caring and never gives up on us?

   _____

4. The fact that the father "ran" towards his son when he saw him returning tells us what about the nature of God?

   _____

LESSON 4
Activity Sheet 7

TYPES OF EVIL AND SUFFERING

When God first created the world and humanity there was no evil and suffering; all was peace, harmony and happiness in Paradise. Evil and suffering only entered the world because of humanity's misuse of freedom – or sin. Following sin came the rupture of our relationship with God, disorder in human relationships, subjection to nature, and the loss of gifts that protected us from pain, sickness, suffering and death. All examples of evil and suffering fall under one of two categories, moral or physical. Moral evils are evils directly resulting from human actions/neglect; physical evils from events beyond human control. Complete the two columns by listing examples of moral and physical evils that you are aware of. To assist students, one example of a moral and physical event is provided.

MORAL EVILS	PHYSICAL EVILS
War	Drought

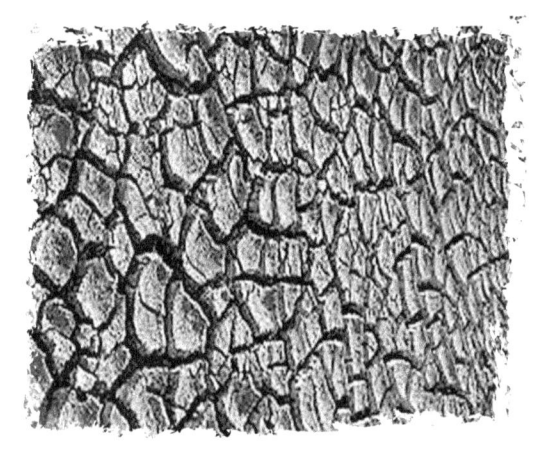

LESSON 4
Activity Sheet 8

THE SUFFERINGS OF JOB

In the Bible there is a wealthy man named Job residing in the land of Uz with his extended family and vast flocks. He is "blameless" and "upright," constantly mindful to live righteously (Job 1:1). God informs Satan of Job's virtue, but Satan responds that Job is only righteous because God has favoured him generously. Satan dares God that, if allowed to inflict Job with suffering, he will change and curse God. God permits Satan to afflict Job to test this claim, but he forbids Satan to take Job's life in the process.

Over the time of one day, Job is given four reports, each informing him that his sheep, servants, and ten children have all died due to thieving intruders or natural disasters. Job rips his clothes and shaves his head in sorrow, yet he still praises God in his prayers. Satan appears before God again and gets permission for another opportunity to test Job. This time, Job is afflicted with terrible skin sores. His wife urges him to denounce God and to give up and die but Job protests, trying to endure his inflictions.

Three of Job's companions, Eliphaz, Bildad, and Zophar, arrive to comfort him, sitting with Job in silence for seven days out of reverence for his grieving. On the seventh day, Job talks, starting a discussion in which each of the four men shares his reflections on Job's troubles in poetic descriptions.

Job damns the day he was born, relating life and death to light and darkness. He wishes that he had never been born, believing that life only increases his suffering. Job's friends conclude that his pain must be due to some sin he has committed that has provoked God's justice. Job reacts to this suggestion with anger and calls his friends "worthless physicians" who "whitewash [their help] with lies" (Job 13:4). Job believes that there is a "witness" or a "Redeemer" in heaven who will testify for his integrity (Job 16:19; Job 19:25). Job becomes bitter, anxious, and scared. He deplores the injustice that allows evil people to thrive while he and many other honest people suffer. Job wants to face God and protest but decides to persevere in fearing God and evading evil.

God eventually intervenes, commanding Job to be brave. Overcome by the appearance of God, Job recognises his infinite power and accepts the limitations of his human understanding. This response pleases God and God then restores Job's health, granting him twice as much property as before, new children, and a remarkably long life.

SAINTS AND SCHOLARS

LESSON 5
Activity Sheet 9

Match the name of the Catholic saint/scholar in Column A with the achievement in Column B. The first one is done to help start you off.

COLUMN A

St Augustine of Hippo (+AD 430)

St Francis of Assisi (+AD 1226)

St Thomas Aquinas (+AD 1274)

St Joan of Arc (+AD 1431)

St Vincent de Paul (+AD 1660)

St Teresa of Calcutta (+AD 1997)

Fr Christopher Clavius SJ (+AD 1612)

Fr Gregor Mendel (+AD 1884)

Louis Pasteur (+AD 1895)

Fr George Lemaître (+AD 1966)

J. R. R. Tolkein (+AD 1973)

Prof. Jerome Lejeune (+AD 1994)

COLUMN B

Medieval saint who lived a life of poverty and humility

Discovered the link between Down Syndrome and chromosomes

Helped to create the modern-day (Gregorian) Calendar

Greatest philosopher and theologian of all time

Founded religious orders to assist the poor in France

Laid the scientific foundations of the 'Big Bang Theory'

Great heroine who helped France win the Hundred Years War

Author of the 'Lord of the Rings' trilogy

Founded the science of genetics

Philosopher who wrote the ancient classic 'City of God'

Founded the science of micro-biology

Devoted her life to assist the poorest of the poor in India

LESSON 5
Activity Sheet 10

GREAT BEAUTY AND SERVICE

Throughout the world, the Catholic Church continues to run and maintain tens of thousands of schools, hospitals and orphanages, looking after the education, health and welfare of tens of millions of people around the world each day of every year. The figures in Africa alone are staggering, with 1,137 hospitals, 1,285 orphanages, 93,315 primary schools, and 42,234 secondary schools run by the Catholic Church.

PAINTING
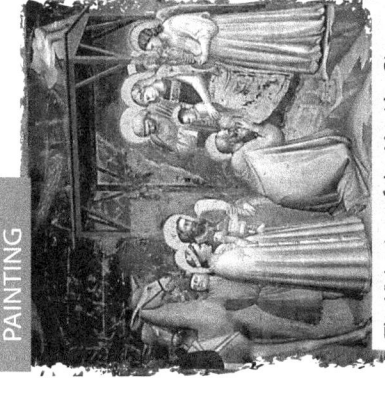
The Visitation of the Magi by Giotto

ARCHITECTURE

Cathedral of Milan

STAINED GLASS WINDOWS

Notre Dame Cathedral in Paris

SCULPTURE

The Pieta by Michelangelo

MUSIC

Gregorian Chant and Manuscripts

HEALTH & WELFARE
Daughters of Charity Health System

LESSON 5
Activity Sheet 11

POPE SAYS SORRY FOR SINS OF CHURCH

THE GUARDIAN, 13 MARCH 2000

Saving one of his most audacious initiatives for the twilight of his papacy, John Paul II yesterday attempted to purify the soul of the Roman Catholic church by making a sweeping apology for 2,000 years of violence, persecution and blunders.

From the altar of St Peter's Basilica in Rome he led Catholicism into unchartered territory by seeking forgiveness for sins committed against Jews, heretics, women, Gypsies and native peoples.

The Pope electrified ranks of cardinals and bishops by pleading for a future that would not repeat the mistakes. "Never again," he said. "We forgive and we ask forgiveness. We are asking pardon for the divisions among Christians, for the use of violence that some have committed in the service of truth, and for attitudes of mistrust and hostility assumed towards followers of other religions."

Wearing the purple vestments of Lenten mourning, the Pope sought pardon for seven categories of sin: general sins; sins in the service of truth; sins against Christian unity; against the Jews; against respect for love, peace and cultures; against the dignity of women and minorities; and against human rights.

https://www.theguardian.com/world/2000/mar/13/catholicism.religion.

1. What was the year of Pope St John Paul II's apology? Why do you think he choose this year for this significant act?
2. What sins did Pope St John Paul II specifically ask forgiveness for?
3. What is the significance of asking for forgiveness for sins "committed in the service of truth"? How could truth have been better served?
4. Do you think Pope St John Paul II's apology improved the image of the Catholic Church? Why/Why not?

LESSON 6
Activity Sheet 12

FR GEORGE LEMAÎTRE AND 'THE BIG BANG'

Ever since the time of the ancient Greeks such as Epicurus and Lucretius (4th century BC) and well into the 20th century it was believed that atoms were eternal and unchanging. They had always existed and were never created. The same was believed for the universe as a whole (the 'Steady State Theory'). For many scientists this meant that there was no room for a creator God. One scientist who defended the 'Steady State Theory' was the famous agnostic astronomer, Prof. Fred Hoyle (1915-2001). This all began to change in 1927 when a Belgian priest by the name of Fr George Lemaître, basing himself on Einstein's Theory of Relativity, announced that the universe was expanding and had a definite calculable beginning to a super dense 'singularity' billions of years ago. The implications of this discovery were profound for both religion and science. It meant that the universe had a beginning akin to the Genesis story and that the 'Steady State Theory' had to be abandoned.

At first Fr Lemaître's theory was ridiculed and rejected. Fred Hoyle mocked it as the so-called 'Big Bang Theory'; the communist-atheist government in Russia called it 'reactionary'. Nevertheless, in short time other famous scientists and astronomers – such as Albert Einstein and Edwin Hubble – confirmed Fr Lemaître's calculations. Eventually, the scientific community as a whole, including Fred Hoyle, came to accept that the universe arose from a singularity with a 'big bang' approximately 13.8 billion years ago.

In 1951, Pope Pius XII acknowledged that Fr Lemaître's work affirmed the Church's teaching that the universe had a beginning in time.

What was the core discovery made by Fr George Lemaître?

_____

Why do you think some scientists were initially hostile to his conclusions?

_____

Fr George Lemaître with Albert Einstein

LESSON 6
Activity Sheet 13

THE ANTHROPIC PRINCIPLE

One strong argument on behalf of a universe created by a rational designer is the so-called 'anthropic principle' (from the Greek word anthropos, meaning human). According to this argument, the universe is so finely tuned that if any of its fundamental forces were differently calibrated, life as we know it would not exist. Looking at our universe, it gives the appearance that it was deliberately arranged by some super-intellect for human life (the 'Big Bloom'); otherwise, it came to be through a series of random events against the most incredible odds.

Examples of 'anthropic coincidences' needed for the existence of life as we know it:

(i) The power of the initial 'Big Bang.'
(ii) The mass of an electron.
(iii) The nuclear force binding protons to the nucleus.
(iv) The cosmological constant governing gravity.
(v) The speed of light.
(vi) The distance of the earth from the sun.
(vii) The position of our solar system within the Milky Way Galaxy.
(viii) The spatial curvature of the universe.
(ix) The genetic pattern of DNA.

NOTE: DNA is one of the building blocks of life. It stores genetic information. The chance of a strand of DNA arising by mere chance is 16^{58}, i.e., the number 16 followed by 58 zeros! For such a thing to occur by chance is practically impossible.

EXTRAORDINARY FINE TUNING IS WHAT ONE WOULD EXPECT OF A UNIVERSE CREATED BY AN INTELLIGENT BEING.

FRED HOYLE:
"A common-sense interpretation of the facts suggests that a super intellect has monkeyed with physics, as well as chemistry and biology, and that there are no blind forces worth speaking about in nature."

LESSON 6
Activity Sheet 14

THE 'CAMBRIAN EXPLOSION'

The oldest fossils are those of ancient bacteria discovered in Western Australia dated to 3,465 million years ago. For the next 3 billion years the only other fossils to appear are single-celled organisms and algae.

Suddenly, 635 million years ago (Ediacarian Period) there occurred a jump in complexity with sponges, worms and molluscs appearing. A hundred million years later, between 530-525 million years ago, there suddenly appeared 16 complete novel phyla and thirty classes of animal forms. These are evident in the Burgess Shale Cambrian fossil bed in Canada.

The Cambrian Explosion poses the following challenges to traditional Darwinianism:

- In the Cambrian Explosion many life forms of vast differences suddenly appear in the fossil record.
- None of the Pre-Cambrian life-forms could have been the common ancestor of Cambrian life-forms.
- The Pre-Cambrian fossil record appears to be complete, so there is very little likelihood of some hidden common ancestor still to be found.
- The six million years of the Cambrian Explosion is too short a time to allow for a slow evolutionary emergence of so many new and complex life forms.

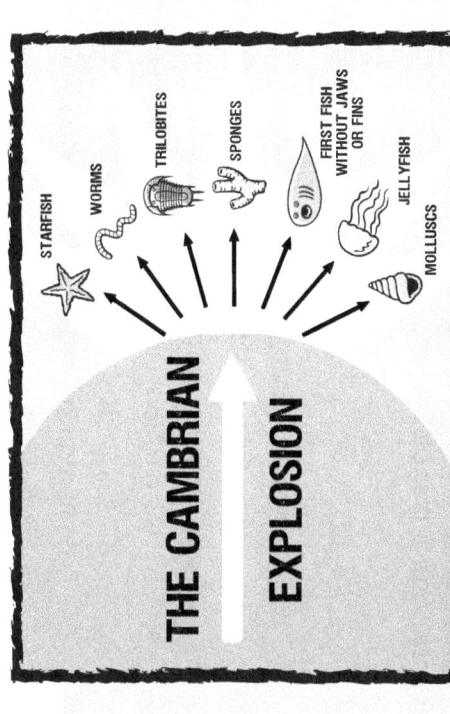

WHAT CONCLUSION CAN BE DRAWN FROM THE 'CAMBRIAN EXPLOSION'?

New life forms appear suddenly on earth rather than through a long and slow evolutionary process. It appears that God suddenly disrupts the stable equilibrium of life by directly creating and introducing new and complete species on earth. This process of direct intervention is called 'punctuated equilibrium.' If evolution occurs, it is only on a 'micro' scale generating genetic changes within a species rather than whole new species altogether.

LESSON 7
Activity Sheet 15

'AFRICAN ADAM' AND 'MITOCHONDRIAL EVE'

A number of modern paleoanthropologists (people who study human fossils, including Rebecca Cann, Chris Stringer and Pamela Willoughby) advance the view that all human beings have a single maternal origin which they call 'African Mitochondrial Eve'. Mitochondria (or mt DNA) are structures within a human cell that contain their own genetic machinery and information and are inherited only from the mother.

The chief reason for believing that all human beings have their origin in one single mother comes from the very small mtDNA variation among humans of all races. Compared to other animal species (orang-utans 5% and gorillas 0.6%), humans have only a 0.3% variation. According to Chris Stringer: *"The realisation that humans are biologically highly homogeneous (the same) has one straightforward implication; that mankind has only recently evolved from one tight little group of ancestors ... We are all members of a very young species, and our genes betray that secret."*

Similarly, recent comparative studies of the human **Y chromosome** (which is uniquely passed down by men) reveal a similar genetic trail parallel to the mtDNA trail, traceable along an unbroken line to an original male ancestor in Africa (**'African Adam'**).

Though still a matter of much debate, a growing number of paleoanthropologists believe that all human beings are members of the same family. Together with recent archaeological discoveries, this family originated sometime between 150,000 and 200,000 years ago in Africa. Later, some 50,000 years ago, members of this family began to leave Africa, gradually spreading to Asia, Europe, the Americas and Australia. According to the geneticist Svante Pääbo, "We are all Africans, either living in Africa or in quite recent exile outside of Africa."

How does the above information address objections to and/or support the Genesis account of humanity's origin from a single set of parents (monogenism)?

LESSON 7
Activity Sheet 16

ADAM AND EVE: EVOLVED OR SPECIALLY CREATED?

Ask the students to read the following arguments relating to whether Adam and Eve evolved or not.

Arguments: When people say they believe that Adam and Eve existed, they mean that they were two individuals involved in real events in a real past, not mythological, legendary or fictional figures. One view, based on a literal reading of Genesis 2, is that God directly created Adam's body from the dust of the earth and then infused the breath of life (a soul) into him. Soon afterwards, God created Eve from a rib taken from Adam's side and likewise breathed a soul into her. Adam and Eve previously had no existence and were unconnected to any past or existing life-forms, namely, pre-human cave men, etc. This is called 'de novo' creation ('new creation'), with Adam and Eve having no continuity with any other life forms. The Catholic Church exclusively held this view of human creation for many centuries and there are many Catholics who still believe the same today. This view preserves the original understanding of Scripture and is certainly not beyond God's creative powers.

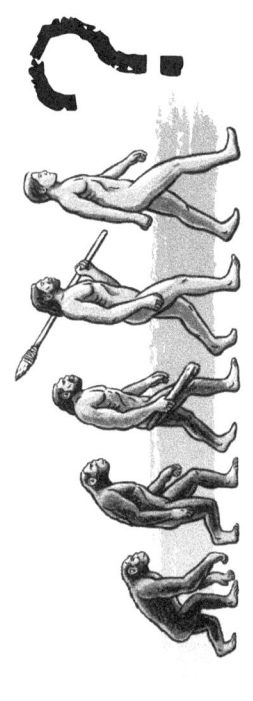

An alternate view believes that Adam and Eve existed as real individuals but seeks to reconcile Genesis 2 with scientific evidence indicating a past evolutionary process of emerging 'cave men.' This view believes that God created the evolutionary process that allows for slow change of physical bodies over time. Eventually, over eons of time the bodies of cave men developed until God intervened to infuse a human soul into one of the existing cave men. The infusion of this soul effectively changed the cave man into a human being (Adam). The same is said to have occurred with Eve's creation. In this view, humans are not entirely separate from cave men but have a 'material continuity' through the body.

In the space provided, write your reasons for which of the above two positions you prefer. If you wish, you will have two minutes to present your reasons to the class.

_____

_____

_____

_____

_____

LESSON 8
Activity Sheet 17

THE HUMAN PERSON: MATERIAL, SPIRITUAL, OR BOTH?

THE THEISTIC/CATHOLIC VIEW OF THE HUMAN PERSON
Created by God in his image and likeness.
Possesses a body and soul.
Has senses and intellect to know and understand.
Possesses a free will.
Has an eternal destiny in the afterlife.

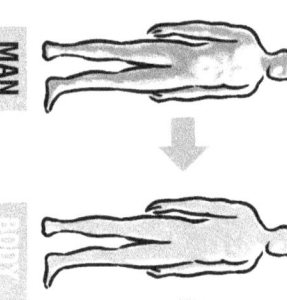

THE ATHEISTIC/POST-MODERN VIEW OF THE HUMAN PERSON
A product of evolution through natural selection.
Possesses only a body.
Is only an intelligent machine. Senses and intellect untrustworthy.
Has no freedom. Free will is illusory.
Has no afterlife beyond the grave.

Read through the following list of human activities and identify which ones are physical/material and which are spiritual/immaterial activities:

Form abstract ideas: _____   Eat and drink: _____   Smell fumes: _____

Make free choices: _____   See and hear: _____   Love others: _____

Understand universal concepts: _____   Taste and touch: _____   Write a poem: _____

Sleep: _____   Exercise self-consciousness: _____   Appreciate beauty: _____

Conclusion: Human beings can do many things physical (material) or spiritual (immaterial). The physical actions are performed by the physical body, which includes the organs that empower humans to taste, touch, smell, hear and see. However, our physical bodies cannot perform spiritual actions, including self-consciousness, knowing, understanding and loving. The power to do spiritual actions can only stem from a distinct spiritual, or immaterial, reality. We traditionally call this spiritual reality the soul, which is the 'principle of life' of each human person. Being spiritual, the soul cannot evolve or change and must therefore be directly created and infused by God. Although united to the body, the soul is independent in its life and actions and can even live on after death. What this means is that humans are both material and spiritual beings comprising body, senses, soul, intellect and will. These powers enable humans to live lives of meaning, truth, freedom and happiness.

xix

LESSON 9
Activity Sheet 18

REVEALED RELIGION

The following are instances when God specially revealed himself and spoke to four chosen persons. Read the words of God in these four instances and in the space below answer the question, *What was God's ultimate purpose in speaking to Adam, Abraham (Abram), Moses and David?*

"And God blessed them (Adam and Eve), and God said to them, 'Be fruitful and multiply, and fill the earth and subdue it ... and have dominion over every living thing'" (Gen. 1:28).

"The Lord said to Abram, 'Go from your country and your kindred and your father's house to the land that I will show you. And I will make of you a great nation' ..." (Gen. 12:1-4).

"Moses ... I have seen the affliction of my people ... I have come down to deliver them out of the hand of the Egyptians and bring them ... to a land flowing with milk and honey" (Exod. 3:7-8).

To David: *"I will appoint a place for my people Israel, and will plant them, that they may dwell in their own place ... I will raise up your offspring after you and I will establish his kingdom"* (2 Sam. 7:9-12).

LESSON 9
Activity Sheet 19

GOD'S PLAN OF LOVING GOODNESS

God reveals his plan of love and salvation for humanity over many centuries, through patriarchs, kings and prophets. This revelation reaches its climax in Jesus Christ. Complete columns A and B with the statements from the Word Bank.

COLUMN A
HOW GOD REVEALS HIMSELF IN JESUS CHRIST . . .

-
-
-
-
-

WORD BANK

- . . . by becoming one of us.
- . . . as the Word who became flesh.
- . . . as the "Emmanuel" – God among us.
- . . . by walking and dwelling among us.
- . . . by teaching us great truths.
- . . . as "my Lord and my God."
- . . . by freeing us from sickness, blindness, diabolical possession, death.
- . . . as the "I Am."
- . . . as "the way, the truth and the life."
- . . . by dying for us on the Cross.

COLUMN B
HOW GOD REVEALS HIS LOVE FOR HUMANITY IN JESUS CHRIST . . .

-
-
-
-
-

LESSON 10
Activity Sheet 20

ABRAHAM, MOSES AND JESUS – DID THEY EXIST?

ABRAHAM

No: Abraham is a mythical figure of later tradition. There is no hard archaeological evidence that he or his family ever existed.

Yes: One should not expect archaeological evidence for private nomadic individuals like Abraham. The story of Abraham is consistent with the literary genre of ancient near eastern biography and does not hesitate to speak of unfavourable moments in his family's history.

MOSES

No: There is no written or archaeological evidence of a mass exodus leaving Egypt and crossing the Sinai in the late Bronze Age.

Yes: Ancient Egyptian historians never recorded military defeats or mistakes made by Pharaohs. Archaeologists have discovered ruins of Canaanite cities destroyed in the 13th century BC, the time when the Israelites forcibly entered Canaan under Moses' successor, Joshua.

JESUS

No: There were 27 major non-Christian authors who lived 100 years within the time of Jesus but none of them mention him at all.

Yes: Jesus is mentioned by name by the Jewish historian Josephus (*Antiquities*, Book 18, AD 93), by the Roman Governor Pliny (*Letters*, 10:96.7, AD 111), and by the Roman historians Tacitus (*Annals of Imperial Rome*, Book 15, AD 116) and Suetonius (*Lives of the Caesars*, chap. 25, AD 121).

What do you think is the most convincing argument for the existence of Jesus and why?

_____

_____

LESSON 10
Activity Sheet 21

MANUSCRIPT EVIDENCE IN SUPPORT OF THE BIBLE

The ancient manuscript copies of the Bible are numerous and include the following:

- **7Q5 Manuscript:** Written pre-AD 70. A fragment of the Gospel of Mark, chapter 6 verses 52-53. Discovered in 1971 among the Dead Sea Scrolls.
- **John Wylands manuscript (P52):** Written c. AD 130. A fragment of St John's Gospel, chapter 18. Discovered in Egypt in 1920.
- **Chester-Beatty Papyrii:** Written c. AD 155 to some time in the 3rd century. Manuscript of 180 leaves of the Old Testament, 30 leaves from the Gospels and Acts and 20 leaves from St Paul and Revelation. Discovered in Egypt in 1931.
- **Bodmar Codex:** Written in Egypt between AD 130 and 200. A 154-page manuscript in Greek of John's Gospel. Contains in full the first 14 chapters and fragments of the remaining 7. Discovered in 1955.
- **Codex Vaticanus:** Written in the 4th century; Gen. 46:28 to Hebrews 9:14; Greek; Egyptian origin.
- **Codex Sinaiticus:** Written in the 4th century; a complete copy of the Greek Septuagint; discovered in 1859 in the monastery of St Catherine in Sinai.
- **Codex Alexandrinus:** Written in the early 5th century; a complete text of the Book of Revelation; Greek-Egyptian origin.
- **Codex Bezae:** Written in the 5th century; complete texts of all four Gospels plus Acts and a part of 3 John; Graeco-Roman.
- **Codex Ephraimi:** Written in the 5th century; contains all books of the New Testament except for 2 Thess. and 2 John.
- **Codex Amiatinus:** Written in the 7th century; earliest Latin copy of the Vulgate; produced in England as a gift for Pope Gregory II.

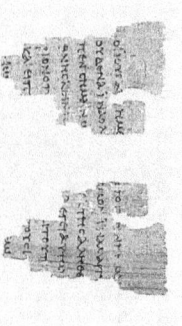

John Wylands Manuscript (P52)

COMPARISON WITH COPIES OF OTHER ANCIENT TEXTS

- **Homer's Iliad – 643** copies (earliest 10th century AD)
- **Sophocles – 193** (earliest mid-10th century AD)
- **Aristotle – 49** (earliest 10th century AD)
- **Tacitus – 280** (earliest 9th and 10th centuries AD)
- **Caesar – 10** (earliest 9th century AD)
- **Herodotus – 8** (earliest 10th century AD)
- **Pliny – 7** (earliest 15th century AD)

There exist no contradictions in any of the above between themselves or with modern-day versions of the Bible with respect to the person, life and sayings of Jesus. This is so even though among the 24,000+ different ancient manuscript copies of the New Testament textual variants exist in 6176 verses out of a total of 7948 (78%). These variations range from simple letters that change a word or its tense, to whole sentences that are missing or significantly different.

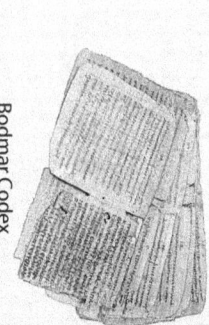

Bodmar Codex

No one seriously questions the authenticity of the above ancient texts even though there are so few and most only date back to the Middle Ages. How does the manuscript evidence for the Bible compare to manuscripts of other ancient non-biblical texts?

LESSON 11
Activity Sheet 22

DEBATING BOETTNER

There have been many anti-Catholic writers over the centuries. One of the most famous is the American Presbyterian minister, Loraine Boettner. In 1962, he published his most important work entitled, Roman Catholicism. The following is a quote from this book against Catholic 'traditions':

"The Church of Rome is following a set of traditions ... which by her own pronouncements she has elevated to equal authority with, or even superiority over the Word of God ... to justify doctrines and practices which have no basis in Scripture, or which are in violation of Scripture" (93).

Task 1: What are the main assertions made by Loraine Boettner in the above quote:

a. _____

b. _____

c. _____

Task 2: How would you respond to Boettner's accusations? (3 points)

_____
_____
_____
_____
_____
_____

LESSON 12
Activity Sheet 23

PARADISE LOST AND REGAINED

The Judeo-Christian narrative is a grand story in four parts that encapsulates the original creation (Paradise), original sin and expulsion (Paradise Lost), the redemption through Jesus' death and resurrection (Paradise Regained), and Jesus' Second Coming and Last Judgement (Paradise Confirmed).

PARADISE

"And God blessed them (Adam and Eve), and God said to them, 'Be fruitful and multiply, and fill the earth and subdue it ... and have dominion over every living thing'" (Gen. 1:28).

PARADISE LOST

"He drove out the man: and at the east of the garden of Eden he placed the cherubim, and a flaming sword which turned every way, to guard the way to the tree of Life" (Gen. 3:24).

PARADISE REGAINED

"When Jesus had received the vinegar, he said, 'It is finished'; and he bowed his head and gave up his spirit" (John 19:30).

PARADISE CONFIRMED

"For the trumpet will sound, and the dead will rise imperishable, and we shall be changed" (1 Cor. 15:52).

How is the Judeo-Christian narrative still relevant?

LESSON 12
Activity Sheet 24

COMPARING THE NARRATIVES

Column A lists the chief characteristics of secular, 'mini' and 'midi' narratives. Complete Column B, which should list the opposing Judeo-Christian characteristic for each point in Column A.

COLUMN A SECULAR, 'MINI', 'MIDI' NARRATIVES	COLUMN B JUDEO CHRISTIAN NARRATIVE
• The universe brought itself into existence. • Humans are the product of evolution/natural selection. • Good education, medicine/science conquers sin and death. • Life is cold, harsh and uncaring. • There is no meaning or purpose to life. • We create our own meaning and purpose. • Life is just about family, friends and myself. • Life is about me and my own pleasure. • 'You only live once.' • Humans can solve all their problems. • Pain and suffering are evils that should be avoided. • Life ends with death and the grave.	

Humans naturally desire a unified vision that provides meaning and purpose to all aspects of life. The Judeo-Christian meta-narrative more than any other meets this fundamental human need.

xxvi

LESSON 13
Activity Sheet 25

UNDERSTANDING THE TRINITY

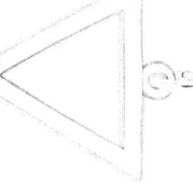

Symbols and art are helpful tools to understand the Trinity. Choose two of the above symbols/pictures and outline how each provides an insight(s) into understanding the Trinity. Are these symbols/pictures adequate to explain the mystery of the Trinity? Why/Why not?

_____
_____
_____
_____
_____
_____
_____
_____
_____
_____
_____
_____
_____
_____
_____
_____

LESSON 13
Activity Sheet 26

COMPARING THE CREEDS

THE NICENE CREED

I BELIEVE IN ONE GOD, THE FATHER ALMIGHTY, MAKER OF HEAVEN AND EARTH, OF ALL THINGS VISIBLE AND INVISIBLE.

I BELIEVE IN ONE LORD JESUS CHRIST, THE ONLY BEGOTTEN SON OF GOD, BORN OF THE FATHER BEFORE ALL AGES. GOD FROM GOD, LIGHT FROM LIGHT, TRUE GOD FROM TRUE GOD, BEGOTTEN, NOT MADE, CONSUBSTANTIAL WITH THE FATHER; THROUGH HIM ALL THINGS WERE MADE. FOR US MEN AND FOR OUR SALVATION HE CAME DOWN FROM HEAVEN, AND BY THE HOLY SPIRIT WAS INCARNATE OF THE VIRGIN MARY, AND BECAME MAN. FOR OUR SAKE HE WAS CRUCIFIED UNDER PONTIUS PILATE, HE SUFFERED DEATH AND WAS BURIED, AND ROSE AGAIN ON THE THIRD DAY IN ACCORDANCE WITH THE SCRIPTURES. HE ASCENDED INTO HEAVEN AND IS SEATED AT THE RIGHT HAND OF THE FATHER. HE WILL COME AGAIN IN GLORY TO JUDGE THE LIVING AND THE DEAD AND HIS KINGDOM WILL HAVE NO END.

I BELIEVE IN THE HOLY SPIRIT, THE LORD, THE GIVER OF LIFE, WHO PROCEEDS FROM THE FATHER AND THE SON, WHO WITH THE FATHER AND THE SON IS ADORED AND GLORIFIED, WHO HAS SPOKEN THROUGH THE PROPHETS.

I BELIEVE IN ONE, HOLY, CATHOLIC, AND APOSTOLIC CHURCH. I CONFESS ONE BAPTISM FOR THE FORGIVENESS OF SINS AND I LOOK FORWARD TO THE RESURRECTION OF THE DEAD AND THE LIFE OF THE WORLD TO COME.
AMEN.

THE APOSTLES' CREED

I BELIEVE IN GOD,
THE FATHER ALMIGHTY,
CREATOR OF HEAVEN AND EARTH.
AND IN JESUS CHRIST, HIS ONLY SON, OUR LORD,
WHO WAS CONCEIVED BY THE HOLY SPIRIT,
BORN OF THE VIRGIN MARY,
SUFFERED UNDER PONTIUS PILATE,
WAS CRUCIFIED, DIED AND WAS BURIED;
HE DESCENDED INTO HELL; ON THE THIRD DAY
HE ROSE AGAIN FROM THE DEAD;
HE ASCENDED INTO HEAVEN,
AND IS SEATED AT THE RIGHT HAND OF
GOD THE FATHER ALMIGHTY;
FROM THERE HE WILL COME TO JUDGE
THE LIVING AND THE DEAD.

I BELIEVE IN THE HOLY SPIRIT,
THE HOLY CATHOLIC CHURCH,
THE COMMUNION OF SAINTS,
THE FORGIVENESS OF SINS,
THE RESURRECTION OF THE BODY,
AND LIFE EVERLASTING.
AMEN.

The Apostles' Creed originates from the second century AD and was originally used as a profession of faith for converts being prepared for baptism. In the early fourth century AD, an Egyptian priest, Arius of Alexandria, began to teach that Jesus Christ was not truly God but only a creature "like in substance" to the Father. In response, the Church in AD 325, inspired by St Athanasius of Alexandria, drafted the Nicene Creed to affirm the divinity of Christ. Later, in AD 381, words were added to the Nicene Creed to affirm the divinity of the Holy Spirit against the teachings of Bishop Macedonius.

Identify the differences between the two Creeds. Highlight which parts of the Nicene Creed relate to God as Trinity, namely, identifies the Father, Son and Holy Spirit as Divine Persons. How significant are the differences?

LESSON 14
Activity Sheet 27

JESUS: GOD, MAN, OR BOTH?

Read through the following verses from the Old and New Testaments and identify which ones apparently support or oppose the divinity of Christ by placing the number of the quote in one of the respective boxes below. The first one is done to help start you off.

Is there a 'Catholic' explanation for the quotes in Column B?

1. "Truly, truly, I say to you, before Abraham was, I am" (John 8:58).
2. "For in him the whole fullness of deity dwells bodily" (Col. 2:9).
3. "I and the Father are one" (John 10:30).
4. "The woman said to him, 'Sir, I perceive that you are a prophet'" (John 4:19).
5. "My Lord and my God" (John 20:28).
6. "The Father is greater than I" (John 14:28).
7. "And this is eternal life, that they know thee the only true God, and Jesus Christ whom thou hast sent" (John 17:3).
8. "In the beginning was the Word, and the Word was with God, and the Word was God" (John 1:1-14).
9. "Behold, a virgin shall conceive and bear a son, and his name shall be called Immanuel (God with us)" (Matt. 1:23).

10. "For to us a child is born, to us a son is given; and the government will be upon his shoulder, and his name will be called 'Wonderful Counsellor, Mighty God, Everlasting Father, Prince of Peace'" (Is. 9:6).
11. "... they began glorifying God, saying, 'A great prophet has arisen among us!' and, 'God has visited his people!'" (Luke 7:16).
12. "... to them belong the patriarchs, and of their race, according to the flesh, is the Christ, who is God over all, blessed for ever. Amen" (Rom. 9:5).
13. "But of the Son he says, 'Your throne, O God, is for ever and ever, and the righteous sceptre is the sceptre of your kingdom'" (Heb. 1:8).

A. God/Equal to the Father/God & Man	B. Only a Creature, Man or Prophet
1.	1.

LESSON 15
Activity Sheet 28

WHO SAW JESUS CHRIST RISEN?

RECORDED APPEARANCES OF THE RISEN CHRIST

Mary, Mother of Jesus, in her home	Unrecorded
St Mary Magdalene and two other holy women at the tomb	Matt. 28:1-10; Mark 16:9-11; John 20:11-18
St Peter alone (place unknown)	Luke 24:34; 1 Cor. 15:5
Cleopas and friend on the road to Emmaus	Mark 16:12-13; Luke 24:13-35
Ten Apostles in the Cenacle on Easter Sunday evening	Luke 24:36-43; John 20:19-23
Ten Apostles in the Cenacle a week later with Doubting Thomas	John 20:24-29
Seven Apostles (including St Peter) at Lake Tiberias	John 21:1-23
Eleven Apostles in Galilee	Matt. 28:16-17; Mark 16:14-15
More than 500 believers together	1 Cor. 15:6
St James the Less alone (place unknown)	1 Cor. 15:7
120 believers (including the Mother of Jesus and the Apostles) on Mt Olivet	Luke 24:50-51; Acts 1:4-11
St Paul on the road to Damascus	Acts 9:5ff.

Jesus Christ appeared to many people after his death. Looking at the above table, answer the following questions:

1. At least how many people saw Jesus Christ after his resurrection?
2. How many times was the Risen Christ seen by more than one person at the same time?
3. What different places and times was the Risen Christ seen?
4. Which witnesses were Apostles, and which were not?
5. Which witness was not initially a follower of Jesus?
6. What does the above variety say about the reliability of the eyewitness accounts?

xxx

LESSON 15
Activity Sheet 29

THEORIES DENYING THE RESURRECTION OF JESUS

Draw a line matching the Title in Column A with the Theory in Column B and the Rebuttal in Column C.

COLUMN A TITLE OF THEORY	COLUMN B THEORY	COLUMN C REBUTTAL
Trash	Jesus only fainted on the Cross and later walked out of the tomb and met up with his disciples, who mistakenly thought he had resurrected.	According to psychologists, illusions are only imagined by one person at any given time, never simultaneously by a group of people.
Hallucination	The disciples only imagined that Jesus had risen from the dead, brought on by the grief of witnessing his arrest, torture and crucifixion.	The Gospels and St Paul record that Jesus was formally buried in the tomb of Joseph of Arimathea, a member of the Sanhedrin.
Swoon	The body of Jesus was thrown into an anonymous grave and was forgotten by his disciples until they claimed they saw him again.	Ancient records indicate that crucifixion was so brutal no one survived the piercing and later suffocation.

LESSON 16
Activity Sheet 30

'INFALLIBILITY' – WHAT IT DOES AND DOES NOT MEAN

The Catholic Church is both a 'mother' and 'teacher' (mater and magistra). The Church teaches to help guide all her children faithfully in the truth of Jesus Christ, to show them the way of happiness in this life and to guide them on the road towards eternal happiness (heaven) in the next. As head of the Church on earth ('Vicar of Christ' and successor to St Peter) the Pope is said to be 'infallible', that is, assisted by the Holy Spirit to ensure that he is a faithful teacher of truth. Does this mean, however, that the Pope is infallible with respect to everything he says and does? The short answer is, No. Four conditions need to be simultaneously satisfied. These four conditions are found below among other statements. Tick the four statements that correctly define and help understand the term 'infallibility' when used in relation to the Pope and put a cross through the other statements that do not.

THE POPE IS INFALLIBLE WHEN:

- Speaking 'ex cathedra', or from the Chair of Peter.
- Acting as the Head of the Church in Italy.
- Defining a question relating to faith or morals.
- Addressing the Universal Church.
- Speaking about politics to the people of America.
- Making a weather prediction.
- Talking to a news reporter on a plane.
- Intending to settle a question once and for all.

LESSON 17
Activity Sheet 31

COMMONALITIES AND COMMON GOOD

Complete the two tables by answering the following questions:

1. Besides our common humanity, what other matters, qualities, characteristics or practices do Catholics share with people of other faiths?
2. What areas can different religions co-operate for the common good?

COMMON CHARACTERISTICS	AREAS OF COOPERATION
 • • • • • • 	 • • • • • •

LESSON 17
Activity Sheet 32

THE 'NON–NEGOTIABLES'

List examples of important religious beliefs that cannot be 'watered down' for the sake of unity. Do this from a theistic, Christian and Catholic perspective. Some examples of 'not negotiable' beliefs are provided in each column as a starting point.

THEISTIC	CHRISTIAN	CATHOLIC
• Belief in one God	• Belief in the Trinity	• The authority of the Pope
•	• Belief in the divinity of Christ	• The Real Presence of Christ in the Eucharist
•	•	•
•	•	•
•	•	•
•	•	•
•	•	•
•	•	•

LESSON 18
Activity Sheet 33

THE 'ANGEL GAP'

WHAT IS THE ARGUMENT FOR THE EXISTENCE OF ANGELS?

The argument for the existence of angels is one of probability. The universe is full of a variety of creatures. Below humans there are higher animals such as lions and lower animals such as frogs. Below these there are plants, then lifeless minerals. These levels of creatures vary in life, power, glory and beauty. It appears to be a hierarchical world of fullness, with no gaps or missing rungs. Above humans there is God. But what exists between us and God? If there were no other creatures above humans, then there would seem to be a huge gap not found below humans. If there exist bodies without spirits (e.g., rocks) why can't there exist spirits without bodies (angels)? Spirits are no less possible than bodies.

What do you think of the above argument? Is it a good one? Can you improve upon it? Can you argue against it? Write your response in the space below.

GOD

ANGELS

HUMANKIND

HIGHER ANIMALS

LOWER ANIMALS

PLANTS

ROCKS

_____
_____
_____
_____
_____

LESSON 19
Activity Sheet 34

MIRACLES – ANSWERING THE CRITICS

Match the arguments against miracles in Column A with the appropriate responses in Column B.
The first one is done to help start you off.

COLUMN A ARGUMENTS AGAINST MIRACLES	COLUMN B APPROPRIATE RESPONSE
"Modern science can today provide reasonable and natural explanations for alleged miracles."	The laws of science tell us how nature normally works but they do not forbid exceptions.
	God did not design a faulty universe; he designed a universe where he is free to intervene when he so chooses.
"Belief in miracles contradicts the laws of nature and science which are fixed and unchangeable."	Science has actually verified, rather than disproved, many miracle accounts.
	Science has explained natural events such as thunderbolts but not the miracles of Jesus in the New Testament.
"Belief in miracles insults God by suggesting that he is an incompetent architect who needs to intervene in nature's regular workings."	As the author of nature, God has the power to suspend its fixed laws if he so chooses.
	God does not perform miracles to repair a faulty universe but to aid humans impacted by a properly functioning universe.

LESSON 20
Activity Sheet 35

THE 'TWO WINGS' OF FAITH AND REASON

Why do you think Pope St John Paul II chose to represent the relationship between faith and reason by two wings?

_____

How does the image of a bird with two wings symbolise the inseparability of faith and reason?

_____

With two wings a bird flies with harmonious balance. What does this say about a person who lives by faith and reason?

_____

In what ways would a person's life be imbalanced if it had only one wing, that is, if it lived only by faith or only by reason?

_____
_____
_____

LESSON 20
Activity Sheet 36

FAITH SEEKING UNDERSTANDING

ST ANSELM
1033–1109 AD

Two famous Catholic saints long ago considered the relationship between faith and reason. In the early 5th century, St Augustine of Hippo said, "Believe so that you may understand"; in the 11th century, St Anselm of Canterbury spoke about, "Faith seeking understanding".

ST AUGUSTINE
354 – 430 AD

"Believe so that you may understand."

"Faith seeking understanding."

Discussion questions: What are St Augustine and St Anselm trying to say? Are their thoughts in agreement or in contradiction?

LESSON 21
Activity Sheet 37

OBJECTIVE VS SUBJECTIVE

Consider the ten statements listed below and categorise each by placing a cross (X) in one of the three columns, Objective Truth, Subjective Truth, Subjective Non-Truth. What are the reasons for your decisions?

STATEMENT	OBJECTIVE TRUTH	SUBJECTIVE TRUTH	SUBJECTIVE NON-TRUTH
1. I am feeling hot.			
2. We live on the planet earth.			
3. I am really a cat.			
4. I believe everything is true.			
5. Red is my favourite colour.			
6. Humans are either male or female.			
7. I like chocolate ice cream.			
8. The earth revolves around the sun.			
9. $2 + 2 = 4$.			
10. There is no objective truth.			

LESSON 21
Activity Sheet 38

HOW DO WE KNOW?

Using the Word Bank below, fill the gaps relating to our knowing powers, where these powers are located in the human person, and what each of these powers can do.

CATEGORY	POWER	LOCATED	WHAT POWER CAN DO
External Sense	Taste		To perceive or experience a flavour
External Sense		Skin	To perceive physical objects through physical contact
External Sense	Smell		To detect odours and aromas around us
External Sense	Hear	Ears	
External Sense	Sight	Eyes	To receive light waves
External Sense	Memory		Stores the information received through the five senses
External Sense	Imagination	Brain	Recalls individual images received through the five senses
Internal Sense		Brain	Co-ordinates the information received through the five senses
Internal Sense	Estimative Sense		
Spiritual Power		Brain	The power to know, understand, judge
Spiritual Power	Will	Soul	The power to love the known good

WORD BANK

External Sense   Soul   Unifying Sense   Tongue   Brain   To receive sound waves   Touch   Nose
Internal Sense   Intellect   Alerts us instinctively to what is safe or harmful

Humans receive data from the outside world through the five external senses of taste, touch, smell, hearing, sight. This data then comes under the influence of the four internal senses of imagination, memory, unifying sense and estimative sense. The intellect then understands the meaning of this data and the will loves what the intellect understands to be good. Realism believes that the information we receive through the external senses is real, our perception of it is accurate, and that the intellect understands this information correctly, allowing us to love properly. This cannot be proven absolutely but to deny the same would make life impossible.

LESSON 22
Activity Sheet 39

WHY WE NEED MORAL ABSOLUTES

Read through the list of actions outlined in Column A and place an X in either Column B or C stating whether the action is always and everywhere right or wrong.

COLUMN A ACTIONS	COLUMN B ALWAYS RIGHT	COLUMN C ALWAYS WRONG
Worshipping more than one God		
Having an abortion		
Telling the truth under oath		
Cheating on your tax returns		
Respecting your parents		
Taking a bribe		
Taking drugs		
Abstaining from sexual activity until marriage		
Committing adultery		
Selling children into slavery		
To drive a car safely		

In your opinion, what would be the consequences for society if morality was changeable or its observance optional?

LESSON 23
Activity Sheet 40

PHYSICAL AND MORAL NATURAL LAWS

Read through the left-hand column and designate with an X whether the listed human actions are governed by physical or moral natural laws.

HUMAN ACTION	PHYSICAL NATURAL LAWS	MORAL NATURAL LAWS
Eating		
Growing		
Speaking truth or lies		
Contracepting		
Reproducing		
Loving neighbour		
Walking		
Judging		
Stealing		
Hearing		

NB: As natures do not change, the natural laws governing natures do not change. All human actions and laws should be consistent with natural laws. When humans freely act contrary to moral natural laws they commit sin.

xlii

LESSON 24
Activity Sheet 41

THE TEN COMMANDMENTS – A COMPLETE WAY OF LIVING

Place the number of the Commandment in Column A with the aspect of human life it governs. Commandment 9 is done to help start you off. Which aspects of life are covered by multiple Commandments? Are there any aspects of life the Commandments do not cover?

COLUMN A COMMANDMENTS	WORSHIP	LIFE	MARRIAGE	FAMILY	PROPERTY	JUSTICE AND TRUTH
1. I am the Lord your God, who brought you out of the land of Egypt, out of the house of bondage. You shall have no other gods before me.						
2. You shall not take the name of the Lord your God in vain						
3. Remember the Sabbath day, to keep it holy						
4. Honour your father and your mother						
5. You shall not kill						
6. You shall not commit adultery						
7. You shall not steal						
8. You shall not bear false witness against your neighbour						
9. You shall not covet your neighbour's wife			9	9		
10. You shall not covet your neighbour's goods						

LESSON 24

Activity Sheet 42

THE TEN COMMANDMENTS — LAWS OF LIBERTY

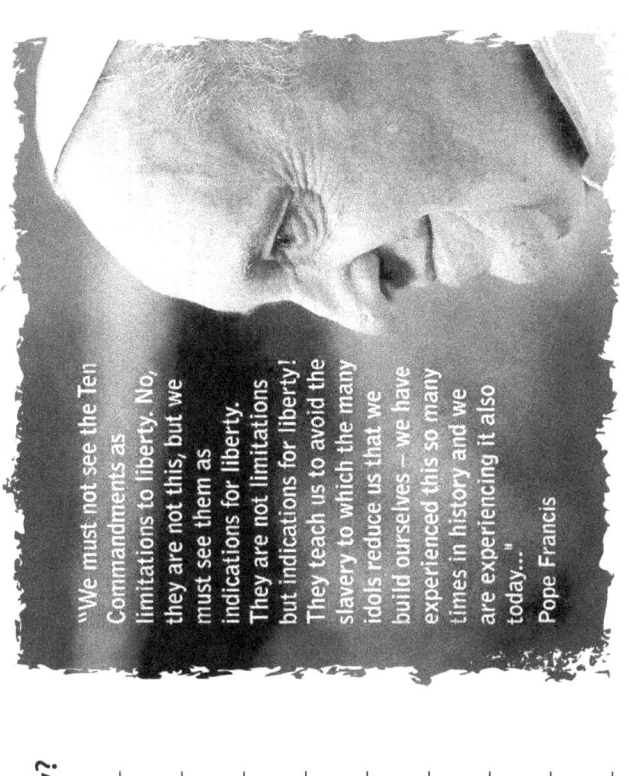

"We must not see the Ten Commandments as limitations to liberty. No, they are not this, but we must see them as indications for liberty. They are not limitations but indications for liberty! They teach us to avoid the slavery to which the many idols reduce us so that we build ourselves — we have experienced this so many times in history and we are experiencing it also today..."
Pope Francis

What does Pope Francis say about the Ten Commandments and human liberty?
Why do you think he says that the Ten Commandments free, rather than restrict, humanity?

_____
_____
_____
_____
_____
_____
_____
_____

Invite the students in the space provided to write down any three new commandments they think are necessary for today.

1. _____

2. _____

3. _____

xliv

LESSON 25
Activity Sheet 43

CONSCIENCE — OUR MOST SECRET CORE

DEFINITION OF CONSCIENCE:

"Conscience is people's most secret core, and their sanctuary. There they are alone with God whose voice echoes in their depths."

(Vatican II, *Gaudium et Spes*, 16).

WHAT DOES CONSCIENCE DO?

(a) It detects a law that holds us to obedience.
(b) It helps us make a judgement about the rightness or wrongness of a specific action.
(c) It calls us to do what is good and to avoid what is evil ("do this, shun that").
(d) It confirms or convicts us when we do or fail to do what we know to be right ('good' or 'guilty' conscience).

Why do you think the voice of conscience is equivalent to the voice of God?

_____

_____

LESSON 26
Activity Sheet 44

SACRAMENTS IN SCRIPTURE

The Catholic Church believes there are seven sacraments: Baptism, Confirmation, the Eucharist, Reconciliation, Anointing of the Sick, Holy Orders and Holy Matrimony. Read through the following quotes from the New Testament and in the spaces provided write which sacrament you think each quote relates to.

(a) "... when the apostles at Jerusalem heard that Samaria had received the word of God, they sent to them Peter and John, who came down and prayed for them that they might receive the Holy Spirit; for it had not yet fallen on any of them, but they had only been baptized in the name of the Lord Jesus. Then they laid their hands on them and they received the Holy Spirit" (Acts 8:14-17).

(b) "Hence I remind you to rekindle the gift of God that is within you through the laying on of my hands ... " (2 Tim. 1:6).

(c) "Is any among you sick? Let him call for the elders of the church, and let them pray over him, anointing him with oil in the name of the Lord; and the prayer of faith will save the sick man, and the Lord will raise him up; and if he has committed sins, he will be forgiven" (James 5:14-15).

(d) "Go therefore and make disciples of all nations, baptizing them in the name of the Father and of the Son and of the Holy Spirit" (Matt. 28:19).

(e) "What therefore God has joined together, let not man put asunder" (Matt. 19:6).

(f) "Now as they were eating, Jesus took bread, and blessed, and broke it, and gave it to the disciples and said, 'Take, eat; this is my body.' And he took a cup, and when he had given thanks he gave it to them, saying, 'Drink of it, all of you; for this is my blood of the covenant, which is poured out for many for the forgiveness of sins'" (Matt. 26:26-28).

(g) "Peace be with you. As the Father has sent me, even so I send you.' And when he had said this, he breathed on them, and said to them, 'Receive the Holy Spirit. If you forgive the sins of any, they are forgiven; if you retain the sins of any, they are retained" (John 20:21-23).

(a) _____
(b) _____
(c) _____
(d) _____
(e) _____
(f) _____
(g) _____

Write one paragraph as to what the following passage from the Old Testament book of Isaiah may mean and why it may relate to the sacraments: *"With joy you will draw water from the wells of salvation"* (Is. 12:3).

_____
_____
_____
_____

LESSON 26
Activity Sheet 45

SACRAMENTS FOR LIFE

Insert the name of the appropriate sacrament into Column B

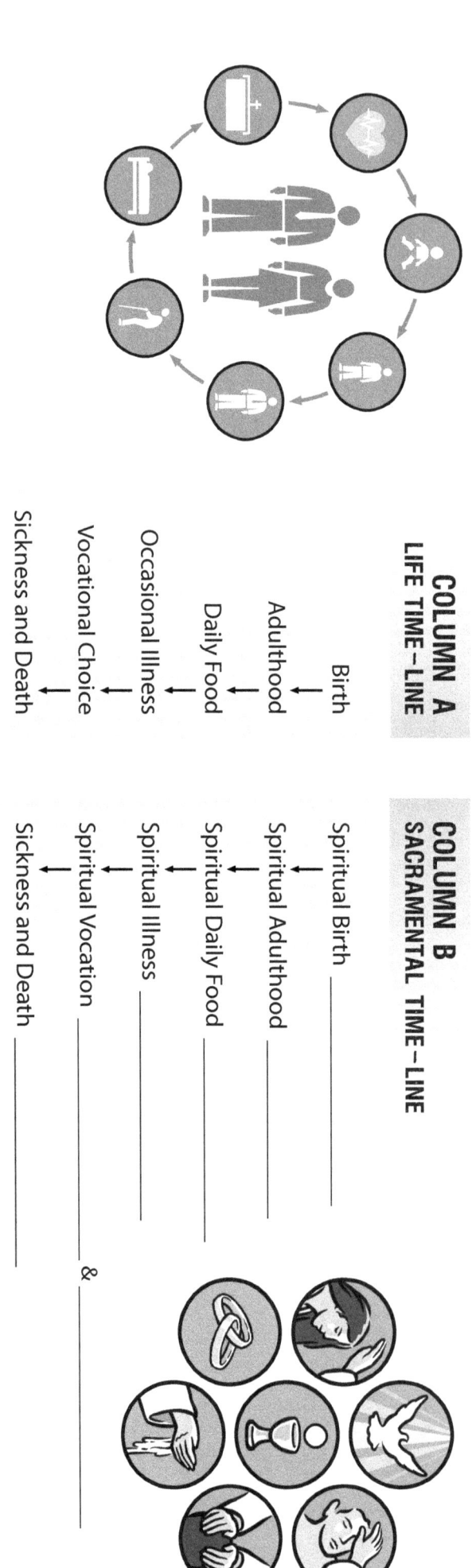

COLUMN A LIFE TIME – LINE	COLUMN B SACRAMENTAL TIME – LINE
Birth	Spiritual Birth _____
Adulthood	Spiritual Adulthood _____
Daily Food	Spiritual Daily Food _____
Occasional Illness	Spiritual Illness _____
Vocational Choice	Spiritual Vocation _____ & _____
Sickness and Death	Sickness and Death _____

The sacraments are ordered to parallel the human life cycle and its spiritual journey towards the heavenly Kingdom. We are all born and there is a sacrament for spiritual birth (Baptism). We grow into adults and there is a sacrament of spiritual adulthood (Confirmation). We require daily food to live and there is a sacrament that provides daily heavenly food for the spiritual journey (the Eucharist). We fall sick from time to time and there is a sacrament that heals us when we fall spiritually sick (Reconciliation). As adults we make vocational choices and there are two sacraments of spiritual vocation (Holy Matrimony and Holy Orders). We all eventually pass from this world and there is a sacrament to assist believers to cross-over into the next life (Anointing of the Sick). This ordering reflects both God's wisdom and his care for the human family.

xlvii

LESSON 27
Activity Sheet 46

THE LAST SUPPER – A SACRIFICE?

Read through the three quotes from the Old and New Testaments and then the three quotes from the first and second-century early Church Fathers. Write out those words/phrases which emphasise sacrifice.

"'I have no pleasure in you, says the Lord of hosts, and I will not accept an offering from your hand. For from the rising of the sun to its setting my name is great among the nations, and in every place incense is offered to my name, and a pure offering; for my name is great among the nations, says the Lord of hosts'" (Malachi 1:10-11).

"And he took bread, and when he had given thanks he broke it and gave it to them saying, 'This is my body which is given for you. Do this in remembrance of me.' And likewise the cup after supper, saying, 'This cup which is poured out for you is the new covenant in my blood'" (Luke 22:19-20).

"We have an altar from which those who serve the tent have no right to eat" (Hebrews 13:10).

The Didache 14, 1 (inter AD 90-150)

"Assemble on the Lord's Day, and break bread and offer the Eucharist. But first make confession of your faults, so that your sacrifice may be a pure one . . . . For this is the offering of which the Lord has said, 'Everywhere and always bring me a sacrifice that is undefiled, for I am a great king, says the Lord and my name is the wonder of nations.'"

St Ignatius of Antioch, Letter to the Philadelphians 4, 1 (c. AD 110)

"Take care, then, to use one Eucharist, so that whatever you do, you do according to God: for there is one flesh of Our Lord Jesus Christ, and one cup in the union of His Blood; one altar, as there is one bishop with the presbyterium and my fellow servants, the deacons."

St Irenaeus of Lyons, Against Heresies 4, 17, 5 (c. AD 180)

"He took that created thing, bread, and gave thanks and said, 'This is My Body.' And the cup likewise, which is part of that creation to which we belong, he confessed to be His Blood, and taught the new oblation of the new covenant, which the Church, receiving from the Apostles, offers to God throughout the world . . . . concerning which Malachi, among the twelve prophets thus spoke beforehand."

_____

_____

The Catholic Mass celebrated today is the same event celebrated by the first and second-century Christians in obedience to Christ's command at the Last Supper. ("*Do this in memory of me*") and is the fulfilment of the prophecy of the Old Testament prophet Malachi, both of which contain sacrificial language.

LESSON 27
Activity Sheet 47

PARTICIPATING IN THE PRIESTHOOD OF CHRIST

Read through the following quotes from the Old and New Testaments and construct an argument for an ordained ministerial priesthood endowed with various functions. Identify prophecy, repeating the Last Supper, ordination, order, forgiving sins, anointing the sick.

How does this priesthood continue Christ's saving work in the world?

"And they shall bring all your brethren from all the nations as an offering to the Lord, upon horses, and in chariots, and in litters, and upon mules, and upon dromedaries, to my holy mountain Jerusalem, says the Lord, just as the Israelites bring their cereal offering in a clean vessel to the house of the Lord. And some of them also I will take for priests and for Levites, says the Lord" **(Isaiah 66:20-21)**.

"And he took bread, and when he had given thanks he broke it and gave it to them, saying, 'This is my body which is given for you. Do this in remembrance of me.' And likewise the cup after supper, saying, 'This cup which is poured out for you is the new covenant in my blood'" **(Luke 22:19-20)**.

"While they were worshipping the Lord and fasting, the Holy Spirit said, 'Set apart for me Barnabas and Saul for the work to which I have called them.' Then after fasting and praying they laid their hands on them and sent them off. So, being sent out by the Holy Spirit, they went down to Seleucia; and from there they sailed to Cyprus" **(Acts 13:2-4)**.

"Jesus has gone as a forerunner on our behalf, having become a high priest for ever after the order of Melchizedek" **(Heb. 6:20)**.

"As the Father has sent me, even so I send you ... Receive the Holy Spirit. If you forgive the sins of any, they are forgiven; if you retain the sins of any, they are retained" **(John 20:21-23)**.

"Is any among you sick? Let him call for the elders of the church, and let them pray over him, anointing him with oil in the name of the Lord; and the prayer of faith will save the sick man, and the Lord will raise him up; and if he has committed sins, he will be forgiven" **(James 5:14-15)**.

LESSON 28
Activity Sheet 48

THE 'BREAD OF LIFE' DISCOURSE

Read the following passage and participate in the classroom discussion led by your teacher.

JOHN 6:27, 47 – 69:

27 Do not labour for the food which perishes, but for the food which endures to eternal life, which the Son of man will give to you; for on him has God set his seal . . . 47 "Truly, truly, I say to you, he who believes has eternal life. 48 I am the bread of life. 49 Your fathers ate the manna in the wilderness, and they died. 50 This is the bread which comes down from heaven, that a man may eat of it and not die. 51 I am the living bread which came down from heaven; if any one eats of this bread, he will live forever; and the bread which I shall give for the life of the world is my flesh." 52 The Jews then disputed among themselves, saying, "How can this man give us his flesh to eat?" 53 So Jesus said to them, "Truly, truly, I say to you, unless you eat the flesh of the Son of man and drink his blood, you have no life in you; 54 He who eats my flesh and drinks my blood has eternal life, and I will raise him up at the last day. 55 For my flesh is food indeed, and my blood is drink indeed. 56 He who eats my flesh and drinks my blood abides in me, and I in him. 57 As the living Father sent me, and I live because of the Father, so he who eats me will live because of me. 58 This is the bread which came down from heaven, not such as the fathers ate and died; he who eats this bread will live for ever." 59 This he said in the synagogue, as he taught at Capernaum. 60 Many of his disciples, when they heard it, said, "This is a hard saying; who can listen to it?" 61 But Jesus, knowing in himself that the disciples murmured at it, said to them, "Do you take offence at this? 62 Then what if you were to see the Son of man ascending where he was before? 63 It is the spirit that gives life, the flesh is of no avail; the words that I have spoken to you are spirit and life. 64 But there are some of you that do not believe." For Jesus knew from the first who those were that did not believe, and who it was that would betray him. 65 And he said, "This is why I told you that no one can come to me unless it is granted him by the Father." 66 After this many of his disciples drew back and no longer went about with him. 67 Jesus said to the twelve, "Do you also wish to go away?" 68 Simon Peter answered him, "Lord, to whom shall we go? You have the words of eternal life; 69 and we have believed, and have come to know, that you are the Holy One of God."

LESSON 28
Activity Sheet 49

FATHERS AND FAVOURS

There are many quotes from the early Church Fathers and accounts of Eucharistic miracles that testify to the Real Presence of Christ in the Eucharist. Below are two examples of each.

ST IGNATIUS OF ANTIOCH, *LETTER TO THE SMYRNAEANS* 7, 1 (C. AD 110)

"They abstain from the Eucharist and from prayer, because they do not confess that the Eucharist is the Flesh of our Saviour Jesus Christ, Flesh which suffered for our sins and which the Father, in his goodness, raised up again. They who deny the gift of God are perishing in their disputes."

ST JUSTIN MARTYR, *FIRST APOLOGY* 66 (C. AD 155)

"For not as common bread nor common drink do we receive these; but since Jesus Christ our Saviour was made incarnate by the word of God and had both flesh and blood for our salvation, so too, as we have been taught, the food which has been made into the Eucharist by the Eucharistic prayer set down by him, and by the change of which our blood and flesh is nourished is both the flesh and the blood of that incarnate Jesus ... The Apostles, in the Memoirs which they produced, which are called Gospels, have thus passed on that which was enjoined upon them: that Jesus took bread and, having given thanks, said, 'Do this in remembrance of Me; this is My Body.' And in like manner, taking the cup, and having given thanks, he said, 'This is My Blood.' And he imparted this to them only."

  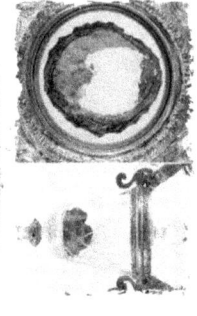 

THE MIRACLE OF LANCIANO (C. AD 700)

During Mass celebrated by a priest-monk of the Order of St Basil around the year 700, the Host suddenly turned into a circle of human flesh and the wine turned into visible human blood. The latter eventually dried into five stone-sized pellets. For the next twelve centuries the Host and the pellets remained housed in an elaborate reliquary in the town of Lanciano, Italy. In 1971, a detailed medical and scientific investigation found that the Host was indeed human heart muscle and the pellets were human blood, both blood type AB. This miracle in currently housed and viewable in the Tabernacle above the high altar of the Church of St Francis in Lanciano.

THE MIRACLE OF BOLSENA, (AD 1263)

"In 1263, a German priest, Peter of Prague, stopped at Bolsena while on pilgrimage to Rome. He was a pious priest but was troubled with doubts about the Real Presence of Christ in the Eucharist. While celebrating Mass in the church of St Christina, blood began to drip from the Host and trickle over his hands onto the altar and the corporal. Fr Peter was confused and attempted to hide the blood, but then ended the Mass and made his way to the neighbouring city of Orvieto, where Pope Urban IV was then residing. The Pope heard Fr Peter's account and absolved him and then ordered an immediate investigation. When all the facts were verified, the Pope ordered that the Host and the blood-stained corporal be brought to Orvieto. Amid great pomp, the relics were placed in the cathedral. One year later, Urban IV instituted the feast of Corpus Christi. The linen corporal bearing the spots of blood is still enshrined and exhibited in the Cathedral of Orvieto, while the blood stains are still visible on the paved floor of the church of St Christina in Bolsena.

LESSON 29
Activity Sheet 50

GROUNDS FOR ANNULMENTS

Look at each of the circumstances listed below and place a tick against those that would provide grounds for an annulment and a cross against those that would not.

CIRCUMSTANCES	GROUND FOR ANNULMENT YES OR NO?
Marrying below the age of consent.	
Not getting on with the mother-in-law.	
Not understanding what marriage is.	
Psychological incapacity.	
Arguing all the time.	
Growing apart.	
Marrying a brother or sister.	
Marrying someone who is already validly married.	
Premature aging.	
Marital consent obtained through force, fear, deceit or fraud.	
Being drunk at the time of the marriage.	
An intention at the time of marriage never to have children.	
Adultery.	
An intention at the time of marriage not to be faithful or marry for life.	
The family business going broke after marriage.	

An annulment does not end a valid sacramental marriage, it is a declaration by the Church that, due to the absence of one or more necessary prerequisites on the day of the wedding vows, no valid marriage took place.

LESSON 30
Activity Sheet 51

HUMAN LIFE – WHEN DOES IT BEGIN?

Those who hold a 'pro-choice' position concerning abortion often claim that what is being terminated is merely a foetus, it does not yet know anything or feel any pain and, therefore, it is not yet a human being deserving of human rights, etc. Those who hold 'pro-life' views believe that life begins at conception, there exists a human life/soul from that moment onwards with the right to life and all other human rights, and that no one, including the mother, has the right to end that life. The following are arguments from Scripture, reason and science concerning the beginning of human life and the status of the foetus.

ARGUMENTS FROM SCRIPTURE . . .

"For thou didst form my inward parts, thou didst knit me together in my mother's womb" (Ps. 139:13).

"Now the word of the Lord came to me saying, 'Before I formed you in the womb I knew you, and before you were born I consecrated you; I appointed you a prophet to the nations'" (Jer.1:4-5).

"When Elizabeth heard Mary's greeting, the child leaped in her womb. And Elizabeth was filled with the Holy Spirit and exclaimed with a loud cry, 'Blessed are you among women, and blessed is the fruit of your womb. And why has this happened to me, that the mother of my Lord comes to me?'" (Luke 1:41-42).

ARGUMENTS FROM REASON . . .

The foetus begins to grow at conception . . .
If it is growing, isn't it alive?
If it has human parents, isn't it human?
If it is human, doesn't it have rights?
If it has rights, doesn't that include the right to life?
If it has the right to life, doesn't that include the time when it is still in the womb?

ARGUMENTS FROM SCIENCE . . .

The foetus in the mother's womb . . .
... has a human genetic code
... has a pumping heart
... has a circulatory system
... has a nervous system
... has electrical signals coming from and to the brain.

After reading the above arguments compose a one-paragraph response to the following question, "Isn't a foetus just a parasite?"

_____
_____
_____
_____

LESSON 30
Activity Sheet 52

IN-VITRO FERTILISATION – PRO-LIFE OR PROBLEMATIC?

The Catholic Church supports the use of reproductive technologies providing they do not lead to the separation of the 'unitive and procreative', meaning they assist but do not replace the natural way of conceiving children via sexual intercourse between the husband and wife. One such technology is in-vitro fertilisation (IVF). Note the various parts of the IVF process and write down reasons why each is morally problematic.

IVF ACTION	MORAL PROBLEMS INVOLVED
Collecting sperm from the husband.	
Fertilising the egg with sperm in a petrie dish.	
Fertilising the wife's egg with sperm from someone other than the husband.	
Fertilising multiple eggs and discarding the ones that are not required.	
Fertilising multiple eggs and freezing them indefinitely or experimenting on the ones that are not required.	
Removing and discarding unwanted fertilised eggs from the womb of the mother.	

Catholic couples should always work with nature when seeking to have children and if children are still not forthcoming to accept such as a spiritual cross and part of God's will for them. Other options for such couples may include fostering or adopting children or giving their lives in service to others.

LESSON 31
Activity Sheet 53

THE DEATH PENALTY – FOR OR AGAINST?

What are the arguments for and against the death penalty? Write your preferred opinions in one of the columns below.

ARGUMENTS FOR	ARGUMENTS AGAINST

Note: Pope St John Paul II, *Evangelium Vitae*, 56:

"This is the context in which to place the problem of the death penalty... The primary purpose of the punishment which society inflicts is to redress the disorder caused by the offence. Public authority must redress the violation of personal and social rights by imposing on the offender an adequate punishment for the crime... In this way authority also fulfils the purpose of defending public order and ensuring people's safety... It is clear that, for these purposes to be achieved, the nature and extent of the punishment must be carefully evaluated and decided upon, and ought not go to the extreme of executing the offender except in cases of absolute necessity: in other words, when it would not be possible otherwise to defend society. Today however, as a result of steady improvements in the organization of the penal system, such cases are very rare, if not practically non-existent."

Do the above words of Pope St John Paul II make any sense? Do they change your thinking on the issue of the death penalty?

_____
_____
_____

LESSON 32

Activity Sheet 54

COMPARING JESUS AND MARY – ARE THEY EQUAL?

Look at the two columns under the respective headings of Jesus and Mary. At first instance they look very similar. Are they really the same?

JESUS	MARY
God	Mother of God
Sinless	Conceived without sin
Virgin	Perpetual Virgin
Ascended into Heaven	Assumed into Heaven
King of Heaven	Queen of Heaven

By way of example, focus on two of Mary's qualities – "Mother of God" and "Conceived without sin." Acknowledging how they appear to be very similar to the corresponding entries in the Jesus column ("God" and "Sinless"), write down below how you as a Catholic would argue that they are nevertheless very different.

_____

_____

N.B.: It should be a matter of celebration that Mary is similar to Jesus in so many ways. This does not mean that Mary is equal to Jesus or in any sense divine. It is the Christian vocation to imitate Jesus; and Mary is the greatest of all Christians. Every privilege Mary possesses was given to her by God and at all times she remains the faithful and obedient *"handmaid of the Lord"* (Luke 1:38).

LESSON 32
Activity Sheet 55

MARY'S IMMACULATE CONCEPTION – ANSWERING THE OBJECTIONS

Read through the various objections to Mary's Immaculate Conception and the Catholic responses to each:

(a) "Believing that Mary was sinless makes her divine like Jesus" Answer – Mary was not the first human to be created without sin. Adam and Eve were so created before they sinned. By believing in Mary's sinlessness, Catholics believe she was the 'New Eve', not divine like Jesus.

(b) "Not even St Thomas Aquinas, the greatest Catholic theologian and philosopher, believed in the Immaculate Conception!" Answer – St Thomas' objections to the Immaculate Conception of Mary were more biological than theological. He believed that the human soul was infused some time after conception, not at the moment of conception. Consequently, as Mary had yet no soul, she could not have received sanctifying grace at conception (hence, no immaculate conception). St Thomas, nevertheless, believed that Mary was born free of all sin and remained sinless all her life.

(c) "The Immaculate Conception of Mary has no support in Scripture" Answer – Note the following two verses:
"I will put enmity between you and the woman, and between your seed and her seed; he shall bruise your head, and you shall bruise his heel" (Gen. 3:15).
"And he came to her and said, 'Hail, full of grace, the Lord is with you!'" (Luke 1:28).
Mary fulfilled these two verses. How? She is the "woman" ("New Eve") in Gen. 3 that will be at "enmity" with the Devil. The enmity God places between the two is sanctifying grace, which frees Mary from sin and the dominion of the Devil. How do we know God did this for Mary? We know from the words of the Angel Gabriel in Luke 1, who greets Mary as "full of grace." God must have placed Mary fully in grace from the moment of her conception to be always at enmity with the Devil.

(d) "The Immaculate Conception makes Mary exempt from needing a Redeemer" Answer – Being a daughter of Adam, Mary needed redemption. Mary's Immaculate Conception, far from exempting her from needing a redeemer, was how God redeemed her. It was an application of the merits of Jesus Christ applied to her in advance, namely, redemption by pre-emption. One can be cured of a disease after having contracted it or one can be spared of that same disease by being inoculated against it in advance. Mary's redemption was affected in this latter manner, sparing her from ever being under the dominion of Satan.

(e) "St Paul in Romans 3 says 'All have sinned and fallen short of the glory of God'. Mary is one of the 'all'." Answer – St Paul's words in Romans 3 do not refer to individuals being in sin but to all races and specifically mentions the Jews and Greeks. While races may be estranged from God, God can sanctify individuals within those races as exceptions. For example, the prophets Jeremiah (Jer. 1:5) and John the Baptist (Luke 1:41) were purified of sin in their mother's wombs. Mary was another and more perfect exception.

Conclusion: Mary's Immaculate Conception was not something that was necessary, it was something that was appropriate, appropriate for Mary as the Mother of God, and appropriate for Jesus who, as King of kings, should dwell in an earthly house free from the dominion of the Devil.

LESSON 33
Activity Sheet 56

THE BROTHERS OF JESUS – WHO ARE THEY?

Read the following passage from Matthew 13:54-57:

"Where did this man get this wisdom and these mighty works? Is not this the carpenter's son? Is not his mother called Mary? And are not his brethren James and Joseph and Simon and Judas? And are not all his sisters with us? Where then did this man get all this?' And they took offence at him."

According to this passage, it seems that Jesus had brothers and sisters. Therefore, Mary could not have remained a virgin all her life and the Catholic dogma of her perpetual virginity is false. Who really are the brothers (and sisters) of Jesus? To find out, read the seven points below and from points 5 to 7 complete Column C, the family of Mary and Clopas.

1. There was an Apostle named James who was "the Lord's brother" **(Gal. 1:19)**.
2. There were two Apostles named James (the Greater & Lesser), their fathers were Zebedee and Clopas (not St Joseph) **(Matt. 10:2; Mark 3:16)**.
3. Mary the mother of Jesus had a "sister" (or sister-in-law) named "Mary the wife of Clopas" **(John 19:25)**.
4. The second century Christian Church historian, Hegesippus, called Clopas "an uncle of the Lord" (i.e., brother of St Joseph).
5. The Apostle James the Less was the son of Clopas **(Matt. 10:2)** and Mary **(Mark 15:40)**.
6. James the Less had a brother named Joseph (Mark 15:40) and another brother named Jude **(Jude 1:1)**.
7. The Church historian, Hegesippus, also says that Simon was "the son of Clopas … a kinsman of the Lord").

COLUMN A 'CATHOLIC HOLY FAMILY'	COLUMN B 'PROTESTANT HOLY FAMILY'	COLUMN C 'FAMILY OF MARY AND CLOPAS'
Mary and Joseph	Mary and Joseph	Mary (sister-in-law to the Virgin Mary)
Jesus	Jesus	Clopas (brother of St Joseph)
	James	
	Joseph	
	Simon	
	Judas	
	(Sisters)	(Sisters?)

If the Protestant Holy Family is the true one, then we end up with the strange scenario whereby Jesus had four brothers named James, Joseph, Simon and Judas as well as four male first cousins with precisely the same names. The reality, however, is that Jesus' four brothers in Matt. 13:54-57 are his first cousins, children of Mary and Clopas, not Mary and St Joseph. It is a case of how in the ancient world the word "brethren" (or "brothers") also meant first cousin.

LESSON 34
Activity Sheet 57

ARE THE DEAD REALLY DEAD?

Read Matthew 17:1-3, Hebrews 12:1 and Revelation 6:9-11 and construct an argument for why the dead in Christ are still alive, know what is happening on earth, and can pray for us. Afterwards, read the two paragraphs below which explain how the saints can hear multiple prayers simultaneously and why praying to the saints is not the same as necromancy.

"And after six days Jesus took with him Peter and James and John his brother, and led them up a high mountain apart. And he was transfigured before them, and his face shone like the sun, and his garments became white as light. And behold, there appeared to them Moses and Elijah, talking with him" **(Matt. 17:1-3)**.

(Referring to the many deceased heroes of the Old Testament):
"Therefore, since we are surrounded by so great a cloud of witnesses" **(Heb. 12:1)**.

"When he opened the fifth seal, I saw under the altar the souls of those who had been slain for the word of God and for the witness they had borne; they cried out with a loud voice, 'O sovereign Lord, holy and true, how long before thou wilt judge and avenge our blood on those who dwell upon the earth?'" **(Rev. 6:9-11)**.

_____
_____
_____
_____
_____

How can a saint respond to the petitions of thousands of different people at the same time? Only God who is 'omniscient' can do this.
Answer: God grants the saints supernatural knowledge of all the petitions directed to them, that is, he makes them 'multiscient.'

Isn't praying to the saints and asking for their prayers akin to contacting the dead, or necromancy, something forbidden in Scripture (Deut. 18:9-12)?
Answer: Praying to the saints does not amount to necromancy, as the latter involves using magic or the occult to directly contact or 'conjure up' the dead for information. This was the sin of King Saul, who engaged the witch of Endor to summon the soul of the prophet Samuel to obtain military and spiritual advice from him (1 Sam. 28:3-20).

LESSON 35
Activity Sheet 58

PROVING PURGATORY

Read the various quotes from Scripture and identify with a tick or cross which ones do/do not provide proof for the existence of a place in the afterlife where people go to complete temporal punishment or receive final purification. Circle the words in each quote which influenced your decision.

| TICK | CROSS | | TICK | CROSS |

(a) *"But if he was looking to the splendid reward that is laid up for those who fall asleep in godliness, it was a holy and pious thought. Therefore he made atonement for the dead, that they might be delivered from their sin"* **(2 Macc. 12:44-45)**.

(b) *"Therefore, do not pronounce judgment before the time, before the Lord comes, who will bring to light the things now hidden in darkness and will disclose the purposes of the heart. Then every man will receive his commendation from God"* **(1 Cor. 4-5)**.

(c) *"As you go with your accuser before the magistrate, make an effort to settle with him on the way, lest he drag you to the judge, and the judge hand you over to the officer, and the officer put you in prison. I tell you, you will never get out till you have paid the very last copper"* **(Luke 12:58-59)**.

(d) *"And that servant who knew his master's will, but did not make ready or act according to his will, shall receive a severe beating. But he who did not know, and did what deserved a beating, shall receive a light beating"* **(Luke 12:47-48)**.

(e) *"For we must all appear before the judgment seat of Christ, so that each one may receive good or evil, according to what he has done in the body"* **(2 Cor. 5:10)**.

(f) *"… fire will test what sort of work each one has done. If the work which any man has built on the foundation survives, he will receive a reward. If any man's work is burned up, he will suffer loss, though he himself will be saved, but only as through fire"* **(1 Cor. 3:13-15)**.

(g) *"But you have come to Mount Zion and to the city of the living God, the heavenly Jerusalem, and to innumerable angels in festal gathering, and to the assembly of the first-born who are enrolled in heaven, and to a judge who is God of all, and to the spirits of just men made perfect"* **(Heb. 12:22-23)**.

(h) *"And just as it is appointed for men to die once, and after that comes judgment …"* **(Heb. 9:27)**.

LESSON 36
Activity Sheet 59

HELL : WHAT JESUS TAUGHT

Read the following four quotes from Jesus – one from each of the Gospels – and then circle or highlight the words that refer to Hell's eternity or the nature of its punishments.

"The Son of Man will send his angels and they will gather out of his kingdom all causes of sin and all evil doers and throw them into the furnace of fire; there men will weep and gnash their teeth"

(Matt. 13: 41-42).

"And if your hand causes you to sin, cut it off, it is better for you to enter life maimed than with two hands to go to hell, to the unquenchable fire. And if your foot causes you to sin, cut it off, it is better for you to enter life lame than with two feet to be thrown into hell. And if your eye causes you to sin, pluck it out; it is better for you to enter the kingdom of God with one eye than with two eyes to be thrown into hell, where their worm does not die, and the fire is not quenched"

(Mark 9:42-48).

"The poor man died and was carried by the angels to Abraham's bosom. The rich man also died and was buried; and in Hades, being in torment, he lifted up his eyes, and saw Abraham far off and Lazarus in his bosom. And he called out, 'Father Abraham, have mercy upon me, and send Lazarus to dip the end of his finger in water and cool my tongue; for I am in anguish in this flame'"

(Luke 16:22-24).

"I am the vine, you are the branches. He who abides in me, and I in him, he it is that bears much fruit, for apart from me you can do nothing. If a man does not abide in me, he is cast forth as a branch and withers; and the branches are gathered, thrown into the fire and burned"

(John 15:5-6).

In addition to the above four examples, Jesus spoke on numerous other occasions about Hell (Matt. 3:10-12; Matt. 5:22; Matt. 7:19; Matt. 8:11-12; Matt. 10:28; Matt. 18:7-9; Matt. 22:11-13; Matt. 25:41ff.). To ignore the teachings of Jesus on Hell is to ignore the main reason why he came and died on the Cross – to deliver us from sin and its consequences.

ABOUT THE AUTHOR

Dr Robert M. Haddad holds qualifications in law, theology, philosophy and religious education, namely, a LL.B (USyd.), Grad. Cert. in RE (Charles Sturt Uni.), Grad. Dip. Ed. (ACU), Grad. Dip. in Teacher Ed. (College of Teachers, London), AMLP (Oxford), MA Theo. Studies (UNDA — University Medalist), MRelEd (UNDA), M. Phil (ACU) and a Ph.D. (UNDA). For his Ph.D Robert researched the 'new apologetics' and constructed an apologetics curriculum for Catholic secondary students.

In addition to his studies, Robert has authored various books, including *Lord of History Series* (2 volumes), *The Apostles' Creed*, *Law and Life*, *The Family and Human Life*, *Defend the Faith!*, *The Case for Christianity — St Justin Martyr's Arguments for Religious Liberty and Judicial Justice*, *Answering the Anti-Catholic Challenge* (ch. 3), *1001 Reasons Why It's Great to be Catholic!*, and *Jesus Played Marbles*.

From 1990-2005 Robert worked at St Charbel's College, Sydney, teaching Religion and History. He held the positions of Year Coordinator and Religious Education Coordinator concurrently for ten years and was Assistant Principal (Welfare) for six years.

From 2006-2008 Robert worked as the Convener of the Catholic Chaplaincy at the University of Sydney. He was also lecturer at the Centre for Thomistic Studies for eleven years (1996-2008), teaching Apologetics, Church Fathers and Church History, a lecturer in the Adult Catholic Education Centre for four years (2010-2013), and assisted part-time with *Lumen Verum Apologetics* from 1996 to 2020. In addition, from 2007 to 2019 Robert worked as a sessional lecturer at the University of Notre Dame (Sydney) in Theology and Religious Education.

From 2009-2012, Robert was the Director of the Confraternity of Christian Doctrine (Sydney) and in that capacity was the chief editor of the revised *Christ our Light and Life* (3rd Edition) religious education K-12 curriculum used by Catholic students in state schools as well as the *Gratia Series* sacramental programs for children preparing for Reconciliation, First Holy Communion, and Confirmation in the Archdiocese of Sydney. In 2014 Robert edited a new RCIA resource for use in Catholic schools in the same Archdiocese entitled *Initiate!*

In 2014, Robert was awarded an Australia Day Award by the Australia Day Council of New South Wales for his overall contribution to education and in 2020 the Dempsey Medal by Archbishop Anthony Fisher OP for his work in evangelisation. Currently, he is the Manager, Network Catholic Identity for Sydney Catholic Schools with responsibility for staff faith formation, family evangelisation and youth ministry in 152 primary and secondary schools.

OTHER WORKS
BY
THE AUTHOR

Introduction to the Greatest Fathers of the Church (Parousia Media, 1999)

A Seat at the Supper (General Editor; author Frank Colyer, self-published, 2001)

Introduction to Early Church History (Parousia Media, 2002)

The Apostles' Creed (Parousia Media, 2004)

Law and Life (Parousia Media, 2004)

The Case for Christianity — St Justin Martyr's Arguments for Religious Liberty and Judicial Justice (Connor Court Publishing, 2009)

The Family and Human Life (2nd Ed. co-authored with Bernard Toutounji, Parousia Media, 2011)

Answering the Anti-Catholic Challenge (General Editor and author of ch. 3, Modotti Press, 2012)

1001 Reasons Why It's Great to be Catholic! (Dynamic Catholic, 2015)

Christ our Light and Life (General Editor 3rd Edition, 2012) religious education curriculum K-12 used by Catholic students in government schools throughout the state of New South Wales.

Gratia Series (General Editor, 2012) sacramental programs for children preparing for Reconciliation, First Holy Communion, and Confirmation in the Archdiocese of Sydney.

Initiate! (General Editor, CEO Sydney Publications, 2014), a RCIA resource for use in Catholic schools in the Archdiocese of Sydney.

Jesus Played Marbles (CEO Sydney Publications, 2015).

Back Cover: **St Paul the Apostle** ~ 5 AD - 64/67

Front Cover
1: **Socrates** ~ 470 BC - 399 BC
2: **Origen of Alexandria** ~ 184 - 253
3: **St Athanasius of Alexandria** ~ 296/298 - 373
4: **St Benedict of Nursia** ~ 480 - 547
5: **St Anselm of Canterbury** ~ 1033 - 1109
6: **St Dominic Guzman** ~ 1170 - 1221
7: **St Thomas Aquinas** ~ 1225 - 1274
8: **St Thomas More** ~ 1478 - 1535
9: **St Pius V** ~ 1504 - 1572
10: **St Peter Canisius** ~ 1521 - 1597
11: **Cardinal Robert Bellarmine** ~ 1542 - 1621
12: **St John Henry Newman** ~ 1801 - 1890
13: **G. K. Chesterton** ~ 1874 - 1936
14: **Hilaire Belloc** ~ 1870 - 1953
15: **Fr Leslie Rumble** ~ 1892 - 1975
16: **Frank Sheed** ~ 1897 - 1981
17: **St John Paul the Great** ~ 1920 - 2005
18: **Archbishop Michael Sheehan** ~ 1939

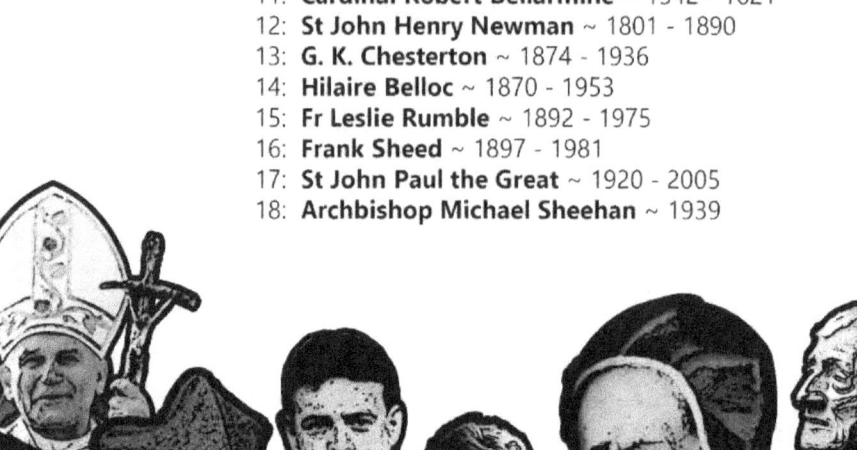

www.ingramcontent.com/pod-product-compliance
Lightning Source LLC
Chambersburg PA
CBHW081919090526
44591CB00014B/2395